The General Crisis of the
Seventeenth Century

The General Crisis of the Seventeenth Century

edited by

Geoffrey Parker

St Salvator's College, University of St Andrews

and

Lesley M. Smith

Brasenose College, Oxford

Routledge & Kegan Paul

London, Henley and Boston

First published in 1978
by Routledge & Kegan Paul Ltd
39 Store Street,
London WC1E 7DD,
Broadway House,
Newtown Road,
Henley-on-Thames
Oxon RG9 1EN and
9 Park Street,
Boston, Mass. 02108, USA
Set in 11/12 Plantin by
Kelly and Wright, Bradford-on-Avon, Wiltshire
and printed in Great Britain by
Lowe & Brydone Printers Ltd
Thetford, Norfolk

British Library Cataloguing in Publication Data

The general crisis of the seventeenth century.

1. Europe—History—17th century—Addresses, essays,
lectures 2. Europe—Politics and government—17th
century—Addresses, essays, lectures
I. Parker, Geoffrey II. Smith, Lesley M.
940.2'52'08   D246   78-40276

ISBN 0 7100 8865 5

For Margaret and Gael

Contents

Preface

The 'General Crisis theory' has been with us now for over twenty years and shows no sign of dying. In 1965 T. S. Aston, editor of *Past and Present*, published a volume of thirteen essays which had previously appeared in that journal and illuminated one or more aspects of the seventeenth-century crisis. That volume, published like this one by Routledge & Kegan Paul, was called *Crisis in Europe 1560–1660*. Since 1965 many more articles have appeared on the subject, often in foreign journals, and from these we have selected seven of the most substantial recent contributions, six of them published abroad. In many ways this volume is a sequel to *Crisis in Europe* since, although none of the material in that collection is reproduced here, most of our contributors review and refine the opinions set down in the earlier work. The two books should be seen as complementary.

The editors are grateful to André Carus, James Coonan, Stephen Davies, Andrew Gailey and Catherine Greenhalgh, with whom they have discussed the problems of the seventeenth century many times, and to Andrew Wheatcroft for his expert help in arranging the publication of this volume. The editors and the publishers are most grateful to the authors and publishers of the contributions included in this book for their permission to reprint the articles.

Chapter one

Introduction

Geoffrey Parker and Lesley M. Smith

I Historians and the 'General Crisis'

According to the latest study of the 'General Crisis' of the seventeenth century, 'Perhaps the first to see this period as a time of fundamental change was Paul Hazard, whose classic *La Crise de la conscience européene* was published nearly half a century ago' in 1935.[1] The concept then passed from a specialist in the history of ideas to political and economic historians: R. B. Merriman's *Six Contemporaneous Revolutions* (Oxford, 1938) looked at six European upheavals in the 1640s; R. Mousnier's *Les XVIe et XVIIe Siècles* (Paris, 1954) characterized the period between 1598 and 1715 as a 'century of crisis', with manifestations in demographic, economic, political, diplomatic, and intellectual spheres; E. J. Hobsbawm's long article, 'The crisis of the seventeenth century' (*Past and Present*, 5 and 6, 1954), studied the problems of the European economy and postulated the existence of a 'general crisis' there too. Then followed a host of other essays in *Past and Present* and elsewhere. Now a full-blown textbook on the subject has been written by T. K. Rabb: *The Struggle for Stability in Early Modern Europe* (Oxford, 1976).

These eminent modern historians, however, were not the first to perceive the unusual instability that characterized the mid-seventeenth century. Some men were struck by the similarities between some of the revolts almost as they happened: the Dutchman Lieuwe van Aitzema compared the Naples uprising of 1647 with the Moscow revolt of 1648; the Italian Count Birago Avogadro published in 1653 a volume of studies on the 'political revolts' of the previous decade. His survey covered the uprisings in Catalonia, Portugal, Sicily, England, France, Naples and Brazil, drawing information from the reports published in newspapers (such as the *Mercure François*).[2]

Nor were Aitzema and Birago Avogadro alone in their perception of a 'general crisis'. The appropriately named Jeremiah Whittaker, a preacher, gleefully informed the English House of Commons in 1643 that they did not stand alone in rebellion. 'These are days of shaking,' he thundered, 'and this shaking is universal: the Palatinate, Bohemia, Germania, Catalonia, Portugal, Ireland, England.' The previous year, a parliamentary pamphleteer, John Goodwin, proclaimed that the 'heate and warmth and living influence' of England's struggle with the King 'shall pierce through many kingdoms great and large, as France, Germany, Bohemia, Hungaria, Polonia, Denmarke, Sweden and many others'. This prediction was largely fulfilled by 1654 when, his patriotic breast bursting with pride, John Milton could imagine 'that from the columns of Hercules to the farthest borders of India, I am bringing back, bringing home to every nation, liberty so long driven out, so long an exile'.[3]

Nor was such interest in foreign developments confined to those at the centre of the Puritan Revolution. At the village of Earls Colne in Essex, the vicar, Ralph Josselin, regularly recorded the 'great actions this yeare' between 1652 and 1664, covering both British and European affairs. One of his earliest surveys, made in January 1652, reveals the wide range of foreign affairs information that came even to a small Essex village. Having dealt with Cromwell's campaigns in England, Scotland and Ireland, Josselin continued:

France is likely to fall into flames by her owne divisions;
this summer shee hath done nothing abroad. The Spaniard
hath almost reduced Barcelona, the cheife city of Catalonia,
and so that kingdome; the issue of that affair wee waite.
Poland is free from warre with the Cossacks but feareth
them. Dane and Suede are both quiet, and so is Germany,
yett the peace at Munster is not fully executed: the Turke
hath done no great matter on the Venetian, nor beene so
fortunate and martial as formerly, as if that people were at
their height and declining rather.[4]

Writing on the other side of the Channel, the French historian, Robert Mentet de Salmonet, prefaced his account of the English Revolution, published in Paris in 1649, with the general statement that he and his fellow Europeans were living in an 'Iron Age' which would become 'famous for the great and strange revolutions that have happen'd in it. . . . Revolts have been frequent both in the East and West.' Salmonet was writing at the height of the crisis, when Frenchmen feared that the fate of Strafford and Charles I would also befall Mazarin and Louis XIV. Writing almost two decades later, Thomas Hobbes could already see that the mid-century troubles were memorable, but isolated. His *Behemoth*, a personal account of the civil war, began with the words, 'If in time, as in place, there were degrees of high and low, I verily believe that the highest time would be that which passed between the years 1640 and 1660.'[5]

But even Hobbes was writing too soon after the events to see the entire 'general crisis' in perspective. It was not until information from all over the world could be gathered and correlated that the magnitude of the upheaval appeared. The first person to advance a 'general crisis' theory was that remarkable luminary of the French Enlightenment, Voltaire. In 1741–2 he took on the task of writing a history book for a lady friend, Mme du Châtelet, who was bored stiff by the past. His *Essai sur les moeurs et l'esprit des nations* was eventually published in 1756. The seventeenth century, with its numerous revolts, wars and rebellions, presented Mme du Châtelet with special problems of boredom, and it was in an attempt to make such anarchy more interesting and comprehensible that he advanced his 'general crisis' theory. Having dealt with political upheavals in Poland, Russia, France, England, Spain and Germany, he turned to the Ottoman Empire where Sultan Ibrahim was deposed in 1648 amid growing anarchy. It was a strange coincidence, he reflected,

> that this unfortunate time for Ibrahim was unfortunate for all monarchs. The crown of the Holy Roman Empire was unsettled by the famous Thirty Years' War. Civil war devastated France and forced the mother of Louis XIV to flee with her children from her capital. In London, Charles I was condemned to death by his own subjects. Philip IV, King of Spain, having lost almost all his possessions in Asia, also lost Portugal.

The early seventeenth century, Voltaire concluded, 'was a period of usurpations almost from one end of the world to the other', and he proceeded to list not only Cromwell in Europe, but also Muley-Ismail in Morocco, Aurangzebe in India and Li-Tsu Ch'eng in China. This 'world dimension' was central to the whole of Voltaire's *Essai*, and he returned to it later on:

In the flood of revolutions which we have seen, from one end of
the universe to the other, there seems a fatal sequence of events
which dragged people into them, just as winds move the sand
and the waves. The developments in Japan are another example.[6]

And so he went on, writing one of the earliest, and most readable,
'global histories' ever composed.

Voltaire drew attention to an important feature of the 'general
crisis' which most later writers have forgotten: the 'crisis' was not
confined to Europe.[7] As Map 1 shows (p. 5), there were upheavals and rebellions in almost all areas of the Old World, and
also in some parts of the New. Simultaneous unrest on a global
scale had certainly happened before. About the middle of the
second millennium BC came the collapse of many of the pre-
Classical civilizations of Eurasia (Shang China, the Indus valley,
Minoan Crete, Mycenaean Greece, the Egyptian Middle Kingdom); in the fourth and fifth centuries AD the main classical
civilizations foundered almost at the same time (the Chin, Gupta
and Roman empires); and in the fourteenth century, even before
the Black Death, the leading states of the High Middle Ages began
to crumble (the Yüan in China, the Minamoto in Japan, the
Ghazni in India, the feudal monarchies in Europe). There was to
be at least one more such 'general crisis' after the seventeenth
century too: between 1810 and 1850 (see page 20 below).

The world-wide extent of these upheavals suggests that,
beneath the more obvious local causes, some very basic and deep-
seated influences were at work, such as a general deterioration of
the global climate leading to relative over-population and food
shortages, to mass migrations (perhaps armed) from poorer to
richer lands, to swift-spreading pandemics, and to frequent wars
and rebellions. If such a climatic explanation of the General
Crisis is to be taken seriously, the evidence of deterioration in the
weather must be sought in many parts of the globe, not just in a
small region such as Europe: parallel manifestations should be
observable over a wide area. And, indeed, in the mid-seventeenth
century, they were. Similarities of experience were sometimes very
close. For example, the peasant revolts in Ming China from 1628
to 1644 had a great deal in common with the simultaneous wave
of popular uprisings in the France of Richelieu: a picture of
increasing military expenditure and growing court extravagance
at a time of economic adversity has been painted in remarkably

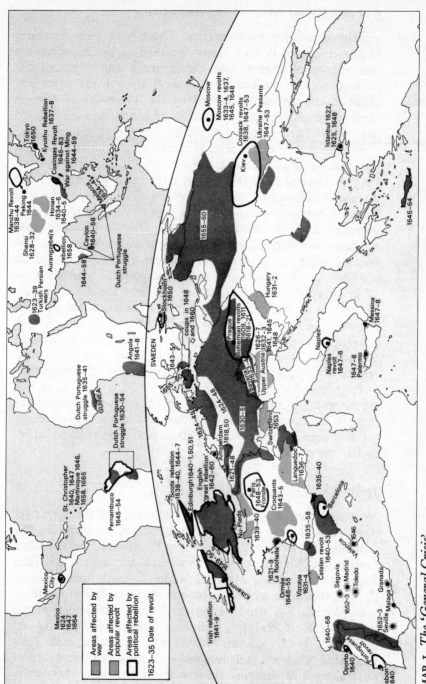

MAP 1 *The 'General Crisis'*

Areas affected by war
Areas affected by popular revolt
Areas affected by political rebellion
1623–35 Date of revolt

Mexico City 1624, 1647, 1664

St. Christopher 1640, 1647 Martinique 1646, 1658, 1665

Pernambuco 1645–54

Dutch Portuguese struggle 1630–54

Dutch Portuguese struggle 1635–41

GUINEA

Angola 1641–8

SWEDEN

Stockholm 1650

coups in 1648 and 1660

1643–5?

1655–60

Moscow

Moscow revolts 1633–4, 1637, 1645, 1648

Cossack revolts 1638, 1647–53

Kiev

Ukraine Peasants 1647–53

Istanbul 1622, 1625, 1648

Hungary 1631–2

Messina 1647–8

Prague

Bohemian revolts 1609, 1611 1618–23

1626–7 1641, 1645, 1648

Upper Austria 1632–3

Bavaria 1633–

Naples

Naples revolt 1647–8 Palermo 1647–8

Switzerland 1653

1630–5

1624–48

Languedoc 1636–7

Manchu Revolt 1638–44, Peking 1644

Shensi 1628–32

Turkish Persian wars 1623–39

Tokyo 1650

Kyushu Rebellion 1637–8

Coxinga's Revolt 1645–83

Honan 1634–5 War against Ming 1640–5 1644–59

Aurangzebe's rebellion 1658

Ceylon 1640–58

1644–58 Dutch Portuguese struggle

1635–40

Amsterdam 1618, 1650

Paris 1648–53 Fronde

Nu-Pieds 1639–40

Scots rebellion 1638–40, 1644–7

Edinburgh 1640–1, 50, 51

English great rebellion 1642–60

1621–48

Barcelona

Valencia 1646

Catalan revolt 1640–53

1635–58

Segovia

Madrid

Toledo

1652–3

Granada

Seville Malaga 1652–3

1640–68

Portugal revolt

Oporto 1640

Lisbon 1640

Vizcaya 1631–4

Ormée 1648–55

La Rochelle 1621–9

1649–50

Kilkenny

Irish rebellion 1641–9

Croquants 1643–5

similar colours for both societies. There were even disastrous plague epidemics in both countries: 1639–44 in China; 1630–2 and 1647–9 in France. One recent study has compared the consequences of the late Ming peasant wars in the 1630s and 1640s to the destruction caused by the Thirty Years' War in Germany, with the population decimated and the area of cultivated land almost halved, from 100 million acres to 58 million acres.[8]

But the similarities end here. There is little resemblance between the events of 1644 in Peking, those of 1648 in Paris and those of 1649 in London beyond the elimination of a sovereign of undisputed legitimacy by 'usurpers' (in Voltaire's phrase). The road from a general economic crisis to a major political upheaval was governed by personalities, local conditions and unforeseen accidents to a degree that makes generalization hazardous. The 'general crisis' is, in fact, two contemporaneous but separate phenomena: one, a series of individual political confrontations, some of which developed into revolutions; the other, a truly 'general crisis' in the demographic and economic development of the world. Each had a somewhat different set of causes. It is prudent to remember the advice of John Selden, the seventeenth-century wit, cynic and antiquarian, to those who were over-zealous in bringing witches to trial: 'The reason of a thing is not to be enquired after, 'til you are sure the thing itself be so. We are commonly at *what's the reason of it?* before we are sure of the thing.'[9] To ensure that we have understood the 'thing' aright, the first step is to keep the 'political' and 'non-political' crises entirely separate.

II An Economic and Social Crisis

Most historians are familiar with the concept of the 'Little Ice Age', remembered, prosaically, in all school textbooks as 'the time the Thames froze'. The problem has always been to find an explanation. The work of an American astronomer, Dr John Eddy, on the so-called 'Maunder Minimum' sheds important new light on this topic, as well as on one of the central problems of solar physics. The notebooks of the leading astronomers of the later seventeenth century – including Johan Hevelius (1611–87) in Poland, G. D. Cassini (1625–1712) in France, and John Flamsteed (1646–1719) in England – all record the almost complete absence of sunspots between about 1645 and 1715, while noting that earlier observers such as Galileo or Scheiner had seen them (see p. 231 below). There was also a failure to observe either aurora borealis (northern lights) or a corona during solar eclipses during this period. These data cannot be dismissed as absence of evidence; they constitute genuine evidence of absence, and they are supported by other facts. First, the detailed drawings of the early astronomers – some of them daily compilations – reveal the sun rotating in a significantly different way in the mid-seventeenth century.[10] Second, measurements of the radioactive isotope of carbon, carbon-14 (^{14}C), deposited in past centuries reveals a notable aberration between 1650 and 1750: there was an enormous increase in ^{14}C deposits, indicating an abundance of carbon in the earth's atmosphere, a circumstance normally associated with a reduction in solar energy. The ^{14}C evidence is extremely important for historians, for it demonstrates that the important observed changes in the sun's behaviour were felt on earth; and it suggests that they were felt in the form of a reduction in the sun's heat. The possibility of some correlation between sunspots and climate was suggested even during the crisis years of the 1640s: a number of astronomers noted the coincidence of sharp fluctuations in the number of sunspots and unusually harsh climatic conditions. Some thought that few sunspots might create drought; others that many sunspots produced cold.[11]

Alas there is no such clear-cut correlation. Nevertheless, an overall decline in solar energy would explain such disparate yet related facts as the advance of glaciers all over the world; the late ripening of grapes in the French vineyards; the late flowering of the cherry trees in imperial Japan; the temperature record of central England in the Northern and of New Zealand in the Southern Hemisphere.[12] All these phenomena have been noted by either historians or meteorologists, and all point to a cooler climate, and in particular to cooler and wetter summers, across the globe in the mid-seventeenth century. In a world dependent largely on vegetable and cereal crops, such changes could not fail to be serious. Everyone in the early modern times was, to some degree, dependent on agriculture, a proportion variously estimated at between 80 per cent and 95 per cent being directly dependent.

> It is generally admitted [wrote Fernand Braudel] that the
> annual consumption per head of wheat (and other cereals)
> was of the order of two (present-day) quintals. . . . If the

population [of the Mediterranean area] was 60 million, the
total annual consumption of wheat or other bread crops
must have been about 120 million quintals. Other foodstuffs,
meat, fish, olive oil, and wine were merely complementary to
the staple diet. If we take the average price of the quintal
in about 1600 to be 4 or 5 Venetian ducats, Mediterranean
consumption (assumed equal to production) must have
reached 480 or 600 million ducats every year. . . . Grain
alone establishes the overwhelming superiority of
agricultural production over all others.[13]

A fall of one degree C in overall temperatures – and that is the
magnitude of the change during the 'Little Ice Age' – restricts
the growing season for plants by three or four weeks and reduces
the maximum altitude for cultivation by about 500 feet.[14] The
expansion of population in the sixteenth century had led to the
cultivation of many marginal highlands: a colder summer would
reduce or perhaps remove the yield of such areas, leaving their
populations on the threshold of starvation. Diminished food
reserves, producing (effectively) serious overpopulation, presented
a favourable terrain for the spread of diseases. Zoologists have
observed that dysentery spreads rapidly among groups of monkeys
when they become too numerous, and it has been suggested that
much the same mechanism operated among early modern human
populations, with dysentery epidemics removing the weaker
members of a community that had outgrown its resources.[15] The
better-known scourge of plague operated in much the same way:
epidemics tended to spread at times when dearth had driven up
the price of basic foodstuffs, placing them beyond the reach of
many ordinary people. At the little town of Ülzen in north-
western Germany plague struck in 1597 and dysentery in 1599,
both at a time when prices were at their highest. At the village of
Heydon in south-east England, in 1564, the harvest was good and
only three families required poor relief, ten families survived by
their own efforts, while nineteen households were prosperous
enough to contribute poor relief. Only four years later, however,
after a bad harvest, more than half the families in the community
were dependent upon poor relief, while roughly a quarter were
'in poverty' (sc. starving).

There was no real escape from this dilemma, which economists
would term a 'high-level equilibrium trap': the inputs and outputs

of the agricultural system had reached a balance that could be broken only by heavy capital investment and new technology. This European agriculture could not provide. As Neils Steensgaard notes on p. 30 below, yield ratios remained stable and even fell: in eastern and central Europe they stood at four grains of corn harvested for every grain sown, which was scarcely enough to feed those who produced it; in Atlantic Europe yields were somewhat better, but until 1700 they were still not high enough to provide a secure basis for economic diversification. And, wherever improved yields were achieved, whether through better methods or increased area of cultivation, the surplus produced was soon swallowed up by the growing population: there was little capital accumulation, therefore little land improvement or technical innovation, and therefore little increase in the supply of daily bread.[16] There were only three choices facing a population caught in this trap: migration, death or revolt.

In May 1597, a chronicler of Aix-en-Provence recorded, 'in the crush of the said poor, six or seven persons died, children, girls and a woman, having been pushed to the ground, trampled and suffocated, for there were more than 1200 poor people there.' In the same year, at Chelmsford, it was reported that 'many men, women and children go out of the town a-begging . . . and . . . there is neither work or victuals unless they beg for it.' Thirty years later, in 1628, 6,000 vagrants from the Limousin crowded the gates at Perigord in search of work or, failing that, charity, while in a town of Lorraine in 1642 one of St Vincent de Paul's helpers wrote, 'At the last distribution of bread we made, there were 1132 poor, without counting the sick, who are numerous, and whom we are helping in many ways.'[17] The majority of these paupers were migrants. Whenever crops failed, or disease threatened, refugees flocked to the towns where there existed the chance of poor relief – a little bread and a little soup. Even in ordinary years, there was a clear trend of population flow away from the smaller villages towards towns and larger settlements. In Spain, this movement was already under way by 1575, and, in the words of a recent study, 'The conclusion appears inescapable: smaller villages located in higher, less fertile regions became overpopulated at an early date, with a consequent migration to larger settlements.' The grain harvest records for the same areas reveal a steady fall in yields from 1615 onwards, while the population declined and entire hamlets in the highlands were abandoned.[18] Many of the 'lost' inhabitants went to the cities, especially to Madrid, which increased in size from 65,000 people in 1597 to 140,000 in 1646, owing to the influx of almost 5,000 migrants per year. But Madrid was one of the few success stories in seventeenth-century Spain; most other towns failed to increase. In some cases, the growth of one town involved the decline of others; in particular, Madrid's gain was Toledo's loss. The history of English towns in the seventeenth century was much the same: in England perhaps 10 per cent of the population lived in towns in 1500 and perhaps 20 per cent in 1700, but over half of this increase was accounted for by London alone, which grew from 25,000 to 575,000 people.[19] Many immigrants were, in fact, part of a floating population, almost permanently mobile. In the small Essex town of Cogenhoe between 1618 and 1628, 52 per cent of the population changed; much the same turnover existed in the much larger town of Southampton.[20] Fear of the 'sturdy beggars' and an awareness of their growing numbers and hidden menace permeates the literature of the period, from the stories about engaging rogues like *Till Eulenspiegel* or *Lazarillo de Tormes* to the more scientific *Il Vagabondo*, an encyclopaedia of the customs and life of the Italian underworld, published by Giacinto Nobile in 1627 and the *Vocabulario di Germania* which listed 1,300 special words used by Spanish beggars in 1609.[21] In the words of W. K. Jordan, 'The most immediate and pressing concern of government . . . for something more than a century (1520–1640) was the problem of vagrancy.'[22] And vagrancy had its roots in the rural depopulation caused by the worsening agricultural situation of the 'Little Ice Age'.

However, not all the 'missing population' had packed their knapsacks and taken to the roads. Many of them had died. Quite apart from the memorable, but widely spread, attacks of a major disease, which could remove between 20 and 30 per cent of a region's population at a stroke, there was during the mid-seventeenth century a stagnation and even a decline, in the birth rate. This phenomenon was particularly pronounced in Castile, where the population appears to have fallen by 50 per cent between 1600 and 1650. It was there that the decline was first noted, and there also that 'modern' methods were first used to plot the decline. A canon of Toledo Cathedral, Sancho de Moncada, consulted the parish registers in his area, and found that 'in the years 1617 and 1618 there were not one half of the marriages which there used to be'. There were therefore fewer children. Subsequent research has vindicated the findings of this pioneer of historical demography: not only in his native Toledo, but all over Spain, parish registers show a steady fall in the rate of baptisms and marriages after about 1610. Moncada also suggested that the primary reason for this persistent fall was not migration, plague or the expulsion of the Moriscos (as other authors had argued), but 'because the people cannot support themselves'.[23] There was, Moncada postulated, not enough food to go round, with the result that the price of essential items such as bread increased beyond the reach of the average wage-earner. There can be no doubt that the price of food did affect directly the vital statistics of early modern Europe. The unpredictable and erratic pulse of the cost of bread controlled the rhythm of births, marriages and deaths: as prices and deaths rose, births and marriages fell. Figure 1.1 shows the experience of Baugé in Anjou (France) from 1691 to 1695.[24]

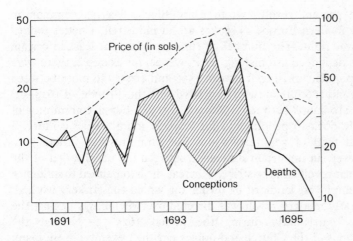

FIGURE I.I *A subsistence crisis in Anjou, 1691–5*

Most areas of Europe seem to have experienced a 'subsistence crisis' of this magnitude about once a decade in the century or so between 1555 and 1665 – lowland England may have been an exception – and in the mid-seventeenth century there were three: one in 1643–4, a second (the worst of the entire century) in

1649–50, and a third in 1652–3. These harvest failures were recorded throughout Europe, from Poland to England and from Sweden to Italy.[25] They were accompanied, in many cases, by industrial and commercial paralysis, for the sharp rise in food prices led to a falling demand for manufactured goods, which in turn led to widespread unemployment among wage-earners. It was therefore not infrequent for a family to find its wages stopped just as the price of essential items was escalating. There is also the evidence, presented by R. Romano in chapter 7, that short-term commercial recessions of this sort were intensified by a general down-turn in the European economy in the half century following the sharp crisis of 1619–20 (although Steensgaard, on p. 42 below, casts some doubt on this, arguing that a failure of distribution, not production, was to blame). It is also the case that between 1620 and 1660, for the reasons noted on p. 14 below, the hardships caused by the harvest failures and trade recessions were made worse by the depredations of troops, or a sudden increase in taxation. In such a situation, a common reaction was rebellion.

'The peasant revolt', wrote Marc Bloch, 'was as common in early modern Europe as strikes are in industrial societies today.' He was right. The number of rural uprisings, at least in certain areas, is indeed astonishing: in Provence, for example, there were 108 popular uprisings between 1596 and 1635, 156 more between 1635 and 1660 (16 of them associated with the 'Fronde' of 1648–53) and 110 more between 1661 and 1715.[26] For a community of barely 600,000 people, and for scarcely more than a century, a grand total of 374 revolts was not unimpressive! There was, however, an important difference between the usual target of the popular revolt and the strike. Whereas the latter aimed to influence the employer, landlord or owner for whom the strikers worked, the early modern revolt was directed overwhelmingly against the State, particularly during the period 1625–75. Neither the exactions of the Church and nobles nor their exemption (in many countries) from taxation seems to have been a leading grievance of the rioters, at least in western Europe. Of course, these matters played their part in generating unrest; but increased seigneurial labour services or the activities of the church courts rarely triggered off a widespread revolt at this time. These burdens were regarded in the same light as the weather, or a bad harvest: inescapable but immutable. Rebellions were directed against grievances that could, in theory, be changed – the policies and demands of government – and the victims of the rioters were normally the officials trying to enforce those policies, especially tax-collectors.

Given the scale of fiscal increase in some areas, the frequency of revolt is scarcely surprising: in the *généralité* of Bordeaux, for example, the *taille* (a direct tax) remained constant from 1610 to 1632, at one million livres; in 1635 it was raised to two million livres, in 1644 to three million livres and in 1648 to four million livres. Small wonder that the area became a centre of rebellion against Louis XIV during the Fronde. The Ormée of Bordeaux lasted from 1651 to 1653 when the city was taken, after a regular siege, by the King's army. New taxes or the increase of old ones played a part in provoking almost every revolt during our period, from the Ship Money of Charles I in England to the *media annata* of Olivares in Castile. Many revolts – those of Naples, Palermo, Normandy, Moscow, to name but a few – were directly triggered by the imposition of a new tax at a time of dearth. They formed part of a long tradition of popular revolts, one that went back at least to the fourteenth century and was to continue to the late eighteenth century, and perhaps beyond. Even the actions of the crowd were the same, as if the oral culture of a community kept alive the traditions of 'proper behaviour' during a riot. The crowd of Naples in 1647 did the same things, in the same ways, as their predecessors during the risings of 1510, 1548 and 1585 and in the same way as their descendants during the rising of 1799. Certain areas had a distinct and long-lasting tradition of revolt: thus the estates of the Schaunberg family were at the heart of each one of the Upper Austrian peasant revolts in 1511–14, 1525, 1560, 1570, 1595–7, 1620, 1626, 1632–3 and 1648. In Aquitaine, in south-western France, no major popular uprising in the seventeenth century was complete without the participation of men from the vicomté of Turenne, the heathland estates of Angoumois or the marshlands around Riez. These areas, partly protected by their geographical location, partly by their privileged status, acted as veritable oases of insurrection. In a lower key, it seems that certain areas might have a tradition of radical thought: Kingston-upon-Thames and the villages around Pendle in Lancashire have been suggested as semi-permanent homes of English radicalism in the sixteenth and seventeenth centuries, which explain the curious survival of certain patterns in popular thought and popular disorder.[27]

However, if this type of analysis can explain away several of the revolts that marked the 'general crisis' it cannot account for them all. There is no way in which the 'Little Ice Age', the bad harvests of the 1630s or even Ship Money can be shown to have caused the English civil wars. The same is true of all the major political crises of western Europe in these years: the Fronde, the revolts of Portugal, Catalonia and the British Isles, the confrontations in Holland and Sweden. In each of them, the cause is to be sought not in the social structure and economic situation of the populations at large, but in the innovative policies of their governments, especially in the fields of finance and religion.

III A Political Crisis

In his elegant essay printed below, Niels Steensgaard presents convincing evidence of the marked increase in government activity and expenditure that took place in the seventeenth century, most of it caused by war. The early modern state was, to a large extent, a military institution. Around half of its income in every year was spent on war, preparation for war, or liquidating the consequences of war. As the State's revenues increased, so its armed forces grew. Table 1.1 makes the development clear:[28]

TABLE 1.1 *Increase in military manpower, 1470–1710*

Date	Spanish Monarchy	Dutch Republic	France	England	Sweden	Russia
1470s	20,000		40,000	25,000		
1550s	150,000		50,000	20,000		
1590s	200,000	20,000	80,000	30,000	15,000	
1630s	300,000	50,000	150,000		45,000	35,000
1650s	100,000		100,000	70,000	70,000	
1670s	70,000	110,000	120,000		63,000	130,000
1700s	50,000	100,000	400,000	87,000	100,000	170,000

Price inflation meant that the cost of putting each of these soldiers in the field rose by a factor of five between 1530 and 1630. The cost of waging war had reached a level that no government could long afford.

And yet, war was more common in Europe during the seventeenth century than ever before: only four complete calendar years were peaceful over the whole continent. Some states spent almost the entire century engaged in war – most notably Spain and her dominions – and hostilities, once commenced, tended to involve several states and indeed continents, thanks to the 'polarization of international politics' that took place (described by Geoffrey Parker in chapter 3). Even in peacetime, most large European states began to maintain a standing army which required payment whether it saw active service or not. In the words of Roland Mousnier:

> There is no strict determinism in the matter of revolt and revolution, no logical sequence, no direct link between the set of circumstances explaining and justifying revolt and the act of revolt itself. The link is a psychological one, a very complex psychological one, and in most cases the historian is unable to enter into the psychology, conscious or subconscious, of the men he studies.[29]

At the back of all the major revolts of our period lay a consciousness that governments were trying to change the *status quo*. This is a crucial point, stressed by Steensgaard, Schöffer and Elliott below. In the words of Niels Steensgaard, 'The six contemporaneous revolutions can only be seen as one if we rechristen them the "six contemporaneous reactions"' (p. 44 below). In every case, it was the 'court', not the 'country', that appeared as the innovator. To take the example of England, it was the initiative of the Crown – whether in matters fiscal (Ship Money) or diplomatic (alliance with Spain), economic (new monopolies) or religious (Arminianism) – that shook the *status quo* and provoked discontent. Even the culture of the Caroline court was new: plays, 'masques', romantic poetry and unrestrained dancing was claimed by some to have 'poisoned the old manners of our Country with foreign delights'.[30] The court had become intellectually isolated. It was the same in France, Spain and the Netherlands, where the court's devotion to stage plays and the theatre provoked widespread criticism (exacerbated in Holland by a linguistic grievance: the House of Orange's players were French and performed in The Hague in French!). This cultural isolation was also common in central Europe, although it was substantially strengthened by religious differences. In the Empire, the Peace of Augsburg of 1555 had given each territorial prince the right to choose his own religion, and enforce it on his subjects; the Confederation of Warsaw introduced a similar scheme in

Poland in 1573. This arrangement placed great power in the hands of territorial rulers, for it made their religious policy the pivot around which the religious policy of everyone else had to turn. It ushered in a period of religious absolutism. In Poland, the lord of Rákow enforced Socinianism on his tenants while in the royal domains of Mazovia the crown enforced Catholicism. Between 1606 and 1620, perhaps two-thirds of Poland's 760 Protestant churches were destroyed by magnates implementing the *cuius regio eius religio* principle. It was the same in the Empire. The Rhine Palatinate changed from Catholic to Lutheran in 1544, from Lutheran to Calvinist in 1559, back to Lutheran in 1576 and back to Calvinist in 1583 simply because its successive rulers were of different religions. In the lands of the Habsburgs, the Jesuit-trained Ferdinand decreed the expulsion of all Protestants from Styria when he came to power there in 1600, from Bohemia, when he had defeated his rival for the territory, Frederick of the Palatinate, in 1620, and from Upper Austria with a special *Reformationskommission* in 1625. 'Confessional absolutism' thus produced results, but success had a high price. In all those areas where the court's Catholic culture was not shared by the population at large, a new gulf was created which allowed disaffection to develop. In Austria it provoked a dangerous peasant revolt in 1626; in Bohemia, where there had already been rebellions in defence of Protestantism in 1609, 1611 and 1618, there was another rising in 1632; in the Ukraine, the Counter-Reformation created a Catholic aristocracy using Latin script and speaking Polish, but it left an Orthodox peasantry using Cyrillic and speaking the traditional language, and this cultural separatism played an important role in providing peasant support for the revolt of the Cossacks under Chmielnicki in 1648.

Although religious passion died away very quickly in the later seventeenth century – Samuel Butler's *Hudibras*, which ridiculed fanaticism in matters of faith, became a best-seller as early as 1663 – the middle decades of the century were a time of acute religious awareness and heightened sensitivity. The Orthodox Church was undergoing a thorough reform of manners and liturgy in the 1640s and 1650s as first Byzantine and then Ukrainian scholars were brought in to improve the texts and Order; in 1653, this enforced 'westernization' provoked a serious split which lasted for some years. The Roman Catholic Church was also moving towards schism over the Jansenist controversy concerning free will and good works, while the Calvinists were split from England through Holland to Hungary by doctrinal disputes (Puritans or Gomarists versus Arminians). But perhaps the most impressive religious divisions of the age occurred in the Jewish community, which was torn in the 1660s by 'the most important messianic movement in Judaism since the destruction of the second Temple'.[31] Sabbatai Sevi, who was proclaimed Messiah and King of the Jews at Smyrna in 1665, found supporters from Scotland to the Yemen and from Morocco to Poland before his apostasy and fall in 1666. Samuel Pepys, in February 1666, found that even the hard-headed London Jews were betting odds of ten to one that 'a certain person now at Smyrna be within two years owned by all the princes of the East . . . as king of the world', while in Aberdeen one Robert Boulter began to publish pamphlets about the imminent redemption of Israel. There were good reasons for this interest so far afield. Boulter was a millenarian, one of those who believed that the end of the world would come in 1666 (according to the prophecy in the Book of Daniel). He was convinced that, before this happened, the Messiah would come and redeem the Jews. Sabbatai Sevi seemed to strengthen the millenarians' case. There was also a Jewish tradition that a redeemer would come in the mid-seventeenth century, a tradition that was strengthened by the appalling persecution that accompanied Chmielnicki's rising in Poland, where the majority of European Jewry lived: some 700 Jewish communities and perhaps 100,000 Jews were destroyed between 1648 and 1658.

IV An International Conspiracy?

It is worth emphasizing this heightened religious awareness because, as many historians have argued, in early modern Europe, it was only religion that was capable of producing an ideology capable of uniting the opponents of a regime. At the same time, it created an alienated élite capable of championing those whose religion seemed threatened. 'Confessional absolutism' was therefore the form of government action most likely to lead to revolution. Possession of religious ideology was something that distinguished the successful revolts of this period (Scotland, England, the Ukraine) from the unsuccessful ones (Catalonia, the Fronde; the exception was Portugal and there King John IV could draw on strong national feeling). Finally, religion was more likely to mobilize a degree of international support for the rebels. It was no accident that the leaders of the anti-Habsburg factions in Austria, Bohemia and Moravia were Calvinists, or that they allied with their co-religionists elsewhere to form a 'Calvinist International' based on Heidelberg, The Hague and Prague to oppose the 'Catholic International' based on Rome, Vienna, Brussels and Madrid (see p. 66 below). There were similar religious links between other groups of rebellions. No one can hope to understand the coming of the English civil war without knowing about the Bishops' War in Scotland and the Confederation of Kilkenny in Ireland. The Stuart monarchy was a personal union of three crowns, and the policies of Strafford were tried out in Ireland before they were attempted in England; those of Laud were implemented simultaneously in England and Scotland. The Protestant opponents of Strafford in Dublin and London thus had as much in common as the Puritans and Presbyterians who opposed Laud. It should therefore come as no surprise if we find Covenanter politicians like Robert Baillie at Westminster, and Covenanting generals like Alexander Leslie fighting beside Cromwell at Marston Moor. It has been correctly pointed out that 'the initiative which the Long Parliament took against the royal prerogative, in 1640 and 1641, depended heavily on the presence of the Scottish army in England. Later, during the civil war, parliament could hardly have carried on without Scottish military help.'[32] And the tie upon which that Scottish assistance depended was the 'Solemn League and Covenant' which undertook to enforce a Presbyterian (i.e. Scottish) religious settlement upon England (and Ireland) 'according to the word of God, and the examples of the best reformed churches'.

Religion, however, was not always the reason for co-operation between rebels.[33] In 1652 the radical Protestant, Colonel Sexby, was sent out by the English Parliament to encourage and advise the Catholic leaders of the Ormée (republic) of Bordeaux, while the revolts against Philip IV – whether in Naples, Catalonia or Portugal – all received substantial aid from either the Catholic French or the Protestant Dutch. The Dutch, according to their official historian, were always ready to acknowledge their *gemeene interesse*, their common interest, with any other enemy of Spain, whether Protestant, Catholic, Orthodox, Moslem or Buddhist. But it was not only the rebels who could see the advantages of cooperation. There were also attempts by governments to co-ordinate their efforts. The 'English Revolution', since it lasted longest, produced the most determined attempts to found a counter-revolutionary league. As early as 1640, Charles I had been vainly trying to raise loans from Spain (£300,000 in May, £100,000 in July, even £50,000 in August), from France, from Genoa, even from the Papacy, in order to buy off the Scots without convoking the English Parliament. After the civil war began, however, aid to the royalists was provided by the Queen Regent of France (Charles's sister-in-law), the city of Hamburg and Frederick Henry, Prince of Orange (whose son had married Charles's daughter). Both of them seemed to have felt that monarchs ought to help each other, acknowledging that there existed (in the words of James I) 'an implicit tie amongst kings which obligeth them, though there be no other interest or particular engagement, to stick unto and right one another upon insurrection of subjects'.[34] Charles II, in exile, also played upon this sentiment. In 1650 he warned the Doge of Venice that: 'If all Christian princes do not make opportune provision . . . there is no doubt that the poisonous breath of rebellion will corrupt all peoples, far and near, wherever malcontents are found.'[35] The same point was made in royalist propaganda, such as the fake translation of a 'decree' issued by Tsar Alexis I of Russia which condemned the 'Rebellion of England as an universall Contagion, [which] being become epidemicall hath poisoned and infected most parts of Christendom' and called for a congress of European monarchs to be held in Antwerp in 1650 in order to form a league dedicated to the destruction of the Commonwealth. But the pamphlet was bogus, just like the intriguing 'Interview between Sultan Ibrahim, Emperor of the Turks, and the King of England, held in the Elysian Fields', published in 1649 and discussing where the two rulers had gone wrong.[36]

The Elysian Fields was almost the only place where Charles I and Ibrahim could have pooled their experiences. Communications in the seventeenth century were too slow to permit a rapid ex-change of resources, or even news. It took weeks for the news of the uprisings in Constantinople, Muscovy and the Ukraine to reach England in 1648, and longer still for any appropriate action to be discussed. The revolt of the Brazil settlers against the Dutch, which broke out on 13 June 1645, was not known in Holland until late August, and a relief fleet was not sent until

April 1646; an adequate fleet was not despatched until 26 December 1647, by which time Dutch Brazil had been lost. A proper account of the events of 1644 in China was not available in Europe until 1654, by which time almost all Ming resistance had collapsed.[37] There was no way in which a 'revolutionary spirit' could connect the revolts in England, France, Austria, Naples, Muscovy and the Ukraine, except that the extreme events in one area made those elsewhere seem more serious.[38]

And there a mere introduction should end. There is, as our contributors point out below, no single model of revolution that unifies all the political upheavals of our period. Both Ivo Schöffer and John Elliott rightly emphasize the exceptions to the 'crisis': Hamburg and north-west Germany largely escaped the Thirty Years' War and prospered, while even areas that were regularly visited by the troops managed to avoid serious damage by skilful adaptation to the soldiers' requirements; the Dutch Republic flourished, and even the South Netherlands managed to recover from the more serious devastation of the later sixteenth century. But these exceptions should not surprise us: even in 1848, the 'year of revolutions', there were many cities that did *not* experience political unrest! And yet, 1848 resembled 1648 in so many ways – as Guizot, fallen idol of the 'year of revolutions', was the first to point out: it came towards the end of a period of adverse climatic conditions, starting with the calamitous years of 1812–17 (again a reduction in received solar energy seems to be the culprit, this time caused by abnormally high volcanic activity ejecting dust into the stratosphere and blocking out the sun's heat); it was a period of repeated lethal epidemics which affected all Eurasia (typhus, and, above all, cholera); and it was a period of popular disturbances and rebellions on an almost unprecedented scale.[39] But the link between these various events remains as tenuous and unproven for the nineteenth, as for the seventeenth, century. A. Lloyd Moote is surely correct to expect greater clarity to emerge only when more comparative studies have been completed. The most obvious candidates for detailed comparative treatment would seem to be: the three revolts against Charles Stuart;[40] the revolts in France and Spain, comparing the Fronde with the *huelga de los grandes* against Olivares in 1641–2, and then the major provincial revolts in the two countries;[41] and the confrontations in Holland, Sweden and Denmark at the end of their 'great wars'. Until this further research has been done, we can scarcely improve on the verdict of Voltaire at the end of his 'global history', written more than 200 years ago. 'Three things exercise a constant influence over the minds of men: climate, government and religion', he wrote; and then added, 'C'est la seule manière d'expliquer l'énigme de ce monde.'[42]

Notes

1 T. K. Rabb, *The Struggle for Stability in Early Modern Europe* (Oxford, 1976), pp. 4–5.
2 Lieuwe van Aitzema, *Saken van Staet ende Oorlog*, III (Amsterdam, 1669), pp. 230–1; G. B. Birago Avogadro, *Delle Historie memorabili che contiene le sollevationi di stato de nostri tempi* (Venice, 1653), reissued the following year in an expanded version: *Tvrbolenze di Evropa dall' Anno 640 sino al 650* (Venice, 1654: the accounts of the English and Portuguese troubles were now expanded so much that they were the subject of separate volumes). Another 'guide to the crisis' for contemporaries was written by Majolino Bisaccioni, *Historia delle Guerre ciuili di questi ultimi tempi* (Venice, 1653).
3 Jeremiah Whittaker, quoted by H. Trevor-Roper, 'The general crisis of the seventeenth century', in T. S. Aston (ed.), *Crisis in Europe* (London, 1965), p. 59; Goodwin by C. Hill, *Puritanism and Revolution* (London, 1959), p. 131; Milton in *Works of John Milton*, VIII (New York, 1933), pp. 14–15 (from *Second Defence of the People of England*, published in Latin in 1654).
4 A. Macfarlane (ed.), *The Diary of Ralph Josselin, 1616–1683* (London, 1976), pp. 269–70.
5 R. Mentet de Salmonet, *Histoire des troubles de la Grande Bretagne* (Paris, 1649; English translation London, 1735), p. ii; T. Hobbes, *Behemoth*, ed. F. Tönnies (London, 1889), p. 1. Hobbes was refused permission to print his scurrilous account of the civil wars.
6 F. M. A. de Voltaire, *Essai sur les moeurs* (Paris, 1963 edn), II, pp. 756–7 and 794. On the originality of Voltaire's vision, see E. J. van Kley, 'Europe's "discovery" of China and the writing of world history', *American Historical Review*, LXXVI (1971), pp. 358–85.
7 One exception among modern writers is the Russian B. F. Porshnev, *Frantzia, Angliskaya Revolutzia i Yevropeiskaya Politika v' CeredinaXVII* (Moscow, 1970), pp. 354–63 ('The crisis on a Eurasian scale'). There is a useful English summary of some of Porshnev's arguments (although not this one) by P. Dukes, 'Russia and mid-seventeenth century Europe: some comments on the work of B. F. Porshnev', *European Studies Review*, IV (1970), pp. 81–8.
8 P. T. Ho, *Studies on the Population of China, 1368–1953* (Cambridge, Mass., 1959), pp. 209, 236, 264–5; M. Elvin, *The*

Pattern of the Chinese Past (London, 1973), pp. 310–11;
J. B. Parsons, *The Peasant Rebellions of the Late Ming Dynasty*
(Tucson, Arizona, 1970). For an attempt to generalize about rural
rebellions at this time, see R. Mousnier, *Peasant Revolts in
Seventeenth-century France, Russia and China* (London, 1972),
which should be read in conjunction with the trenchant
criticism of A. L. Moote, M. O. Gately and J. E. Wills in *Past
and Present*, LI (1971), pp. 63–80.

9 John Selden's *Table Talk* (1689) quoted in K. V. Thomas,
Religion and the Decline of Magic (London, 1971), p. 517.

10 See J. A. Eddy, P. A. Gilman and D. E. Trotter, 'Solar rotation
during the Maunder Minimum', *Solar Physics*, XLVI (1976),
pp. 3–14. See also J. A. Eddy, 'The case of the missing sunspots',
Scientific American (May, 1977), pp. 80–92, and especially the
figure on page 88 which calibrates the rise and fall of human
civilizations with fluctuations in glacial activity, temperature
changes and the sunspot and ^{14}C records in a fascinating way.

11 Opinions collected by G. B. Riccioli, *Algamestum novum,
astronomiam veteram novamque* (Bononiae, 1651), p. 96 (book III,
chapter 3 is all about sunspots). For an interesting but mistaken
attempt to tie the sunspot cycle into human history, see J. H.
Biraben, *Les Hommes et la peste en France et dans les pays
européens et méditerranéens*, I (Paris, 1975), pp. 120, 128 and
133–4, where plague cycles are correlated with a presumed
sunspot cycle which, as Eddy shows, did not exist!

12 Information may be found on these matters in: H. Arakawa,
'Climatic change as revealed by the blooming dates of the cherry
blossom at Kyoto', *Journal of Meteorology*, XIII (1956), pp. 599–
600; H. H. Lamb, *Climate: Past, Present and Future*, I (London,
1972) and II (London, 1977); E. Le Roy Ladurie, *Times of Feast,
Times of Famine: A History of the Climate Since the Year 1000*
(London, 1973).

13 F. Braudel, *The Mediterranean and the Mediterranean World in the
Age of Philip II*, I (London, 1972), pp. 420–1. The quintal is
100 kg (220.5 lbs).

14 D. Pimental *et al.*, 'Energy and land constraints in food protein
production', *Science*, CXC (1975), p. 760. In the United States
today, one day's delay in harvesting reduces the yield of cereals
by 63 kilos per hectare. For proof that a similar equation actually
existed in early modern times, see A.-M. Piuz, 'Climat, récolte et
vie des hommes à Genève, XVIe–XVIIIe siècles', *Annales E.S.C.*,
XXIX (1974), pp. 599–618.

15 The suggestion is made by E. Le Roy Ladurie, 'L'histoire
immobile', *Annales E.S.C.*, XXIX (1974), p. 685; there is an
interesting illustration of it (apparently unknown to Le Roy) in
E. Woehlkens, *Pest und Ruhr im 16. und 17. Jahrhundert.
Grundlagen einer statischetopographischen Beschreibung der
grossen Seuchen, inbesondere in der Stadt Ulzen* (Hanover, 1954).

16 See the useful equation in J. de Vries, *The Economy of Europe in an Age of Crisis 1600–1750* (Cambridge, 1976), pp. 35–6, and the data on yield ratios in G. Parker and C. H. Wilson, *Introduction to the Sources of European Economic History, 1500–1800*, I (London, 1977), pp. 10–11 and 121. For the 'high-level equilibrium trap' in China at this same time, see M. Elvin, *The Pattern of the Chinese Past* (London, 1973), Ch. 13 (e.g. pp. 310–11).

17 Braudel, *The Mediterranean*, p. 460; J. Samaha, *Law and Order in Historical Perspective: the Case of Elizabethan Essex* (London, 1974); H. Kamen, *The Iron Century* (London, 1971), p. 409; R. Mousnier, 'The Fronde', in J. P. Greene and R. Forster, *Preconditions of Revolution in Early Modern Europe* (Baltimore, 1970), p. 135.

18 M. Weisser, *The Peasants of the Montes: the Roots of Rural Rebellion in Spain* (Chicago, 1976), pp. 62–70.

19 Figures on Spanish towns from D. R. Ringrose, 'The impact of a new capital city: Madrid, Toledo and New Castile, 1560–1660', *Journal of Economic History*, XIII (1973), pp. 761–91; on England, see P. Clark and P. A. Slack, *Crisis and Order in English Towns, 1500–1700* (London, 1972), p. 6.

20 On Cogenhoe, see Kamen, *Iron Century*, pp. 49–50; on Southampton, see T. B. James, 'The geographical origins and mobility of the inhabitants of Southampton, 1400–1600' (St Andrews University PhD Thesis, 1977).

21 Data about beggars come from Kamen, *Iron Century*, pp. 401–3. See also A. A. Parker, *Literature and the Delinquent: the Picaresque Novel in Spain and Europe, 1599–1753* (Edinburgh, 1967).

22 W. K. Jordan, *A History of Philanthropy in England* (London, 1959), p. 78.

23 S. de Moncada, *Restauración política de España* (Madrid, 1619; ed. J. Vilar, Madrid, 1974), pp. 135–8. There are further data in Weisser, *Peasants of the Montes*, Ch. 4.

24 F. Lebrun, *Les Hommes et la mort en Anjou aux 17e et 18e siècles. Essai de démographie et de psychologie historiques* (Paris–Hague, 1971), p. 341.

25 See the diagram prepared by F. Braudel and F. C. Spooner in: E. E. Rich and C. H. Wilson (eds), *Cambridge Economic History*, IV (Cambridge, 1967), p. 468. The suggestion that England was a special case is made by P. Laslett, *The World We Have Lost* (2nd edn) (London, 1971), Ch. 5 – 'Did the peasants really starve?'. They certainly did in the North: see A. B. Appleby, 'Disease or famine? Mortality in Cumberland and Westmorland, 1580–1640', *Economic History Review*, XXVI (1973), pp. 403–31; and so they did in Scotland: see M. Flinn (ed.), *Scottish Population History from the Seventeenth Century to the 1930s* (Cambridge, 1977), 109–32.

26 R. Pillorget, *Les Mouvements insurrectionnels de Provence, entre 1596 et 1715* (Paris, 1975), p. 988.

27 R. Villari, *La Rivolta antispagnola a Napoli. Le Origini (1585–1647)* (Bari, 1967); A. Hoffmann, 'Zur Geschichte der Schaunbergischen Reichslehen', *Mitteilungen des Oberösterreichischen Landesarchivs*, III (1954), pp. 381–436; Y. Bercé, *Histoire des croquants. Etude des soulèvements populaires au XVIIe siècle dans le sud-ouest de la France* (Geneva, 1974), pp. 648–51 – Bercé notes at least 450 popular revolts in Aquitaine between 1590 and 1715; C. Hill, *The World Turned Upside Down* (London, 1972), pp. 65–8 and 89–90; in general concerning patterns of popular behaviour during revolts see E. P. Thompson, 'The moral economy of the English crowd in the eighteenth century', *Past and Present*, L (1971), pp. 76–136.

28 G. Parker, 'The "military revolution, 1560–1660" – a myth ?', *Journal of Modern History*, XLVIII (1976), p. 206; see also the remarks of P. Goubert, *L'Ancien Regime*, II (Paris, 1973), pp. 112–33.

29 R. Mousnier, 'The Fronde', in: R. Forster and J. P. Greene (eds), *Preconditions of Revolution in Early Modern Europe* (Baltimore, 1970), pp. 157–8, cited and developed in the important review article by H. G. Koenigsberger in *History*, LVII (1972), pp. 394–8, as well as by A. Lloyd Moote on pp. 134–64 below.

30 Stephen Gosson quoted in P. W. Thomas, 'Two cultures ? Court and country under Charles I', in: C. Russell (ed.), *The Origins of the English Civil War* (London, 1973), p. 173.

31 G. Scholem, *Sabbatai Sevi – the Mystical Messiah, 1626–76* (London, 1973), p. ix, on which the following paragraph is based. On religious conflict in seventeenth-century Hungary, see L. Makkai, 'The Hungarian Puritans and the English revolution', *Acta Historica* (Budapest), V (1958), pp. 13–44.

32 H. G. Koenigsberger, *Dominium Regale or Dominium Politicum et Regale. Monarchies and Parliaments in Early Modern Europe* (inaugural lecture, University of London King's College, 1975), amplified by C. Russell, 'Parliamentary history in perspective', *History*, LXI (1976), pp. 1–27. See also p. 129 below.

33 Some contemporaries, indeed, believed that religion only served as an excuse in such matters. On 21 February 1649, in a discussion at the Swedish Council of State, Queen Christina (then 23 years old) resisted pressure to support Charles II's projected expedition to Scotland. Marshal Jakob de la Gardie argued first that in a period of such manifest *spiritus virtiginis* all monarchs should co-operate, and then that co-religionists should support each other. 'People use religion as a pretext,' replied Christina, 'and it is used by us against Calvinists and Papists alike.' 'The Pope, the Spaniards and the rest of the House of Austria have always sought to make use of religion,' de la Gardie reminded her. 'Like a raincoat when it's wet,' quipped Christina. 'But one which may be put on in case of necessity,' added de la Gardie.

See S. Bergh, ed., *Svenska riksrådets protokoll*, XIII (Stockholm, 1925), p. 17.

34 James VI and I, quoted by Hill, *Puritanism and Revolution*, p. 126; information on Charles I's loans from S. R. Gardiner, *History of England*, IX (London, 1884), pp. 131–2, 157, 175 and 184, and from P. Geyl, *Orange and Stuart* (London, 1969), Ch. 1. See also, on support for the Crown in Hamburg, G. Schilfert, 'Zur Geschichte der Auswirkungen der englischen bürgerlichen Revolution auf Nordwestdeutschland', in: F. Klein and J. Streisand (eds), *Beiträge zum neuen Geschichtsbild, zum 60. Geburtstag von Alfred Meusel* (Berlin, 1956), pp. 105–30.

35 Quoted in Hill, *Puritanism and Revolution*, p. 123, at the beginning of his stimulating essay, 'The English revolution and the brotherhood of man' (first published in 1953).

36 See L. Loewenson, 'Did Russia intervene after the execution of Charles I?', *Bulletin of the Institute of Historical Research*, XVIII (1940), pp. 13–20; and Porshnev, *Frantzia*, p. 118.

37 W. J. van Hoboken, 'Een troepentransport naar Brazilie in 1647', *Tijdschrift voor Geschiedenis*, LXII (1949), pp. 100–9; C. R. Boxer, *The Dutch in Brazil, 1624–1654* (Oxford, 1957), pp. 169–88; E. J. van Kley, 'News from China: seventeenth-century European notices of the Manchu conquest', *Journal of Modern History*, XLV (1973), pp. 561–82; and *ibid.*, 'An alternative muse: the Manchu conquest of China in the literature of seventeenth-century northern Europe', *European Studies Review*, VI (1976), pp. 21–43. See also: A. A. M. Adshead, 'The Seventeenth-century General Crisis in China', *France–Asie*, XXIV (1970), pp. 251–65.

38 A point made by P. A. Knachel, *England and the Fronde* (Ithaca, New York, 1967), Ch. 1.

39 See J. D. Post, 'Meteorological history', *Journal of Interdisciplinary History*, III (1973), pp. 730–1. Guizot's analogy was expertly demolished by Karl Marx, *Selected Essays* (ed. H. J. Stenning) (Edinburgh, 1926), pp. 196–208.

40 A point made with great eloquence by J. G. A. Pocock, 'British history: a plea for a new subject', *Journal of Modern History*, XLVII (1975), pp. 601–28. One could make much the same plea for the history of almost any early modern European country.

41 See the important pioneer article of C. S. L. Davies, 'Peasant revolts in France and England: a comparison', *The Agriculture History Review*, XXI (1973), pp. 122–34.

42 Voltaire, *Essai*, II, 806. An attempt to link the revolts together in a new typology will be made in G. Parker, *Europe in Crisis, 1598–1648* (a volume in the 'Fontana History of Europe' Series due to appear in 1979).

Chapter two

The Seventeenth-century Crisis*

Niels Steensgaard

In his introduction to the anthology, *Crisis in Europe 1560–1660*, published in 1965, Christopher Hill maintained that agreement now seemed to have been reached that there was an economic and political crisis all over western and central Europe in the seventeenth century. This is undoubtedly correct: the crisis has been an undisputed fact among those historians who are occupied with early modern Europe; it has become the hallmark of the seventeenth century in the same way as the Renaissance and the Reformation characterize the sixteenth century and Enlightenment and Revolution the eighteenth century. But agreement does not lie very deep; historians are agreed about the existence of the crisis, but not about its character. Since it first became recognized in the middle of the 1950s, the term 'seventeenth-century crisis' has been employed in at least four different senses.

1 A general economic crisis, i.e. a retrogression in European production, or at any rate a fall in the rate of growth of the European economy. This aspect has especially concerned recent French historians engaged in the economic field of research,[1] but forms a part of all versions of the crisis theory.

2 A general political crisis, i.e. a crisis in the relationship between state and society. This theory, conceived by Trevor-Roper, takes as its point of departure the contemporaneous revolutions in the middle of the century, the economic crisis being regarded as an established fact. According to Trevor-Roper the crisis was the result of a conflict between a puritanically minded opposition (the 'country') and a parasitic bureaucracy created by the Renaissance state during the boom of the sixteenth century, but which became unendurable during the period of decline and the lengthy wars in the seventeenth century.[2]

* Originally published as 'Det syttende Arhundredes Krise' in *Historisk Tidsskrift* (Dansk), XII (1970), pp. 475–504. Translated by Paula Hostrup-Jessen.

3 A crisis in the development of capitalism. For Eric Hobsbawm the crisis was a symptom of the decisive break between the feudal order of society and the capitalist production forms.[3] This theory is developed in the framework of Marxist terminology, though it cannot be regarded as *the* Marxist interpretation of the crisis.[4]

4 A crisis comprising all aspects of human life. For Roland Mousnier, the crisis is not so much a problem demanding a special explanation, as a useful term with which to describe a chaotic century.[5]

Finally, a fifth group might be said to comprise those historians who express doubts as to the justifiability of such a concept as the seventeenth-century crisis. A. D. Lublinskaya has been the one to reject the various versions of the crisis theory the most emphatically and in the most detail, but the Dutch historian, Ivo Schöffer, has also expressed his misgivings in describing the 'golden century' of the Netherlands as the century of the European crisis.[6]

Since the versions of the crisis theory summarized above were elaborated, our knowledge of the seventeenth century has grown considerably; inspired to some extent by the crisis theory, a number of historians have worked on the problem within the fields of both economic and political history. Despite the fact that they have often taken one or other of the original formulations of the crisis theory as their starting-point, the concept cannot be said to have been clarified. It must be realized that nowadays the crisis is often merely an affirmation of the undisputable fact that something happened in the seventeenth century; the crisis has become a synonym for what historians concerned with other centuries call 'history'. It has therefore become necessary to reconsider the very concept of crisis; to seek – in the light of recent research – clarification as to whether the economic and political conditions of the seventeenth century justify speaking of a general crisis; and, if this is the case, to attempt to define the nature of this crisis more narrowly.

I The Economic Crisis

'Et le XVIIe siècle n'est un siècle "triste" qu'à condition de définir scientifiquement une tristesse de longue durée, s'il en existe.' ('And the seventeenth century is only "sad" provided that we can define in scientific terms what we mean by "long-term sadness", if such a thing exists.')[7] But how does one define a 'tristesse de longue durée'? The answer, presupposing unlimited access to statistical material, is simple: the definition must be bound up with the series concerned with consumption, production, employment, economic growth, etc.; and the detection of both long- and short-term fluctuations must be based on these series.

Such a procedure is excluded in the study of the seventeenth century. The idea of a prolonged economic depression originates from the statistical era, but the method must be adapted to the conditions of the pre-statistical era; we cannot procure the statistical series we need, so we must use what we have. It must nevertheless be an elementary requirement as to method that the indicative facts from which we arrive at the European fluctuations must be drawn from the whole of Europe, or that we at least have a fairly certain knowledge as to the extent of the gaps. Conclusions about the general fluctuations of the European economy drawn from isolated or specialized series are *a priori* inadmissible. This is something that historians have often forgotten,[8] but it should be added that only the most recent research has made it possible to comply. In what follows, I shall examine the present state of research in five sectors – population, agriculture, industry, international trade and the public sector – taking heed of the necessity of covering (or almost covering) the total European development.

POPULATION

Of especial interest for the detection of a prolonged crisis are the changes in the total population figures. There is scarcely any doubt now that the increase in population during the sixteenth century was followed in the seventeenth century by a decline, by stagnation, or at any rate by a retardation in the rate of growth. The demographic peak seems to have been reached earlier in southern Europe than in the north, so that throughout the century a shift in the balance of the population occurred from the Mediterranean towards the Channel regions. Castile, the Italian peninsula (though not the islands) and Germany suffered a considerable decline in population in the first half of the seventeenth century.[9] The population of Catalonia continued to increase slightly in the first part of the seventeenth century, but from about 1630 onwards it stagnated.[10] Both the south and the north of the Netherlands seem to have suffered a corresponding fate, the turning-point nevertheless lying nearer the middle of the century.[11] Denmark and Poland suffered a considerable loss of population in connection with the Northern War at the end of the 1650s.[12] England's population is supposed to have increased in the seventeenth century, but it is probable that the increase took place chiefly in the first half of the century.[13] As far as France is concerned the century began with an increase in population, which must nevertheless be seen in the light of the losses incurred during the Wars of Religion at the close of the sixteenth century. Further development shows quite considerable regional variations, but the general impression is nevertheless that of a moderate increase in population until the middle of the century in northern France, continuing until 1675–80 in southern France, and thereafter stagnation or a decline.[14] In 1693, after the 'hunger year', France is said to have had the same population as she had a century earlier at the close of the Wars of Religion.[15]

It has previously been the general opinion that the death rate was the most important variable in the pre-industrial population figures, and it has therefore been possible to bring the population trends in direct relation to the general economic development only in connection with the great catastrophes: famine, plague and war, i.e. within the short run only. Therefore, the fact that it has been possible to demonstrate far greater fluctuations in the birth rate than previously supposed awakens considerable interest. There is evidence of such a considerable span, both in time and from place to place, that historians have dared without hesitation to speak of deliberate family planning.[16] The most important variable in this respect is women's age on first entering marriage, but the number of pregnancies within marriage also shows fluctuations, which must be the outcome of decisions founded upon either economic considerations[17] or *mentalités collectives*.[18] This observation paves the way for a more human and less mechanical form of demography. Wrigley has suggested that the Malthusian model, under which populations tend to approach a maximum with regard to accessible foodstuffs, is an exception, fluctuations *below* maximum being the rule;[19] and he has expressed the opinion that birth control created the basis for an increase in real incomes in England between the middle of the seventeenth century and the middle of the nineteenth century.[20]

AGRICULTURE
In order to undertake a comprehensive evaluation of agricultural

trends during the seventeenth century (as opposed to detailed local studies), there are at present only two possible methods, based either upon price history or upon the study of the yield ratios. Supplementary information may be gained from the data concerning the corn trade.

Already several years ago, on the basis of price historical information derived from all over Europe, Abel painted a picture of the long-term trends in European agriculture that he has by and large been able to maintain in the revised edition of the book published in 1966.[21] He pointed out that the turning-point of the sixteenth-century boom had already been reached in the years immediately following 1600. The outbreak of the Thirty Years' War again brought rising prices, which continued in Denmark, France and northern Italy until the 1620s, in Germany and Holland until the 1630s and in England, Belgium and Austria until the 1640s. Prices thereafter were low all over Europe until the middle of the eighteenth century, although in Germany a tendency to rise can be demonstrated somewhat earlier. Abel seeks the explanation of this prolonged depression first and foremost in demographic developments.

Abel's material is not always as reliable as his methods (for instance, as far as France is concerned he relies on d'Avenel's out-dated price figures), but in the main his results have been confirmed by recent studies of the history of prices.[22] There is, however, no agreement concerning the time when agricultural prices began to fall; French historians have ardently discussed the exact date;[23] while Abel himself has advocated that, instead of seeking a definite turning-point, the reversal should be regarded as having taken place over a longer period.[24]

In the yield ratios calculated by the Dutch historian Slicher van Bath, we have obtained a valuable supplement to the price-historical investigations.[25] Van Bath operates with fifty-year periods – so there is no question of a search for turning-points in this case – and he argues for a decline in the yield ratio in Germany in the second half of the sixteenth century; in England, Germany, France and eastern Europe in the first half of the seventeenth century; and in England, France, Germany and Scandinavia in the second half of the seventeenth century.[26] Several historians have expressed misgivings concerning van Bath's extremely hetero-geneous material,[27] and it is indisputable that more data and a more penetrating criticism of the material gathered would increase confidence in his conclusions. On the other hand, the fluctuations established appear so significant that even on the present basis it is safe to assume that the demonstrated tendencies are in agreement with the actual development. The fact that the decline in the yield ratio coincided with stagnating or falling prices indicates that the cause must be sought on the side of demand.[28]

Abel's and van Bath's results are confirmed by the information available concerning the extent of the international corn trade. Aksel E. Christensen demonstrated considerable short-term fluctuations but no sign of a lasting retrogression in the transport of corn through the Sound before the end of the 1630s.[29] On the other hand, Faber and Jeannin have proved that, after the middle of the seventeenth century, there was a considerable reduction in the export of corn from the Baltic region.[30] Faber, too, chooses to seek the operative factor on the side of demand, i.e. in the demographic conditions, but he also points out that the cultivation in western Europe of new crops like maize, rice and buckwheat may have been increasing. This latter hypothesis is supported by the French historian Jaquand.[31] It would also be reasonable in this connection to consider the fact that England, after the introduction of the bounty in 1673, began to assert herself as an exporter of corn to the west European market.[32]

INDUSTRY

If we are to fulfil the requirement that the data utilized should be applicable to Europe as a whole, then there is in this case only one suitable industry. However, it is one of the most important: the weaving of woollen textiles. The available figures have to a large extent already been taken into account in the discussion concerning the chronological limits and the very existence of the crisis. A survey of the available material, however, suggests that the conclusions reached on the basis of isolated series have been hasty: although the material shows great fluctuations, I do not believe that it supports the theory of a general European crisis.

The decline of the traditional centres of the Italian wool industry starts around 1600 and is indisputable some decades into the new century.[33] The Castilian wool industry stagnated from about the end of the sixteenth century, but there seems to have been no question of a real depression until the middle of the seventeenth century.[34] The Catalan industry seems to have been in difficulties from about 1620.[35]

Corresponding to this recession in the Mediterranean region, there was an increase in north-west European production and in the export of woollen textiles to southern Europe, the Levant and Asia.[36] The production of the most important Dutch textile centre, Leiden, was growing until 1654, the value of annual production rising from 1630 until that date from about 4 million fl. to 9 million fl. Lying concealed behind this overall development in Leiden's production, there is however a qualitative reorganization. The Netherlands was concentrating to an increasing extent on the production of more expensive goods; the production of the cheaper new draperies began to decline as early as the 1620s.[37] However, total Dutch textile exports to the Baltic continued to increase up to the 1640s.

There are no proper production data as far as England is concerned, the most valuable statistics being those concerning the export of cloth from London.[38] Although the series is not complete (seventeen years within the period 1601–40), it is clearly characterized by stagnation after the peak year of 1614. It ought, however, to be added that the value of the consignments undoubtedly was increasing, since a steadily larger proportion of the cloth was exported finished and dyed and not – as previously – as half-finished white cloths.[39]

But these export figures that show stagnation comprise cloths alone; they do not include the lighter and cheaper 'new draperies', which were produced and exported in increasing quantities during the same period and which by 1640 are thought to have constituted almost as large a percentage of English exports as the traditional broadcloths.[40] On the basis of Hinton's survey of all the cloth exported through the Sound, Romano asserts (p. 187 below) that the peak period of English exports, not just of cloth but of woollen textiles as a whole, came in the second decade of the century.[41] This may be an overstatement, but there was certainly a prolonged rise in Dutch textile exports to the Baltic (which continued up to the 1640s). The changeover from production of broadcloths to production of new draperies constituted a decisive structural crisis in the development of the English textile industry, but there is absolutely no justification for interpreting this as a symptom of a European regression: the opposite trends in English and Dutch industry point to the contrary. Wilson finds the causes of the complementary development chiefly in the English manufacturers' easier access to cheap long-staple wool as well as in the higher production costs (especially wages) in the Netherlands. In cheaper goods, the Netherlands were unable to compete with the English rural industry.[42]

In the southern Netherlands the century also began with a rapid advance for the wool industry. Lille prospered until about 1620, but suffered a recession in the 1630s.[43] The most important production centre, Hondschoote, trebled its exports between the 1590s and the 1630s, the peak point of the seventeenth century being reached in 1630; not until the years 1640–5 was there any question of a catastrophic recession.[44] In Ghent and Bruges the production of cheaper-quality textiles ceased, because the town weavers could not compete as regards price with the rural industry; but on the other hand they demonstrated a considerable adaptability by switching over to the production of luxury textiles. According to Craeybeckx the textile industry continued to prosper in both these towns until the last decades of the seventeenth century when the increased protectionism on the export market was largely responsible for reducing sales.[45]

It is not possible to procure any reliable production or export statistics for France, but with the aid of other quantitative sources French historians have been able to assess the development of the wool industry of northern France in the seventeenth century. Until 1610 there was a rapid advance, albeit in part no more than a recovery after the slump that accompanied the last stage of the Wars of Religion. Progress continued at a slower rate until the 1620s but in about 1630 the industry suffered a severe crisis which continued until the mid-1640s. There was some recovery in 1648 and 1659, and from 1660 onwards there was a slow and hesitant progress characterized by a changeover to luxury production. In France, too, the manufacture of cheaper goods was transferred to country districts.[46] A corresponding development can be detected in the relationship between Aachen and its surrounding countryside.[47]

There are many missing details in this picture of the European wool industry, but one thing is certain: it is not possible to reach any conclusions regarding the general European trends on the basis of isolated local or national statistical series. It is not difficult to demonstrate local crises, or crises in the production of specific qualities, but where is one to place the general European crisis of the seventeenth century? In the first years of the century –

if we are to go from the Italian or Castilian data; in 1614 – if we are to go from the export of English cloth; at the beginning of the 1630s – if we are to go from the northern French industry; in 1640–5 – if we accept Hondschoote as a norm; in 1654 – if we are to go from Leiden. But at that time the reconstruction of the French textile industry was drawing near, and Ghent's and Bruges's difficulties did not come about until after the revival of the French textile industry. Finally, the English export of new draperies seems to have been steadily increasing, and it is probable that throughout the century there was an increase in the production of woollen materials in northern and eastern Europe.[48]

Two structural alterations in the textile industry appear just as significant as the demonstrable fluctuations in production: the conversion to rural industry, and the changeover to the production of lighter textile materials. Everywhere, the seventeenth century was an important phase in the development of rural industry on a 'putting-out' basis,[49] and it is thus probable that the stagnation or retrogression of industry in the towns often concealed a transference of production to the country districts. But since one of the chief motives for such a transference was precisely the wish to dodge the guild regulations and taxation of the towns – i.e. the institutions that have provided us with the bulk of the quantitative sources – we shall scarcely ever with any certainty be able to determine the extent and chronology of this transference. Nor can we determine precisely the other structural change – the altered taste with regard to cloth – but the general tendency is clearly from the heavier cloth towards the lighter woollen or mixed cloths, worsteds and silk, and – in the second half of the century – the Indian cottons.

INTERNATIONAL TRADE

Nor do the statistics available for international trade allow un-equivocal conclusions regarding the overall trends. Let us begin with the trade between Seville and Spanish America. The decline demonstrated by Chaunu is indisputable: the peak was reached in 1608, the thirteen-year moving average culminated in 1614–15, and thereafter there was a drop until the middle of the century in the annual tonnage dispatched to a level somewhat below half of the maximum.[50] But Chaunu stopped at 1650 and Hamilton collected figures on the import of American silver to Spain only up to 1660; and both assumed, with little evidence, that the depression continued throughout the second half of the seventeenth century.[51] However, Morineau has subsequently demonstrated that the import of silver from Spanish America to Seville between 1661 and 1700 was far greater than previously reckoned; it even equalled the record figures from the end of the sixteenth century.[52] Moreover we must remember that these figures are limited to *Spanish* America. As Chaunu himself has pointed out, from the beginning of the seventeenth century onwards there were 'other Americas'. The production and export of sugar from Brazil was increasing rapidly, and the English and the Dutch began to interest themselves to a greater extent in America precisely in those years when the Spanish trade was in decline. The new competitors could scarcely make up for the decline in the trade of Seville in the first decades of the century, but it is probable that they did so shortly after the middle of the century.[53]

The Sound Toll Registers, as is well known, are difficult to interpret; exceptions and smuggling limit the value of the information given by the tables, and only after correction for these and other sources of error are they of interest as a barometer registering fluctuations. Aksel E. Christensen found no signs of permanent recession in the period he investigated, i.e. until 1639.[54] This impression is confirmed by Jeannin, who has carried the critical analysis of the Sound Toll Registers further by means of a comparison with the toll registers from Königsberg.[55] In his corrected series there are signs of a trade depression in the Baltic only from about the middle of the century. The years between 1620 and 1650 may have been characterized by violent fluctuations, but according to Jeannin there is no question of a lasting depression, as the setbacks can be traced to short-term production crises, i.e. crop failure in the Baltic regions, or to political conditions. On the other hand, the 1650s and 1660s exhibit signs of real depression; not until the years between 1668 and 1680 do the various commodities, individually, show signs of recovery. Not all groups of commodities were equally badly hit by the recession. Hardest hit was corn, whereas raw materials for industry and ship-building materials did not manifest nearly the same retrogression, either in price or in turnover.[56] Jeannin concludes that the adverse trend did not hinder a considerable advance in important industrial sectors.[57]

The trade to Asia has also been drawn into the discussion concerning the economic crisis.[58] The same applies here as in other places, however: all argument based on isolated series is mis-leading. If the total number of ships sent out from Europe in the sixteenth and seventeenth century with an Asian harbour as destination is counted up, a trend that runs more or less counter to the other known series for the total European trade is revealed. Stagnation or a slight increase from the middle of the sixteenth century is succeeded by a rapid expansion from 1600 to 1620, i.e. coinciding with the Seville trade recession. A period of stagnation, 1621–50, is then succeeded by a new large-scale expansion, 1651–70, i.e. coinciding with the greatest difficulties in the Baltic trade. An interesting feature disclosed by the survey is that, just as in the case of the wool industry, a clear com-plementary relationship between the English and the Dutch activity can be detected, at any rate in the last four decades of the seventeenth century.[59]

This complementary relationship, so obvious at the time, has perhaps been underestimated by the historians of our age who are more used to analysing economic life in terms of growth or fluctuations.[60] The decades in the middle of the century, when the greatest economic difficulties were to be found in Spain, Germany, France and England, were at the same time the golden age of the Netherlands.[61] When the Dutch trade began in the last years of the century to show signs of weakness – the decline may be dated from 1672 at the earliest[62] – there were others prepared to step in: the advance of English foreign trade after 1660 is a well-known phenomenon. According to R. Davis, during the last four decades of the century English exports rose by about 50 per cent, imports by about 30 per cent;[63] and according to Delumeau, French foreign trade and shipping were also expanding from 1660 to 1690 to an extent which makes it unreasonable to connect France as a whole with '*la conjoncture méridionale*'.[64] Finally, Danish–Norwegian shipping and trade were also advancing in the last decades of the century.[65]

THE PUBLIC SECTOR

In the relevant literature concerning the seventeenth century's economic crisis, a description of the public sector may be sought in vain. This omission appears unjustified: a modern analysis would not be able to avoid including public consumption and public investments, and when an economy like that of seventeenth-century Europe with its poorly developed market sector is concerned, the omission is fatal. Not only were the governments in seventeenth-century Europe undoubtedly the strongest buyers in the market, but there is also every probability that they had proportionately a greater share in the total market transactions than has been the case in the industrialized economies until quite recently. Moreover, the redistribution that was effected by the State was of such an extent that it would necessarily affect the standard of living within the separate regions and groups: it is therefore of additional interest in interpreting the production and price data we have at our disposal.[66]

That historians have nevertheless tended to avoid this complicated problem may possibly be due to the nature of the material. The budgets and surveys of revenue and expenditure, which either have been or can be unearthed from the various European states in the seventeenth century, may be correct enough within their own limitations, but they are seldom comparable over a long period of time and they give only an incomplete picture of the economic impact of the State. To the money at the disposal of governments should be added the legitimate remunerations and perquisites of governmental officials, tax collectors and tax farmers, monopoly profits, payments for delegated state services, corruption, looting of conquered towns and countryside, etc.

Many historians have indicated in general terms the possibility that wars and taxes were contributory causes of the economic difficulties and social conflicts of the seventeenth century,[67] but only a few have tried to estimate the extent of the taxes in relation to the total production. Fernand Braudel tentatively estimated the gross product of the Mediterranean region in the years approaching 1600, with a population of about 60 million, at about 1200–1500 million ducats. The total state budgets during the same period he estimated at about 48 million ducats, i.e. less than a ducat per head per annum – about the same as the average contribution to the seigneur. Braudel is of the opinion that the part of the 'product' that was administered through the public sector was astonishingly small: 'Was the mighty state, striding across the stage of history, no more than this?' he asks.[68] Of course it was. As Braudel himself points out, the greatest part of the estimated product never reached the market: it was consumed locally. Annual grain consumption alone was equivalent to between one-third and one-half of the total estimated product. Moreover, we must remember that up to 90 per cent of the population lived in rural areas. Early modern Europe was, to a large extent, a 'subsistence economy', and the role of the State as an entrepreneur was correspondingly greater.

Domínguez Ortiz has attempted a corresponding calculation for Castile alone, in the middle of the seventeenth century. He estimates the gross national product at about 180 million ducats, and the total amount demanded in taxes at about 20 million ducats or approximately 11 per cent of the latter. Nor is Domínguez Ortiz impressed by the size of the share – the twentieth century has toughened us – but on the other hand he is in no doubt that taxation was disastrous for the Castilian economy. He finds the most important reason for this is the unequal distribution of taxes and in the fact that, over and above the Crown's demands, the Castilian population was saddled with a number of other expenses in what we would call today the public sector. The foremost of these extra burdens was the tithe.[69]

Braudel has also tried to collect information concerning the development of the states' budgets during the sixteenth century. He emphasizes the shortcomings of the available information but nevertheless discerns a connection between the economic trend and the state budgets. 'Despite their lacunae, these curves show that fluctuations in state revenues corresponded to fluctuations in the price sector', he wrote.[70] The two curves certainly move in the same direction, but Braudel seems to underestimate the increase in the budgets in relation to the rise in prices. On the basis of his own figures, in the second half of the sixteenth century we find a trebling of the Venetian and Spanish state budgets and a doubling of the French, expressed in real terms; but at the same time the index for Spanish prices, also reckoned in real terms, rose in the same period only from about 80 to about 130.[71]

Did the State's share of the national product in the seventeenth century increase? We shall never possess the statistical information that would permit an exact answer to this question, but we may maintain without any hesitation that the seventeenth century, crisis or no crisis, witnessed an enormous growth in public expenditure. In the seventeenth century the largest armies since the time of the Roman Empire were established,[72] and before the end of the century most of the states also had standing armies in peace-time.[73] Military organization was one of the century's most advanced forms of enterprise:[74] fortresses, navies and royal palaces constituted the century's biggest efforts in planning and organizing and its most precious investments.[75] These facts cannot be left out of account in a discussion of the seventeenth-century crisis. Braudel advocates a 'public vices = private benefit' viewpoint; i.e. state expenditure stimulated the economy as a whole.[76] But this point of view can be correct only if the resources that were used in establishing the armies or in undertaking the year-long campaigns and erecting the fortresses were previously lying idle. If on the other hand the resources were transferred from other sectors, there is no reason for surprise when we find that these other sectors manifested symptoms of crisis.

The problem should also be seen from the taxpayer's point of view. That the seventeenth-century wars had a depressive effect on those areas directly involved in the fighting (e.g. the greater part of Germany) is well known, but it is worth emphasizing that there were also countries – like Sweden,[77] Castile[78] or Naples – [79] in the seventeenth century that largely avoided warfare on their own territory but which, on account of the wars, had to carry a heavy tax burden for long periods, causing a decrease in living standards for large sections of the population. Goubert's estimates of a normal budget in Beauvaisis in the second half of the seventeenth century gives an impression of the effect that even a moderate increase in taxes could have. Of the gross product, rent amounted to about 20 per cent; tithes, etc., to about 12 per cent; taxes, etc., to about 20 per cent; and seed and sundry expenses to an average of 20 per cent. For the farmer and his family there remained about 30 per cent of the yield if he was a tenant, about 50 per cent if he owned his own land. According to Goubert's estimates, this distribution of the crop meant that up to three-quarters of the farms in the area investigated were too small to support a family. 'Were they, then, condemned to suffer hunger or even to starve to death ? The answer is most definitely in the affirmative.'[80] Beauvaisis was still marked by a moderate prosperity right up to the middle of the 1630s. Retrogression first began around the outbreak of war, the years of crop failure around the middle of the century, 1647–15, being particularly catastrophic. It is difficult to avoid the conclusion that the years of crop failure hit a population that was already taxed to starvation level. That taxation in France at the middle of the seventeenth century increased more rapidly than production is scarcely to be doubted. In the case of Languedoc, Le Roy Ladurie has reckoned the part played by direct taxation in the gross product at a little over 6 per cent in the years approaching 1620, rising to about 13 per cent at the middle of the century. At the same time a corresponding increase in indirect taxation occurred.[81]

We cannot draw any general conclusions on the basis of local investigations, but they illustrate the effect that increased taxation might have on a local level, and the numerous peasant revolts in the France of Richelieu and Mazarin leave no doubt that this fiscal pressure was felt nearly everywhere. Increased taxation pressure in the areas not directly affected by the great wars may be one of the most important causes of the demographic and agrarian crises that hit Europe in the seventeenth century; it may also have contributed towards disruptions within other occupations, either directly – by forcing craftsmen to emigrate and merchants to invest in privileged undertakings such as land, state loans or offices – or indirectly – by accentuating the rural population's competition with the urban industries. Goubert has described the desperate search of the rural population for other means of income, 'the incessant search for other forms of income, for piece work and such like, hunting for vacant leases, for wool to spin, for lace to manufacture, for wood to chop, carve or sell, for any small job on the larger estates'.[82] The pressure on the rural population might be a ruthless, growth-promoting measure by enforcing the utilization of unused manpower reserves or overlooked resources. It is probable that the expansion of the rural industry in suitable areas reflected the need for procuring cash or credit.[83] But the competition from the rural industries mentioned above, which could be observed nearly everywhere in Europe, certainly contributed just as much to the difficulties of the urban industries as the loss of their rural customers.

THE ECONOMIC CRISIS

This survey of the most important economic sectors indicates that the seventeenth-century crisis was not a universal retrogression, but that it hit the various sectors at different times and to a different extent. The long-term trends in trade and industry are unclear: there were crises at one time or another in every European production centre and in all branches of European trade, but it is impossible to pin-point a time or a period when European trade and industry as a whole was hit by a depression.

On the other hand, the demographic trends and agricultural prices and production indicate that there was something seriously the matter with the European economy, and the low relative prices combined with the falling yield indicate that we should seek the explanation not solely in poorer climatic conditions or in population pressure – for in that case the prices would have been rising – but in the inability of the population to buy corn and their inability to survive. Finally, if we take a look at the public sector and reckon protection to be a service, in the economic–theoretical meaning of the word, the whole question of a seventeenth-century crisis falls to the ground. Never before was Spain so thoroughly protected as under Philip IV; never before was Germany so thoroughly protected as during the Thirty Years' War; and never before was France so thoroughly protected as under the cardinals and Louis XIV! The production of protection was the seventeenth century's 'leading sector'.

It would be reasonable to suppose that these phenomena were interrelated. An increase in taxation in the widest sense, which exceeded the increase in production in an economy still chiefly based on subsistence agriculture, would have precisely these effects. Part of the population was always living at or near subsistence level, and an increase in the tax burden would reduce their chances of surviving an especially difficult year. Furthermore, it may be regarded as probable that a population would react to a drop in its available income by a reduction in the birth rate, e.g. by raising the age at first marriage. The effect in the agricultural sector would, with the exception of a few privileged localities, be purely negative, as the decrease in private demand would not be compensated for by an increase in public expenditure. For industry and trade the effects would be more complicated. Increased public demand would probably more than compensate for the reduced private demand, but not necessarily within the same production areas. Moreover, the difference in the level of taxes and in the tax systems would have different effects on the production costs and thereby on the ability to compete in the various production centres.

'Taxes are not a *deus ex machina* to explain everything.'[84] On the other hand, every attempt to understand the seventeenth-century economic crisis without taking account of the distribution of income that took place through the public sector is doomed to failure. What appears to be a '*renversement de la tendance majeure*' was in reality the result of an altered pattern of demand precipitated by the transfer of income through taxation. The seventeenth-century crisis was a distribution crisis, not a production crisis.

This conclusion has methodical implications affecting problems other than the one treated here. The last generation of economic historians has followed the economic theoreticians by interesting themselves more in the production of the goods than in their distribution. But this isolation of the object of investigation, however fruitful it may be in an economic analysis, has turned out to be destructive in an historical investigation. Quantification and the drawing up of series provide sure results within the given framework, but do not permit us to draw up either global fluctuations or quadri- or quinquaecyclic systems.[85]

II The Political Crisis

Trevor-Roper's 'general crisis' – i.e. one in the relations between State and society – may be left uncontested, for it is so general as to be applicable to every revolt. On the other hand, as already pointed out by several of the contributors to the symposium on Trevor-Roper's thesis in 1960,[86] the pair of concepts, court–country, has scarcely any European validity. The dualism between a parasitic bureaucracy and an indignant, puritanically minded country opposition does not explain the revolts in the middle of the seventeenth century, which formed the starting-point of Trevor-Roper's discussion. The revolts were by no means directed against a stagnating parasitism, but against a dynamic absolutism which, with its taxation policy, violated the customary laws and threatened to disrupt the social balance or deprive parts of the population of their livelihood. In Catalonia and Portugal the revolts were precipitated not by dissatisfaction with the established order, but by dissatisfaction with Olivares's attempt to alter the established order when he demanded that the vice-royalties should contribute towards the costs of Spain's foreign policy side by side with Castile.[87] The revolt in Naples followed after a number of years of large contributions to the Spanish war chest, which not only had been economically devastating, but also had created chaos in the traditional distribution of authority and wealth.[88] The revolt in Palermo took place under the slogan, 'Long live the King and down with the taxes', a slogan that is to be found time and time again during the revolts of the French peasants.[89] The opposition of the Parlement of Paris in the 1640s had no ideological aim, but was concentrated against the Crown's fiscal legislation; and the Fronde of the Parlement was triggered by a legislation that would have decreased the Parlement's own privileges.[90] In England the trends are less clear, but even in this case there is an apparent conflict between the monarchy's attempt to strengthen its economic independence and the taxpayer's defence of his customary rights. Even in the coup d'état in the Netherlands the fiscal element is present, though in this case the conflict was precipitated by the states of the province of Holland refusing to continue payment of the soldiers they had to maintain, which were under the command of the Stadtholder.[91]

The common factor in the contemporaneous revolutions is thus something far less subtle than Trevor-Roper's dualism between court and country. We do not need to look for abstract similarities between the social structures of the societies in revolt, for there is a concrete similarity between the policy of the governments concerned, that is in their attempts to increase their income or to secure control over the state revenue regardless of customary rights. This statement, which is supported both by our knowledge of the revolts and by the analysis of the economic crisis presented above, can be further substantiated if we extend the comparative investigation to include those countries that did not suffer internal armed conflict in the middle of the seventeenth century. In Bavaria the power of the Estates was broken during the Thirty Years' War; their attempts to regain control of taxation after 1648 led to no result.[92] In the Hohenzollern possessions the electoral independence was achieved step by step between 1653 and 1667; when the conflict with the Estates' institutions and towns was over, the Elector had made sure of a regular annual income which enabled him to maintain a standing army.[93] In 1655 in Hessen-Kassel, the Landgrave out-manoeuvred the Estates, thereby obtaining a standing army, which made him and his successors independent of Estates grants.[94] In Saxony and Württemberg we find the same problem again, but without any clear victory for either the Prince or the Estates.[95] In Denmark the formal introduction of the absolute monarchy in 1660 was coupled with the financial crisis following the Northern War, and it was succeeded by a comprehensive modernization of finance and administration.[96] In Sweden a battle over the state finances started in 1655 and stretched over several decades, but the final result was once again a strengthening of the monarchy's fiscal position.[97]

All this is well known; but it is necessary to emphasize it at this point in order to show that Trevor-Roper started in the wrong place in taking for his point of departure the revolts. That it came to armed conflict in some states is not a valid criterion; the chosen starting-point should be the conflict, be it armed or unarmed, that is common to all the states. Behind the conflict we find the same thing everywhere: the State's demand for higher revenues. In some cases the tax demands were coupled with financial reforms that were not necessarily unfair, but which undermined customary rights; in other cases the increased burden of taxation came to rest on the population groups already living below the bread line. The different reactions in different countries, regardless of whether or not it came to armed conflict, or whether the protests led to any results, depended on the social and economic situation of the country in question and on the policy chosen by the governments (not least upon the choice of the social groups with which they chose to co-operate and the social groups upon which they chose to lay the burden of the increased taxation). But in every case it was the governments that acted in a revolutionary manner: the tax demands disrupted the social balance. They did not create a revolutionary situation: they were in themselves a revolution.[98] The six contemporaneous revolutions can only be seen as one if we rechristen them 'the six contemporaneous reactions'.

III The Problem of Absolutism

Behind the symptoms of economic crisis, and behind the internal conflicts in the European countries in the middle of the seventeenth century, we find the same factor: the growth of state power and the increased fiscal demands. The problem of the crisis is therefore the problem of absolutism.

Naturally the observation of a connection between the taxation pressure and the revolts is not original – it is an interpretation that in many respects approaches Mousnier's view of the seventeenth-century crisis. Mousnier has pointed out that increased fiscal demands hit all groups of society, and in his later writings he has pointed out repeatedly and with ever-increasing emphasis the decisive importance of taxation pressure for the peasant revolts in seventeenth-century France. In *Peasant Uprisings* he says, concerning the taxes: 'The lists that can be made from the records of these impositions on the people are still capable of causing the scholar who draws them up to clench his fists, however *blasé* about poverty and wretchedness he may be.'[99] Nevertheless, he undertakes a defence of absolutism, at least where France is concerned, which blocks the way for further analysis. The State for Mousnier is part of the fight against the crisis, not its initial cause. It is the guarantee of order and progress, of freedom itself, and absolutism is a fulfilment of the people's wishes: 'Absolutism was the wish of the masses who saw their salvation through concentrating all powers in the hands of one man.'[100] 'France adopted the goal of saving European liberties from the Habsburg claims of a universal monarchy.'[101] 'French governments of the seventeenth century were governments of war, economic stagnation and social unrest. They thus grew increasingly dictatorial.'[102] Even in *Peasant Uprisings*, in which Mousnier particularly emphasizes the importance of taxation pressure for popular revolts, pointing out that it was the State and not the fighting populace that violated the customary rights, he defends the Government's foreign policy as being a political necessity: the wars were national and France had long frontiers to defend.[103] The wars are treated in this book as a *circonstance*, something external, on a par with climatic changes and international price conditions.

The importance of taxation pressure in generating the French peasant revolts has been just as strongly emphasized by the Soviet historian Porshnev. But whereas the wars, for Mousnier, are an unavoidable calamity and the governments the defenceless victims of pressures within the international system, Porshnev regards the wars as a governmental red herring concealing their true function: the subjugation of the exploited classes.

During this period, French absolutism pursued four vital aims. In descending order of importance, they were, firstly and above all, the subjection of the exploited classes. . . . Then, to induce a substantial part of the bourgeoisie to support the state in the conflict, . . . thirdly, to ensure a centralised income for the bulk of the nobility, via taxes . . . finally, the protection, and, if possible, the extension of the borders of France.[104]

Or, expressed more briefly in another context, 'Absolutism was an institution for the repression and oppression of the peasantry in the interests of the nobility.'[105] But this identification of the ruling class with the nobility is either meaningless or incorrect. It is incorrect if we postulate a continuity between the ruling class before and after the victory of absolutism for, as both Porshnev's own and Mousnier's investigations have proved, the dividing line in the internal French conflict of the seventeenth century did not run between the classes, but within them. As regards both recruiting and function, the nobility that flocked around Louis XIV was a different group from the nobility that had fought in the Wars of Religion. It is meaningless to define the nobility merely as the class that exploited the peasants – there was not much else to exploit; even with Porshnev's own theoretical background the interest must lie in the actual *nature* of the exploitation during the later stages of feudalism.

It is scarcely accidental that the two collections of Chancellor Séguier's papers that finally landed in Leningrad and Paris, respectively, have been able to lead two eminent historians to opposite conclusions. By virtue of their professional scepticism, most historians would scarcely be able to avoid the iconoclastic thought that Mousnier and Porshnev are fighting out the twentieth-century ideological battle on seventeenth-century ground. We can accept Mousnier's conclusions only if we believe with him that the nation is more than a sum of its individuals, that the masses could have a common wish and 'France' could have a goal. We can accept Porshnev's conclusions only if we believe with him that the government was a tool in the service of one particular class, and that the most radical division between the classes in seventeenth-century France lay between the nobility, the bourgeoisie and the peasants. But the more we know about the seventeenth century – not least through the publication of the two antagonists' own research – the more difficult it becomes to believe that the social grouping that came into being at the close of the eighteenth century was identical with that of the seventeenth century.

It is impossible to harmonize these two viewpoints, but perhaps is it not really necessary to make a choice, for behind both of them lies the idea of the government as an institution that acts rationally, in the interests either of the nation or of a social class. One might invoke the support of political science against such a simplified conception of governmental functions, but it would be more appropriate to seek a more subtle approach among those historians who have been concerned with the European *ancien régime*. J. H. Elliott [pp. 114–19 below] has criticized the use modern historians have made of the concept of revolution where the seventeenth century is concerned. He pointed out that the French Revolution has become, as it were, a paradigm for revolution as a whole, and that historians have even attempted to analyse older revolts and upheavals in accordance with this model. But, he says,

> it is open to question whether our persistent search for
> 'underlying social causes' has not led us down blind alleys. . . .
> Political disagreement may, after all, be no more and no less
> than political disagreement – a dispute about the control
> and exercise of power.

Perhaps historians are just as dependent on the nineteenth century for their view of governments as for their view of revolutions, though with the difference that, as far as governments are concerned, there are not one but two models available – the 'conservative national' and the 'conservative sociological'. A third possibility, which might constitute the first step towards an emancipation from these models, has been outlined by Lane and van Klaveren, but has apparently gone unnoticed by those historians concerned with the seventeenth century – perhaps because their theories are too destructive of well-loved myths both on the Right and on the Left.

For Lane, governments are to be regarded as institutions specializing in the organized exercise of violence; they may be regarded as producers of a particular service, that of protection. Normally the production of protection will yield a profit over and above the costs of production – the producer has a natural monopoly – and a policy that aims at reducing production costs and the sales price is unlikely to be encountered unless the government concerned is controlled by the customers, which – as Lane points out – is an historical exception.[106] Independently of Lane, though on somewhat similar lines, van Klaveren has investigated the part played by corruption in the pre-industrial socioeconomic system. Government officials used their power and influence as a matter of course to enrich themselves at the expense of the prince or the public. Corruption during the *ancien régime* was not a criminal action, but a part of the constitution.[107]

It is clear that this model does not exclude the two models characterized above as the 'conservative national' and the 'conservative sociological'. The government may act on behalf of all consumers of protection, i.e. for the nation, or in the interests of a single social class; but both these possibilities must be regarded as extreme cases. By bringing the actual wielders of power into focus, and by presuming that they act primarily in their own interest, what may be described as the Lane–van Klaveren model opens up very important analytical possibilities. As a consequence of their outlook it will be possible to extract the question of absolutism from its sterile deadlock and to deepen our understanding of it as a political system.

IV Conclusion

In this essay I have attempted to review the concept of the seventeenth-century crisis in the light of our present knowledge of that century's economy and of internal political conflicts in the middle of the century. Both from an economic and from a political point of view, the tracks pointed in the same direction; those symptoms of crisis that may be demonstrated lead to an already well-known phenomenon: the growing power of the State, frequently characterized by the introduction of absolutism. The crisis was not a production crisis but a distribution crisis; the revolts were not social revolutionary, but reactionary against the demands of the State. According to preference, we can reject the concept of crisis altogether or couple it with the problem of absolutism. But this very coupling of the two problems seems to provide possibilities for a fruitful resumption of the discussion. If the governmental actions were revolutionary and the revolts reactionary, if we are to seek the dynamic factor in conjunction with the State and not with the people, we must abandon the stereotype conception of absolutism as a passive instrument for the nation or a class, and resume the analysis of early modern monarchy as a political system, on the assumption that governments were not only products of that society in which they arose, but were also instrumental by means of their policy – i.e. in the choice of whom they taxed and whom they subsidized – in forming that society.

Notes

1 P. Chaunu, 'Le renversement de la tendance majeure des prix et des activités au XVIIe siècle', *Studi in onore di Amintore Fanfani*, IV (Milan, 1962); and 'Réflections sur le tournant des années 1630–1650', *Cahiers d'Histoire*, XII (1967); R. Romano, 'Tra XVI e XVII secolo. Una crisi economica: 1619–1622' (printed on pp. 165–225 below); and 'Encore la crise de 1619–1622', *Annales E.S.C.*, XIX (1964).

2 H. R. Trevor-Roper, 'The general crisis of the seventeenth century', *Past and Present*, XVI (1959), reprinted in Trevor Aston (ed.), *Crisis in Europe, 1560–1660* (London, 1965).

3 E. Hobsbawm, 'The crisis of the seventeenth century', *Past and Present*, V–VI (1954), reprinted in Aston, op. cit.

4 Hobsbawn's thesis has been sharply and expertly criticized within his own theoretical framework in A. D. Lublinskaya, *French Absolutism: The Crucial Phase, 1620–29* (Cambridge, 1968), pp. 38–75.

5 R. Mousnier, *Les XVIe et XVIIe siècles*, 3rd edn (1961), p. 159 (quoted p. 15 above).

6 A. E. Lublinskaya, *French Absolutism*; Ivo Schöffer, 'Did Holland's Golden Age coincide with a period of crisis?', pp. 83–109 below.

7 Romano, 'Encore la crise', p. 37.

8 Such important series as John U. Nef's estimates of the extent of the English coal production in *The Rise of the British Coal Industry* (London, 1932), I, pp. 19–21 and II, pp. 379–89, and Ralph Davis's esimates of the English merchant navy in *The Rise of the English Shipping Industry* (London, 1962) pp. 7–15, which show considerable advance throughout the seventeenth century, have been ignored, whereas far less important series, such as the soap production in Amsterdam, have been taken up for discussion. Another example is the argumentation based upon the number of ships sent out to Asia from one single country – see my 'European shipping to Asia, 1497–1700', *Scandinavian Economic History Review*, XVIII (1970).

9 Ivo Schöffer, 'De demografie van het oude Europa', *Tijdschrift voor Geschiedenis*, LXXIV (1961), pp. 1–31; K. J. Beloch, *Bevölkerungsgeschichte Italiens* (3 vols, Berlin, 1937–61), particularly vol. III pp. 350–4; Carlo M. Cipolla, 'Four centuries of Italian demographic development', *Population in History*, D. V. Glass and D. E. C. Eversley, eds (London, 1965), p. 573; Günther Franz, *Der Dreissigjährige Krieg und das Deutsche Volk*, 3rd edn (Stuttgart, 1961). Uncertainty is greatest where Castile is concerned, but it is most probable that the population figures reached their peak before the plague of 1599–1600; E. J. Hamilton, 'The decline of Spain', *Economic History Review*, 1st series, VIII (1937–8); J. H. Elliott, 'The decline of Spain', *Past and Present*, XX (1961), reprinted in

Aston, op. cit.; Hermann Kellenbenz, 'The impact of growth on government: the example of Spain', *Journal of Economic History*, XXVII (1967); J. Vicens Vives (ed.), *Historia Social y Económica de España y América* (Barcelona, 1957), pp. 251–5.

10 J. Nadal and G. Giralt, *La Population Catalane de 1522 à 1717* (Paris, 1967), pp. 19–23; according to P. Vilar, *La Catalogne dans l'Espagne Moderne* (Paris), I, pp. 617–20, 635, moderate growth continued throughout the century, only interrupted by the plague of 1650–3.

11 J. A. Faber *et al.*, 'Population changes and economic developments in the Netherlands: a historical survey', *A.A.G. Bijdragen*, XII (1965); R. Mols, 'Die Bevölkerungsgeschichte Belgiens im Lichte der heutigen Forschung', *Vierteljahrschrift für Sozial- und Wirtschaftgeschichte*, XLVI (1959).

12 S. Hoszowski, 'the Polish Baltic Trade in the 15th–18th centuries', *Poland at the 11th International Congress of Historical Sciences in Stockholm* (Warsaw, 1960), p. 119; Aksel Lassen, *Fald og Fremgang* (Aarhus, 1965).

13 E. A. Wrigley, 'Family limitation in pre-industrial England', *Economic History Review*, XIX (1966).

14 Denis Richet, 'Croissance et blocage en France du XVe au XVIIIe siècle', *Annales E.S.C.*, XXIII (1968); P. Goubert, 'Recent theories and research in French population between 1500 and 1700', *Population in History*, op. cit., p. 472.

15 P. Chaunu, *La Civilisation de l'Europe Classique* (Paris, 1966), pp. 254–5.

16 Wrigley, op. cit., pp. 86ff.; Chaunu, op. cit., pp. 189ff.

17 Chaunu, op. cit.

18 P. Goubert, 'Disparités de l'ancienne France rurale', *Cahiers d'Histoire*, XII (1967).

19 Wrigley, op. cit., p. 103.

20 E. A. Wrigley, 'A simple model of London's importance in changing English society and economy, 1650–1750', *Past and Present*, XXXVI (1967), p. 98.

21 Wilhelm Abel, *Agrarkrisen und Agrarkonjunktur*, 2nd edn (Stuttgart, 1966).

22 See the recent survey by F. Braudel and F. C. Spooner in *Cambridge Economic History of Europe*, IV (Cambridge, 1967), Ch. vii.

23 Richet, op. cit., pp. 760–3.

24 Abel, op. cit., p. 143.

25 B. H. Slicher van Bath, *The Agrarian History of Western Europe, 500–1850* (London, 1960); 'De oogstopbrengsten van verschillende gewassen, voormelijk graanen, in verhouding tot het zaazaaid, ca. 810–1820', *A.A.G. Bijdragen*, IX (1963); 'Yield ratios 810–1820', ibid., 10 (1963); 'Les problèmes fondamentaux de la société pré-industrielle en Europe occidentale', ibid., XII (1965); and 'Die europäischen Agrarverhältnisse im 17. und der ersten Hälfte des 18. Jahrhunderts', ibid., XIII (1965).

26 B. H. Slicher van Bath, 'Oogstopbrengsten', pp. 74–80.

27 Cf. e.g. Fridlev Skrubbeltrang in (Danish) *Historisk Tidsskrift*, 12.rk. i (1964), pp. 391–4.

28 Slicher van Bath, 'Agrarverhältnisse', p. 145.

29 Aksel E. Christensen, *Dutch Trade to the Baltic about 1600* (Copenhagen, 1941), p. 420 and diagrams xvi–xviii.

30 J. A. Faber, 'The decline of the Baltic grain trade in the second half of the seventeenth century', *Acta Historiae Neerlandica*, I (1966); P. Jeannin, 'Les comptes du Sund comme source pour la construction d'indices généraux de l'activité économique de l'Europe', *Revue Historique*, CCXXXI (1964); cf. S. Hoszowski, 'The Polish Baltic trade in the 15th–18th centuries', *Poland at the 11th International Congress of Historical Sciences* in Stockholm (Warsaw, 1960) and A. Soom, *Der Baltische Getreidehandel im XVII Jahrhundert* (Stockholm, 1961).

31 Faber, op. cit., p. 131; J. Jaquand, 'La production agricole dans la France du XVII siècle', *Dix-Septième Siècle*, LXX (1966), p. 32.

32 C. Wilson, *England's Apprenticeship, 1603–1763* (London, 1965), pp. 146ff.; R. Davis, 'English Foreign Trade, 1660–1700', *Economic History Review*, 2nd series, VIII (1954), reprinted in W. E. Minchinton (ed.), *The Growth of English Overseas Trade* (London, 1969).

33 Carlo M. Cipolla, 'The decline of Italy: the case of a fully matured economy', *Economic History Review*, 2nd series, V (1952); Domenico Sella, 'Les mouvements longs de l'industrie lainière à Venise', *Annales E.S.C.*, XII (1957). Revised versions of both these articles are reprinted in Brian Pullan (ed.), *Crisis and Change in the Venetian Economy* (London, 1968); Domenico Sella, *Commerci e Industrie a Venezia nel Secolo XVII* (Venice and Rome, 1961); R. Romano, 'A Florence au XVIIe siècle', *Annales E.S.C.*, VII (1952).

34 Hermann Kellenbenz, 'The impact of growth on government: the example of Spain', *Journal of Economic History*, XXVII (1967), pp. 356–7; Felipe Ruiz Martin, *Lettres Marchandes Echangées entre Florence et Medina del Campo* (Paris, 1965), pp. cviii–cix.

35 Vilar, *La Catalogne dans l'Espagne moderne*, op. cit., I, pp. 593–4.

36 C. Wilson, 'Cloth production and international competition in the seventeenth century', *Economic History Review*, 2nd series, XIII (1960); F. J. Fisher, 'London's export trade in the early seventeenth century', *Economic History Review*, 2nd series, III (1950); Davis, 'English foreign trade'.

37 N. W. Posthumus, *De Geschiedenis van de Leidsche Lakenindustrie*, III (Leiden, 1939), pp. 924–7 and table 114, p. 941; Wilson, 'Cloth production', p. 214. R. Romano interprets Posthumus in an entirely opposite way, maintaining that a reduction in quality occurred from the 1620s; R. Romano, 'Tra XVI e XVII secolo', p. 190 below, referring to Posthumus, op. cit., pp. 941–6. This, however, must be the result of a misreading. It is correct that the

manufacturers of the cheaper qualities tried to meet the
competition by a further reduction in quality, but of far greater
importance was the expansion in the production of the more
expensive cloth (especially in the years around 1635–55) and
mohair (especially after 1650).

38 B. E. Supple, *Commercial Crisis and Change in England, 1600–1642*
(Cambridge, 1959), p. 258.

39 ibid., pp. 149–52.

40 W. E. Minchinton in his introduction to *The Growth of English
Overseas Trade*, op. cit., p. 9; Fisher, op. cit., reprinted in
Minchinton, op. cit., pp. 66–8.

41 R. W. K. Hinton, *The Eastland Trade and the Common Weal*
(Cambridge, 1959), pp. 226–9.

42 Wilson, 'Cloth production', pp. 217–21.

43 Pierre Deyon and A. Lottin, 'Evolution de la production textile à
Lille aux XVIe et XVIIe siècles', *Revue du Nord*, XLIX (1967).

44 E. Coornaert, *La Draperie-sayetterie d'Hondschoote* (Paris, 1930),
pp. 48–9, 56–7, 493–5.

45 Jan Craeybeckx, 'Les industries d'exportation dans les villes
flamandes au XVII siècle, particulièrement à Gand et à Bruges',
Studi in onore di Amintore Fanfani, IV (1962).

46 Pierre Deyon, 'Variations de la production textile aux XVIe et
XVIIe siècles: sources et premiers résultats', *Annales E.S.C.*,
XVIII (1963); 'La production manufacturière en France au
XVIIe siècle et ses problèmes', *Dix-Septième siècle*, LXX (1966),
pp. 53–6; and *Amiens: Capitale provinciale* (Paris and The Hague,
1967), p. 170; P. Goubert, *Beauvais et le Beauvaisis de 1600 à
1730* (Paris, 1960), pp. 585–92.

47 Herbert Kisch, 'Growth deterrents of a medieval heritage: the
Aachen woollen trades before 1790', *Journal of Economic History*,
XXIV (1964), pp. 524ff.

48 Hinton, op. cit., pp. 104 and 156; Supple, op. cit., pp. 137–42.

49 Hermann Kellenbenz, 'Industries rurales en Occident de la fin du
moyen âge au XVIIIe siècle', *Annales E.S.C.*, XVIII (1963),
pp. 877–8; E. L. Jones, 'Agricultural origins of industry', *Past
and Present*, XL (1968); Slicher van Bath, 'Agrarverhältnisse',
p. 147; Vilar, op. cit., I, pp. 596ff.; D. Sella, 'Industrial
production in seventeenth century Italy', *Explorations in
Entrepreneurial History*, 2nd series, VI (1969), pp. 236–8; Deyon,
Amiens, pp. 206–10.

50 P. Chaunu, *Séville et l'Atlantique*, VIII[2:1] (Paris, 1959 edn),
pp. 15ff.

51 E. J. Hamilton, *American Treasure and the Price Revolution in
Spain 1501–1650* (Cambridge, Mass., 1934), p. 34.

52 Michel Morineau, 'D'Amsterdam à Séville: de quelle réalité
l'histoire des prix est-elle le miroir?', *Annales E.S.C.*, XXIII
(1968), p. 196. Already from 1656–60 to 1661–5 imports rose
from 3.4 million *pesos de mina* to 28.8 million *pesos de mina*. The
record from 1591–5, 35.2 million pesos, was exceeded in 1676–80,

1686–90 and 1696–1700. In no five-year period after 1661 was the import less than 22 million *pesos de mina.*

53 Wilson, *England's Apprenticeship*, pp. 56ff.; Davis, *The Rise of the English Shipping Industry*, Ch. 13.

54 Christensen, op. cit., p. 358, cf. diagram xiii.

55 P. Jeannin, 'Les comptes du Sund comme source pour la construction d'indices généraux de l'activité économique en Europe', *Revue Historique*, CCXXXI (1964).

56 Hinton, op. cit., pp. 105–12.

57 Jeannin, op. cit., pp. 337, 340.

58 Romano, p. 203 below, refers to the Dutch figures; Chaunu, 'Le renversement de la tendance majeure', refers to the Portuguese figures. The series selected in both cases support the chronology preferred by the author.

59 Niels Steensgaard, *The Asian Trade Revolution of the Seventeenth Century* (Chicago and London, 1974), pp. 169–74.

60 Francis Bacon's classic formulation, 'the increase of any estate must be upon the foreigner (for whatsoever is somewhere gotten is somewhere lost)', *Essays* (London, 1962 edn), p.45, expresses a train of thought common to most Mercantilist theoreticians and statesmen; cf. E. F. Heckscher, *Merkantilismen*, 2nd edn, II (Stockholm, 1953), pp. 18–22.

61 On pp. 83–109 below, Ivo Schöffer criticizes the concept of a seventeenth-century crisis from this point of view.

62 It is probable that the definite decline of the Netherlands should be placed even later: C. Wilson, 'The economic decline of the Netherlands', *Economic History Review*, 1st series, IX (1939), pp. 111–27.

63 Davis, 'English foreign trade'.

64 J. Delumeau, 'Le commerce extérieur français au XVIIe siècle', *Dix-septième Siècle*, LXX (1966); also P. Goubert, *Louis XIV et vingt millions de Francais* (Paris, 1966), pp. 141f.

65 Jørgen H. P. Barfod, *Danmark-Norges Handelsflåde, 1650–1700* Helsingór, (1967).

66 Strangely enough, it is the economic historians who are most liable to overlook the economic importance of the public sector. Is this the result of the influence of an economic science that has preferred to dwell on the production of goods rather than on their distribution? Cf. Gunnar Myrdal, *Economic Theory and Underdeveloped Regions* (London, 1963), pp. 115–16. The most paradoxical is Chaunu's attitude. He maintains that there was a far more rapid growth in government revenue than in production in the seventeenth century, and adds, 'de là à affirmer qu'il est le moteur de la croissance il n'y a qu'un pas à franchir prudemment': *La Civilisation de l'Europe Classique*, p. 59. But out of the more than 600 pages in this book only half a page is used for a discussion of the finances, and Chaunu's numerous articles dealing with the short- and long-term fluctuations of the sixteenth and seventeenth centuries may be searched in vain for a

reference to the public sector. The interrelation between
fiscalism and popular revolts has been emphasized most strongly
by R. Mousnier, e.g. in his *Peasant Uprisings* (London, 1971),
pp. 305ff., and by B. Porshnev in *Les Soulèvements populaires en
France de 1623 à 1648* (Paris, 1963).

67 Of course there is also the opposite viewpoint that the militarist
policy created the demand, which formed the basis for the
development of the modern economy: Werner Sombart,
Krieg und Kapitalismus (Munich, 1913), John U. Nef, in
War and Human Progress (Cambridge, Mass., 1950), has disputed
Sombart's viewpoint, but apart from this one case the problem
seems to have vanished from the field of recent historical research.
A French economist, Gaston Imbert, has indicated the
possibility of a connection between a pre-industrial Kondratieff
cycle and the wars: *Des Mouvements de longue durée Kondratieff*
(Aix-en-Provence, 1959), pp. 394–8, 420–4.

68 F. Braudel, *The Mediterranean and the Mediterranean World in the
Age of Philip II*, I (London, 1972), p. 451.

69 Antonio Domínguez Ortiz, *Política y Hacienda de Felipe IV*
(Madrid, 1960), pp. 180–5.

70 Braudel, op. cit., II, pp. 684–6.

71 ibid., p. 33.

72 Quincy Wright, *A Study of War*, 2nd edn (Chicago, 1965),
pp. 232–7, and appendix XXI table 49; G. Parker, 'The
"military revolution 1560–1660" – a myth?', *Journal of Modern
History*, XLVIII (1976), pp. 195–214.

73 Hans Delbrück, *Geschichte der Kriegskunst im Rahmen der
Politischen Geschichte*, IV (Berlin, 1920), pp. 255–7.

74 Fritz Redlich, *The German Military Enterpriser and his Work
Force* (Wiesbaden, 1965).

75 The royal palaces (constructions, etc.) were entered at well over
15 million livres on the debit side of the French budget for
1685: Werner Sombart, *Luxus und Kapitalismus* (Munich, 1913).
We may compare this amount with the share capital of the French
East India Company after its reconstruction in the same year,
1.6 million livres: Paul Kaeppelin, *La Compagnie des Indes
Orientales et François Martin* (Paris, 1908), p. 195.

76 Braudel, op cit., I, pp. 409–10.

77 Eli F. Heckscher, *Sveriges Ekonomiska Historia*, I^2 (1950),
pp. 420–2.

78 J. H. Elliott, 'The decline of Spain', in Aston, op. cit., pp. 182f.;
op. cit., pp. 176ff.

79 R. Villari, *La Rivolta antispagnola a Napoli, le origini (1585–1647)*
(Bari, 1967), pp. 6–7.

80 Goubert, *Beauvais et le Beauvaisis*, pp. 180–2; and 'The French
peasantry of the seventeenth century: a regional example', *Past
and Present*, X (1956), reprinted in Aston, op. cit., p. 156; cf.
however, the more conservative estimate in his *L'Ancien
Régime*, I (Paris, 1969), pp. 100, 119–30.

81 E. Le Roy Ladurie, *Les Paysans de Languedoc* (Paris, 1966), pp. 294, 481–2.
82 Goubert, 'The French peasantry', p. 157; cf. *Beauvais et le Beauvaisis*, pp. 131f.
83 Kellenbenz, 'Industries rurales en Occident', pp. 877f.
84 C. Wilson, 'Taxation and the decline of empires, an unfashionable theme', *Bijdragen en Mededelingen van het Historisch Genootschap*, LXXVII (1963).
85 The expression is taken from P. Chaunu, 'Le XVIIe siècle, problèmes de conjoncture, conjoncture globale et conjonctures rurales françaises', *Mélanges Antony Babel* (Génève, 1963), p. 354. For a more detailed criticism of the theory of cyclic fluctuations especially championed by Chaunu see my 'Det syttende arhundredes krise' (Danish), *Historisk Tidsskrift*, 12.rk.iv (1970), pp. 488–92.
86 'Trevor-Roper's "general crisis", symposium', *Past and Present*, 18 (1960), reprinted in part in Aston, op. cit.
87 J. H. Elliott, *The Revolt of the Catalans* (Cambridge, 1963), pp. 512–15 and *passim*.
88 Villari, *La Rivolta Antispagnola*, pp. 124–38, 144–9.
89 H. G. Koenigsberger, 'The revolt of Palermo in 1647', *Cambridge Historical Journal*, VIII (1944–6), p. 133; Porchnev, *Les Soulèvements Populaires en France*.
90 E. H. Kossmann, *La Fronde* (Leiden, 1954), Ch. 2.
91 Pieter Geyl, *The Netherlands in the Seventeenth Century*, II (London, 1964), pp. 15–17; *Algemene Geschiedenis der Nederlanden*, VII (Utrecht, 1954), pp. 4–7.
92 F. L. Carsten, *Princes and Parliaments in Germany* (Oxford, 1959), pp. 400ff.
93 F. L. Carsten, *The Origins of Prussia* (Oxford, 1964), pp. 185ff., 207ff., 243ff.
94 Carsten, *Princes and Parliaments*, pp. 182ff.
95 ibid., pp. 72ff., 228ff.
96 Johan Jørgensen, 'Bilantz 1660, Adelsvaeldens bo', *Festskrift til Astrid Friis* (Copenhagen, 1963), pp. 153ff.; C. O. Bøggild-Andersen, *Hannibal Sehested, En Dansk Statsmand*, II (Aarhus, 1970), pp. 57ff.
97 Hans Landberg, 'Kungamaktens emancipation. Statsreglering och militärorganisation under Karl X Gustav och Karl XI', *Scandia*, 35 (1969).
98 At the 13th International Congress of Historical Sciences in Moscow, 1970, discussion of the viewpoints put forward here revealed a fundamental disagreement concerning the definition of the concept of revolution. In order to prevent misunderstandings I wish to make it clear that I define a revolution as every comprehensive alteration of custom and law put into effect by violent means, or under threat of violence.
99 Mousnier, *Peasant Uprisings*, p. 307.
100 Mousnier, *Les XVIe et XVIIe Siècles*, p. 245.

101 ibid., p. 281.
102 R. Mousnier, 'La participation des gouvernés a l'activité des gouvernants dans la France de XVIIe et XVIIIe siècles', *Etudes Suisses d'Histoire Générale*, XX (1962–3), p. 216.
103 Mousnier, *Peasant Uprisings*, pp. 308–9.
104 Porshnev, *Les Soulèvements Populaires*, p. 458.
105 B. Porshnev in *XIIe Congrès International des Sciences Historiques*, V, Actes (Vienna, 1965), P. 679.
106 F. C. Lane, 'Economic consequences of organized violence', *Journal of Economic History*, XVII (1958), reprinted in *Venice and History, the Collected Papers of Frederic C. Lane* (Baltimore, 1966).
107 J. van Klaveren, 'Die historische Erscheinung der Korruption', *Vierteljahrschrift für Sozial- und Wirtschaftsgeschichte*, XLIV (1957) and XLV (1958); and 'Fiskalismus, Merkantilismus, Korruption. Drei Aspekte der Finanz- und Wirtschaftspolitik während des Ancien Régime', ibid., XLVII (1960).

[*Editors' note:* Many of the series of economic data discussed in this article are now available in G. Parker and C. H. Wilson, eds, *Introduction to the Sources of European Economic History, 1500–1800* (London, 1977).]

Chapter three

The Dutch Revolt and the Polarization of International Politics*

Geoffrey Parker

I Introduction

'During the whole course of the seventeenth century,' wrote Sir George Clark in 1929, 'there were only seven complete calendar years in which there was no war between European states: the years 1610, 1669–71, 1680–2. . . . War, therefore, may be said to have been as much a normal state of European life as peace.'[1] There were, as far as the present writer can see, even fewer complete calendar years without war in Europe during the sixteenth century. However, an important difference separated the hostilities which took place in the two centuries. Until the 1580s, at least, most European wars involved only two powers fighting a simple duel; thereafter, wars that involved rival blocs of allies were more common. In the seventeenth century, hostilities were so widespread, and the allies so numerous, that making peace became extremely difficult. The despair of Germany during the seemingly interminable Thirty Years' War was given ironic but effective expression by the novelist Hans Jakob Christoffel von Grimmelshausen. In his famous novel about the war, *Simplicissimus*, he put his plan for peace into the mouth of a wandering madman, 'The great God Jupiter'.[2]

There are a number of developments that help to explain why the various states of Europe allowed themselves to be drawn into war more frequently after 1580 than before. There were the significant improvements in diplomatic organization, with more (and more skilful) resident ambassadors, closer co-operation between neighbours, and firmer commitments between allies.

* This article originally appeared in *Tijdschrift voor Geschiedenis*, XXXIX (1976), pp. 429–44, and is reprinted here by permission of the publishers of the journal, H. D. Tjeenk Willink. I am most grateful to Dr Hugo Soly, my friend for many years, and to Mr André Carus, one of my students, for making some very valuable suggestions concerning this paper.

There was the emergence of a number of dogmatic but antipathetic Christian churches in Europe, with adherents in one country willing and ready to go to the aid of their co-religionists elsewhere. These developments were facilitated by improvements in communications – better roads, faster ships, more (and more regular) postal services – which made it easier to co-ordinate diplomatic and, when necessary, military contacts across continents. Equally important, but less obvious, there was the appearance of a semi-permanent pole of political and religious ferment in north-western Europe: the Low Countries. The wars in the Netherlands tended to exert an influence on all other conflicts in Europe. As Gustavus Adolphus observed to a Dutch ambassador in 1625: 'The Hague was the stage on which all the negotiations and actions of Europe took place.' It is the argument of this paper that the war between Spain and her Netherlands 'rebels' between the 1560s and the 1640s played a crucial role in the polarization of international politics, both inside and outside Europe, into two hostile camps.[3]

II The Struggle for Survival, 1565–85

> Our guarantees that we shall not become the conquered
> province of another kingdom are as follows: God, the water,
> Batavian heroism [den Bataafschen heldenmoed], the balance
> of power in Europe, the mutual jealousy of our neighbours,
> and the fact that our Republic has survived for several centuries.[4]

This verdict of Johannes Meerman, a Dutch statesman of the later eighteenth century, was largely true. But it did not apply to the early years of the Dutch struggle against Spain. In the sixteenth century there was no 'balance of power' in Europe, and the survival of an independent state in the North Netherlands owed more to God, the water and 'Batavian heroism' than to the jealousy of foreign powers. Nevertheless, from the earliest days, the leaders of the Netherlands opposition to Philip II had appreciated the need to take account of the attitudes and deeds of Spain's enemies elsewhere.

Many of the Netherlands nobles were related to the leading families of other countries. Montigny and Hornes were close relatives of the Constable of France, Anne de Montmorency (indeed, Montigny had been brought up in the Constable's household); William of Orange, himself the son of the Count of

Nassau, married Anna, niece of the Elector of Saxony and grand-daughter of the Landgrave of Hesse; Egmont married the sister of the Elector Palatine; Brederode and Hornes married into the family of the counts of Neuenar. With such strong family con-nections, the Netherlands nobles naturally took a keen interest in the affairs of France and the Empire. However, foreign affairs in the 1560s were dominated by the Ottoman Turks. The 'Grand Seigneur' was, after 1559, the only ruler capable of challenging the power of Spain in open combat, and for twenty years after the peace of Cateau-Cambrésis Philip II's principal preoccupation was the defence of the Mediterranean against the power of the Ottoman Sultan. It seems clear that the Netherlands nobles exploited this preoccupation in their opposition to the King. The Turkish siege of Malta in 1565, in particular, was undoubtedly used by Orange, Egmont and Hornes to secure concessions from the King. Brederode was not the only Netherlander to wish that the Turks 'were in Valladolid already'; he well knew that a Turkish victory would have made royal concessions in the Low Countries inevitable.[5]

But Malta did not fall, and there were no royal concessions. In 1566, therefore, serious attempts were made by the Nether-lands opposition to draw together these random contacts and 'polarize' opinion and policies in neighbouring states. Montigny and Hornes took steps to establish a common front between the French Huguenots and the 'Gueux'.[6] In Germany a major propaganda campaign was mounted to whip up support for the opposition's cause: letters were written to leading princes, pamphlets were composed and printed, envoys were sent to the emperor (Count Hoogstraten) and to friendly princes (Gillis le Clercq), the Reichstag was petitioned when it met at Augsburg.[7] But the response to these initiatives was disappointing: the German princes stood aloof and the Huguenots never managed to send an army. The Dutch cause was offered active support, paradoxically enough, only by the Ottoman Turks.

Since 1526 the Sultan had had an understanding with the kings of France that, whenever possible, both would attack the Habsburgs together. In 1543 the Turkish fleet had even wintered in the ports of southern France. At about the same time, the *entente* had been extended to include the German Protestant princes, the leader of whom was the Landgrave of Hesse, later to become the grandfather-in-law and close correspondent of

William of Orange.[8] The Landgrave's letters throughout the 1560s gave Orange news of Turkish developments. In 1566, however, it seems that the Sultan took the initiative and established direct contact with the Netherlands opposition to Philip II. The Catholic historian, Famiano Strada, who based his work on documents from the (now destroyed) private archive of Margaret of Parma, asserted that in October 1566 a letter from one of the Sultan's principal advisers, Joseph Miques, Duke of Naxos, was read out to the Calvinist consistory of Antwerp, pledging that 'the forces of the Ottomans would soon hit King Philip's affairs so hard that he would not even have the time to think of Flanders'.[9] It proved an empty promise. The death of Sultan Suleiman the Magnificent in September 1566, and the provincial rebellions and military mutinies that followed, prevented the Ottomans from attacking Spanish power for some years. However, in 1568 the Prince of Orange sent a special envoy to Constantinople to renew contact with the Duke of Naxos (who had resided in Antwerp in the 1540s), and to persuade the Turks to attack Spain.[10] The Sultan's advisers were unmoved: they had already decided upon an attack on Ivan the Terrible, and in 1569 the Sultan's armies rolled northwards and attempted to dig a canal between the Don and Volga Rivers. The Netherlands, like the *Moriscos* of Granada, were neglected.[11]

To a large extent, the first revolt of the Netherlands, in 1566–8, had failed for lack of foreign support, and the opposition leaders decided that any future attempt to overthrow Spanish power in the Low Countries could take place only with full foreign backing. William of Orange and his brother Louis therefore laboured ceaselessly and, on the whole, successfully to persuade France, England, Sweden, and certain German and Italian princes to support their project to invade the Netherlands during the spring of 1572. The Sultan and the King of Algiers were also involved.[12] The outcome of all these plans is well known: England and Sweden stood back, French support was destroyed by the massacre of St Bartholomew; only the Count Palatine (ruler of a small state of 400,000 souls) and the Count of Nassau (ruler of an even smaller state of only 50,000 people) sent substantial support. Again, as in 1566–8, without foreign support the rebellion foundered. Only about thirty towns in Holland and Zeeland carried on their resistance after 1572. The Prince of Orange and the other exiles perforce threw in their lot with them, but the outcome of their desperate stand against Spain still depended upon aid from abroad. In May 1574, the Prince of Orange informed his brother:

> I see very little chance of being able to finance any special undertaking unless we find someone to help us. And in this connection I remember something which I said to you some time ago: that one could defend this country against all the forces of the king of Spain for the space of two years, but that we would then stand in need of help . . . and as the two years will soon be up, it is high time that some princes and potentates lent us a hand.[13]

In fact, Orange did not have long to wait. Already in 1573, Charles IX of France began to supply the Prince with a subsidy to finance his struggle against Spain, and in 1574 both Orange and Charles IX endeavoured to interest the Ottoman Sultan, Selim II, in a co-ordinated attack on Spain. The Prince sent a special envoy to Constantinople; Theodore de Beza, from Geneva, sent letters; and the French king worked through his ambassador, the pro-Huguenot Bishop of Dax.[14]

The result of these initiatives was the dispatch of a special messenger to the 'Lutheran sect' of 'Filandara', bearing an expression of the Sultan's support. The messenger, 'who knows the military affairs and conditions of that area', was also to put the Dutch in contact with the still-discontented *Moriscos* of Granada and with the pirates of Algiers. Meanwhile the Sultan himself sent a great fleet into the western Mediterranean which reconquered Tunis in October 1574.[15]

The fall of Tunis, as both the French and the Dutch were quick to realize, inevitably reduced Spanish pressure on the Dutch.[16] In 1575, Philip II even held formal talks with his 'rebels' about a possible settlement to the revolt (the conference of Breda). But the talks broke down after three months, and once more foreign aid dried up. The death of Charles IX of France in May 1574 removed the crucial intermediary between Orange and the Sultan; after 1574 there was little direct contact. Although the Sultan was said to have encouraged Dutch resistance in 1576–7, and although a Turkish consulate ('De Griekse Natie') was established in Calvinist Antwerp in 1582, the Ottoman Sultan was no longer interested in the Netherlands.[17] In April 1577, Spain and the Turks reached a provisional agreement to cease hostilities and a formal truce was signed in 1580. All the Sultan's efforts after that were directed against Persia, and even the frenzied pleas of England, France and the Dutch in the Armada year, 1588, failed to provoke the Turks to attack Philip II again.[18]

III The Netherlands at Bay, 1585–1609

For a decade after the death of Charles IX, the Dutch were unable to win over any great power to their cause. The Palatinate sent one army to the Netherlands in 1578; the French Huguenots sent another. In 1581 a third French army arrived, under the Catholic Duke of Anjou, who agreed to become sovereign ruler of the Low Countries in place of the now-deposed Philip II.

All these interventions were ill-starred, however. In 1583 the French, led by the 'sovereign' Duke of Anjou, tried to wrest control of the country from the States-General by staging an armed attack on the major cities of Flanders and Brabant. It failed, and Anjou retired disconsolate to France, where he died in June 1584. Almost at once, the situation was transformed.

Anjou may have proved a miserable failure as ruler of the Netherlands, but he had fulfilled a vital role in France: as the nearest male relative of the childless Henry III (his brother), he was the personal guarantee that the next king of France would be a Catholic. After his death, Henry III's nearest male relative was the Protestant leader, Henry of Navarre (later to be Henry IV). The prospect of a Protestant succession so alarmed Philip II that he entered into a formal alliance with the league of French Catholics created by the Guise family: the Sainte Union. The King of Spain promised to pay a regular subsidy to the Union, and between 1585 and 1588 the Guise family received over a million ducats (almost three million florins) from Spain.

There seems to be no doubt that this alliance, the Treaty of Joinville (signed on 31 December 1584), frightened England. Queen Elizabeth had already been alarmed by the rising tide of Spanish success: the conquest of Portugal in 1580, the annexation of the Azores in 1582–3 in the teeth of tough local opposition (supported by France and England), and the steady subjugation of the South Netherlands. In the autumn of 1584, Lord Burghley, Elizabeth's chief adviser, impressed upon his sovereign the need to make common cause with Spain's other enemies. 'Your strength abroad', he told the Queen, 'it must be in joining in good confederacy, or at least intelligence with those that would willingly embrace the same.' Burghley proposed alliances with the Turks, Morocco, Florence, Ferrara and Venice; but above all he counselled the dispatch of immediate aid to the Low Countries, to make sure that Spain would not reconquer the provinces still in revolt. 'If he [Philip II] once reduce the Low Countries to absolute subjection, I know not what limits any man of judgment can set unto his greatness.'[19] After deep thought and protracted negotiations, Queen Elizabeth became the first sovereign ruler to make a formal alliance with the Dutch. The Treaty of Nonsuch, which guaranteed substantial English aid to the Dutch 'rebels', was signed on 17 August 1585. The situation of the two allies did not improve overnight. In August 1587, a correspondent of the Earl of Leicester, English governor-general in the North Netherlands, lamented

> the alliance and understanding of the duke of Parma with
> the Catholic League and the House of Guise; and we, on
> the contrary, have no league or alliance with the princes of our
> religion but, what is worse, we antagonize them from day to day.[20]

As the Spanish Armada sailed up the Channel in the summer of 1588, England and Holland found themselves alone: no foreign power would lend them money or material support. The Catholic–Habsburg domination of Europe was complete.

The diplomatic isolation of Queen Elizabeth and the States-General only ended when the assassination of Henry III, the last of the Valois (1 August 1589), intensified the struggle between the Protestants, led by Henry of Navarre, and the Catholic league for control of France. The Catholic states of western Europe sent massive aid to the Sainte Union. Spain provided 15,000,000 florins in cash subsidies between 1588 and 1595; she invaded Languedoc and sent a permanent military force to Catholic Brittany; and she mounted four major campaigns in northern France, using the army of Flanders (1590, 1592, 1594, 1596). The Catholic Duke of Savoy, aided by a Spanish subsidy, invaded and occupied part of Provence. The Pope sent an army of 10,000 men to fight in France in 1591–2, at a cost of 1,500,000 florins.[21]

This grand alliance of the Catholic powers was soon matched by a similar association of Protestant states. Henry of Navarre received important military and financial support from several German princes, particularly the Elector Palatine, and from Queen Elizabeth.[22] The Dutch sent him 90,000 florins in 1588, 90,000 more in 1589, and 120,000 in 1591; they also dispatched arms and munitions in 1591 and an expeditionary force in 1592, 1594, 1596 and 1597. The Dutch also collaborated closely with England: a Dutch contingent assisted in the capture of Cadiz in 1596, and Queen Elizabeth continued to provide a share of the Dutch war-budget. In Germany, the Dutch took advantage of a rising, engineered by Calvinist refugees in the city, to place a garrison in Emden 'to prevent anything untoward . . .' (April 1595);[23] in 1597 they attacked and captured several Spanish-held strongholds in the archbishopric of Cologne. Most of these gains could not be held however. Diplomatic efforts were more fruitful. In 1594, Oldenbarnevelt sent Dr L. Myller to 'Duytslandt' to enlist the support of the princes of the Empire 'against the Spanish claims to universal monarchy or overlordship'. He failed.[24] An attempt by Maurice of Nassau in 1599 to enlist the aid of the princes of the Westphalian Circle of the Empire, whose lands had been plundered by Spanish troops the previous winter, also failed.[25] A new diplomatic offensive in 1602 produced better results: the Dutch occupation of Emden was made permanent and negotiations were begun with the Elector of Brandenburg. In April 1605, the Elector signed a treaty with the Dutch which promised a subsidy and an expeditionary force; much to Olden-barnevelt's surprise, the Brandenburg 'hulptroepen' arrived in May and took part in the campaign.[26]

Despite this diplomatic success, however, the Dutch were again becoming isolated. In May 1598 Henry of Navarre made peace with Spain, achieving universal recognition as lawful king of France (albeit, since 1593, a Catholic one). Although Henry continued to provide the Dutch with a large annual subsidy (in all, almost 13 million florins were sent 1598–1610), this scarcely equalled the value to the Republic of the war in France, which had distracted Spain for almost a decade.[27] In August 1604 England, now ruled by James VI of Scotland (no friend of Calvinists), also made peace with Spain. Left on their own to oppose the might of Spain single-handed, the Dutch concluded first a cease-fire (April 1607) and then a twelve-year truce (April 1609) with Spain.

IV *The Dutch Take the Offensive*

Although concluded largely through weakness and exhaustion, the Twelve Years' Truce was a major success for the Dutch.

Apart from the economic benefits brought by peace, the truce conferred complete political respectability on the Republic. The truce talks at The Hague in 1608-9 were attended by representatives from France, England, Denmark, Hesse, the Palatinate and Brandenburg; and in the end the Republic was recognized by Spain 'as if it were a sovereign power'. Almost immediately, other states followed suit: in July 1609 the Dutch envoy in London was recognized as a full ambassador representing a sovereign power, and in September James VI and I accorded his agent in The Hague similar promotion.

Later in the year the same thing happened in the Republic's diplomatic contacts with France and Venice.[28] Before long, 'We can see all Christian nations, large and small, and even the Turks and Muscovites, becoming concerned about the fate of our Netherlands.'[29] The Republic was in the process of forming alliances 'with all the princes and potentates who . . . opposed the tyranny and the claims to universal monarchy of Spain, such as the kings of France, England, Denmark and Sweden, with the Republic of Venice, the Hanseatic League and others'.[30] The 'others' included Brandenburg (after 1605), Muscovy (after 1631), Transylvania (after 1626), the Turks (after 1611), Morocco (after 1608), and Algiers and Tunis (after 1622). These allies were not idly chosen. The motive for the treaties was often explicitly admitted to be 'because the same towns or kingdoms had . . . a powerful hostility towards Spain'.[31]

Spain was still a menace. She emerged during the decade following the signing of the truce, as she had in the 1590s, as the backbone of a militant Catholic alliance. The Protestant states of Europe again began to fear that Spain headed a 'Catholic international' which sought to 'plant the Popes Law by Armes, as the Ottomans doe the Law of Mahomet'.[32] In August 1610 the King of Spain agreed to become the 'Protector' of the League of German Catholic princes, and he engaged himself to provide 30,000 *escudos* (about 75,000 florins) every month for two years, to enable the League to raise and maintain an army. In 1611 this army, financed by Spain, invaded Bohemia; in 1614, aided by troops from the Spanish Netherlands, it invaded and occupied parts of the disputed duchies of Cleve and Julich. In 1616-17 Spain paid for a part of the Habsburg army fighting against Venice in Dalmatia.[33] In 1618, following the outbreak of rebellion in Bohemia, Spain promised the immediate dispatch of men and money to the Emperor: in the course of 1619 some 10,000 Spanish troops and about 500,000 florins were sent to Vienna and in 1620 another Spanish army was sent from the South Netherlands to occupy the lands of the Elector Palatine, who had rashly agreed to become the king of the Bohemian rebels.[34] Other Catholic potentates soon intervened in the struggle to help the Emperor and Spain: Louis XIII of France persuaded the German Protestant princes to remain neutral while Maximilian of Bavaria, the greatest Catholic prince in the empire, loaned his army to the Habsburgs. Above all the Pope sent large sums of money: between 1619 and 1623, the Curia sent 400,000 *escudos* (1,000,000 florins) to the Emperor, almost 350,000 *escudos* to the Duke of Bavaria, and a further 16,000 *escudos* to another ally of the Habsburgs, the King of Poland.[35] Of course this Catholic aid to the Emperor did not end in 1623. The Papacy continued to send regular subsidies to the Emperor and the League until at least 1635.[36] Spanish forces continued to occupy the Rhine Palatinate until the 1640s while in 1634 a major army, commanded by the King of Spain's brother Ferdinand (the Cardinal-Infante), invaded Germany and routed the Protestants at the battle of Nördlingen. Following this victory, Spain sent enormous sums of money to the German Catholics: 5,339,985 Rhine *gulden* (about 8,500,000 Dutch florins) were spent by the Spanish Treasury in Germany between April 1635 and March 1643.[37] In return for such substantial assistance, in 1629–31 the Emperor sent troops to fight in Italy for Philip IV, and in the 1620s, 1630s and 1640s, imperial troops fought periodically in the Netherlands against the Dutch.

In the face of this militant Catholic axis, linking Madrid, Brussels, Vienna, Munich and Rome, the rest of Europe felt threatened. Several opposition groups were formed. In the west, there was the ancient 'triple alliance' of England, the Dutch, and the French Protestants; in the east, a looser association of Calvinists existed, led by the Elector Palatine Frederick V, his ministers Christian of Anhalt and Ludwig Camerarius, the Prince of Transylvania Bethlen Gabor, and the leaders of the Protestant minorities in the Habsburg hereditary lands (Georg Erasmus Tschernembl in Austria, Peter Vok Rožmberk and Václav Budovec of Budov in Bohemia, and Karel Zerotin in Moravia).[38] To the south of this Calvinist network lay the traditionally anti-Habsburg Republic of Venice and the Islamic states of the

Mediterranean; to the north were the Lutheran kingdoms of Denmark and Sweden and the Orthodox tsardom of Muscovy. The overriding problem facing those who wished to oppose the might of the Catholic axis after 1609 was, therefore, not where to find support, but how to weld the numerous enemies of Spain into a coherent rival 'international' or axis.

The first efforts at active co-operation were the Dutch attempt to mediate a peace between Sweden and Russia in 1615, the dispatch of 3,000 Dutch troops and twelve warships to fight for Venice against the Habsburgs in Dalmatia and the proposal to send more military aid to Savoy in 1617.[39] The strength of the anti-Habsburg forces, however, lay in the groups of allies in the east and the west of Europe. Everything depended on the extent to which they could be united. The revolt of Bohemia in 1618 seemed to provide the perfect opportunity for alliance. Frederick of the Palatinate was the nephew of Maurice of Nassau and the son-in-law of James VI and I; the Bohemians had a long tradition of association with both England and the Netherlands. It has even been suggested that the three countries were linked by a 'secret culture' of magic, alchemy and cabbalistic lore – the 'Rosicrucian enlightenment' – which was actively patronized by Frederick of the Palatinate.[40] Unfortunately for Frederick's cause, however, in 1618 King James was allied to Spain and refused to help either the Bohemians or his son-in-law, and Dutch aid was paralysed by the fall of Johan van Oldenbarnevelt, the minister who for thirty years had directed the Republic's foreign policy. Only in September 1619 did the Dutch leaders promise to send men and money to Bohemia and to 'take such a course by way of divertion that the Spanish troopes in those provinces under the Archduke shall not be spared or have commoditie to be employed into Germanie'. And in the end only 5,000 men and 550,000 florins actually reached Bohemia, while the Archduke was left free to send not one army but two against the rebels in the Empire.[41] In November 1620 the main army of the Bohemians was defeated by the Catholic allies of the Emperor at the battle of the White Mountain.

After the victory of the Habsburgs, the Calvinist remnants from central Europe took refuge in The Hague. From there, the 'government-in-exile' of Frederick V laboured to create a new network of alliances which would be capable of defeating the Madrid–Vienna axis. England, Denmark and Sweden were successively enmeshed; eventually France and a host of lesser potentates were also involved. By the 1630s, according to T. K. Rabb:

All the upheavals were regarded as variations on the theme of confessional struggle. An international Catholic diplomatic network, centred in Brussels, fought single-mindedly against a parallel Protestant network centred in Amsterdam. The tentacles of the one extended from Portugal to Poland, of the other from Scotland to Hungary.[42]

Although, however, one of these 'networks' was centred in the North Netherlands, the Dutch had done little to create it. The list of treaties made by the Republic included several that were not the work of Dutch diplomats. In many cases the groundwork was done by the Palatine and Bohemian exiles. Just as the exiles from Flanders and Brabant strengthened the militant foreign policy of the Republic in the 1590s, so the exiles from central Europe acted as a 'general staff' for the anti-Habsburg alliance in the 1620s and '30s.[43] The Dutch provided a headquarters, funds and respectability, but they lacked the singleminded determination to organize and co-ordinate a European struggle. They also lacked the means. On the one hand they found it difficult to recruit a sufficient number of suitable diplomats; on the other they were reluctant to spend money without evident cause.[44] In 1628 and 1631, because the Brussels government was known to have no money to mount a campaign, the States-General economized and in the *Staten van Oorlog* we read 'There was no campaign this year.' In 1640–1, although a fleet and an expeditionary force were sent to aid the Portuguese rebellion against Philip IV, they sent none to the Catalans, even though they recognized their 'common interest' with any other rebels against the King of Spain.[45]

The Republic thus tended to fight shy of all foreign commitments that might cost money, although they fully realized the advantages that accrued from the diplomatic efforts of others to polarize European politics into a mutually hostile balance of power.

The preservation of this state depended on the jealousy of its neighbours. Are there not many small states in Germany and Italy which maintain their independence thanks to the same jealousy, and have they not always done so ? Why, therefore, should this powerful republic not continue to exist and maintain itself in the same way ? Everything, indeed, has been due to the jealousy of Spain, France and England.[46]

But that 'jealousy' was not, in the seventeenth century, entirely of Dutch making. They also reaped a harvest sown by others.

The distinctive contribution of the Dutch to the polarization of international politics in the seventeenth century was not, in fact, made in Europe at all, but in Africa, Asia and America. Overseas, the Dutch were far more 'positive' in their foreign policy, creating enemies for the Iberian world empires where none had existed before. In this they followed the policy of Queen Elizabeth of England, who had ever believed that:

If you touch him [the king of Spain] in the Indies, you touche the apple of his eye, for take away the treasure which is *nervus belli*, and which he hath almoste [all] out of his west Indies, his old bandes of souldiers will soone be dissolved, his purposes defeated, his power and strengthe diminished, his pride abated, and his tyranie utterly suppressed.[47]

However, where the English had been content to sink Spanish shipping and plunder isolated colonies, the Dutch set out more systematically to create a rival colonial and commercial empire and to discover 'in what ways we could injure this powerful enemy with his own resources'.[48]

Inspired by Willem Usselincx, one of the Flemish exiles, attempts were made to foment discontent among Spain's Indian vassals, while in the Netherlands public opinion was stirred up by a 'Black Legend' propaganda campaign against Spanish 'atrocities' in America. A Dutch edition of Bartolomé de las Casas's *Brevíssima relación de la destrucción de las Indias*, published at Amsterdam in 1620, asserted that the Dutch (in view of Spanish brutality) had a manifest destiny to liberate the Indians from their Iberian oppressors.[49] Already steps had been taken to achieve this. In 1614 a fleet under Joris van Spilsbergen left the Netherlands with orders to make contact with the Indians of America, especially with those of Chile who were known to be hostile to the Spaniards. This initiative failed (the Indians were as suspicious of the Dutch as they were of the Spaniards), but more substantial efforts followed the foundation of the West India

Company in 1621 (inspired by Usselincx). Since 1619 a purpose-built fleet had been under construction ready to sail to South America and capture a major port, provoke a native rising against the Iberian settlers and create a Dutch colony in its place.[50] In this they could count on the assistance of a 'fifth column' of Jewish residents, most of them Portuguese 'marranos', some of whom had reached America only after a period of exile in Holland, who 'would rather see a couple of Dutch pennants than an inquisitor'.[51] Some of these 'marranos' appear to have acted as secret agents.[52]

Despite the long preparations and the advantage of surprise, the Dutch attack on Callao (capital of Spanish Peru) failed totally, and the occupation of Bahía (capital of Portuguese Brazil) lasted only a year (May 1624–May 1625).[53] The Dutch did not give up, however. In 1630 they again made use of Jewish and other anti-Portuguese elements in Brazil to seize the province of Pernambuco, the most populous area of the viceroyalty and the centre of its sugar production. By 1644 the invaders controlled over 1,000 miles of the coastal plain of Brazil, and an expedition from the province gained control of most of Angola, the region that provided the slaves needed to farm the sugar plantations.[54] Dutch Brazil became a thriving concern until the revolt of the settlers in 1645. Even before this, however, the Dutch had lost much of their credibility in South America. Once she had herself become a colonial power, the Republic could not pose convincingly as the liberator of the oppressed Indian. A new effort under Admiral Hendrik Brouwer to interest the Araucanian Indians in concerted action against the Spaniards (1642–3) proved a failure, even though Brouwer's men founded a small post in Chile in the hope of establishing permanent contact.[55]

More sustained and more successful efforts were made by the Dutch to sap the Kings of Spain and Portugal's power in Asia. Although the admirals of the 'voorcompagnieën' were instructed to avoid armed conflict with other Europeans in the Far East, after 1602 and the merger of the companies into the Vereenigde Oostindische Compagnie, aggression against the Portuguese and the Spaniards became an established feature of Dutch operations in Asia.[56]

In 1602 a Dutch expedition under Joris van Spilsbergen arrived in Ceylon, the centre of cinnamon production, bearing an offer from Prince Maurice of Nassau to aid the King of Kandy against the Portuguese. The offer was renewed in 1612 and it was eventually taken up in 1636: for twenty years the Dutch and the King of Kandy co-operated to expel the Portuguese from the island.[57] Much the same pattern of anti-Iberian activity was repeated elsewhere: on the Coromandel coast of India (where the Dutch established trading contacts in 1605, thanks to the intervention of a local Jewish resident), in Indonesia, in China and above all in Japan.[58]

The first Dutch trading mission to Japan arrived in 1609 and at once the 'merchants' set about discrediting the Iberian powers, which had conducted trade with the Japanese for sixty years. They played upon the fears of the Japanese Court that Portuguese missionaries were trying to 'Christianize' the country. (The Dutch themselves never flouted their religion and the Japanese, like the Turks, were said to prefer the Dutch to their competitors because they were 'less Christian'.) Partly due to Dutch insinuations, the Spaniards were expelled from Japan in 1624, the Portuguese in 1636. This was a major success for the Dutch, for they became the sole middlemen in Japan's lucrative trade with the outside world, but there was a price to be paid for continued Japanese favour. In 1637 a civil rebellion broke out among the largely Christian population of Kyushu island. The Japanese government decided, partly at the suggestion of the Dutch, that the revolt was the work of the Portuguese (whose factory was at Nagasaki, on Kyushu). The government therefore decided to end all contact with the Portuguese and to extirpate all Christian worship in Japan. By 1638 the rebels, most of them Christians, were driven back and forced to take refuge in Hara castle on the coast. The imperial government ordered the Dutch factor in Japan to send his warships to attack Hara. He obeyed, and from 24 February until 12 March 1638 the Dutch ships aided the blockade of the castle. Shortly afterwards Hara surrendered and the defenders, including thousands of Christians, were massacred. The Dutch thus proved that they were 'safe', and so retained their control over Japanese foreign trade (worth 4 million florins a year). For two hundred years, thanks to the massacre of Hara, the Dutch provided the only contact between Japan and Europe.[59]

The motives of the Dutch in Japan, and in many other situations overseas, were obviously political and economic rather than religious. A measure of 'polarization' was advantageous to the interests of the Dutch economy and was bound to follow in the wake of Dutch trade. And yet there was undoubtedly an element of crusading zeal, of 'godliness' in many seemingly spiteful attacks made by the Dutch on their fellow-Europeans. Many Dutchmen clearly regarded any blow struck against Spain, whether or not it aided their struggle for 'liberation', as a blow against Roman Catholicism and therefore as something good in itself. Piet Heyn, who captured the New World silver fleet off Cuba in 1628, seems to have been seen by some as God's instrument to scourge the Catholics.[60] The efforts of the Spaniards – 'maraens' as the Dutch normally called them – to defeat or subjugate the Calvinist Republic were viewed as some sort of *crimen lesae majestatis divina*, treason to God. In the words of one of the *Geuzenliederen* ('Sea Beggar Songs'), '"Maraen" how dare you raise your sword and musket against God!'[61] This, however, was a song composed in the Netherlands. It did not reflect the sentiments of Dutchmen actually fighting in the colonies where, as Oliver Cromwell observed, gain was preferred to godliness, politics to religion.

Yet was there any alternative? Throughout their struggle with Spain, the Dutch were at a disadvantage in terms of population, size and resources. As Cornelis Pieterszoon Hooft wrote in 1617, 'Our origins were very small and modest. In comparison with the king of Spain we were like a mouse against an elephant.'[62] And although the mouse grew to formidable size, it was never really the equal of Spain or any of the other 'great powers' of Europe. The basic problem of the Republic was:

> The ambiguity of the Dutch position as a first-rate commercial power without a corresponding territorial and demographical basis. It was the problem of a nation seeking security in peace, in a world which granted no profit without power, no safety without war.[63]

I have tried to show in this paper that the preferred solution of the leaders of the Republic to this problem was to 'polarize' the vague diplomatic forces both inside and outside Europe for their own ends. In that, perhaps, lay the most significant achievement of the Dutch Revolt. As John Lothrop Motley wrote over one hundred years ago:

> The Rise of the Dutch Republic must ever be regarded as one of the leading events of modern times. Without the birth

of this great commonwealth, the various historical
phenomena of the sixteenth and following centuries must
have either not existed, or have presented themselves under
essential modifications.[64]

Motley's judgement, like his prose, has stood the test of time.

Appendix

A DUTCH SPY IN SPANISH AMERICA: ADRIAAN RODRÍGUEZ

In his *Toortse der Zee-Vaert* of 1623 Dierick Ruiters (who had
lived in South America between 1617 and 1621) drew attention
to the large number of Jews resident there, who might serve as
allies of the Dutch. Although he mentioned no names, one of these
discontented Jews was undoubtedly Adriaan Rodríguez, living
in Callao, the principal port of Peru. Rodríguez was a Portuguese
Jew who had taken refuge in Leiden in Holland, working as a
carpenter. In 1599 he set sail as a ship's carpenter aboard the
fleet of van Noort, which was to circumnavigate the globe, but
his ship was wrecked off Peru. Rodríguez and twenty-five other
Dutch survivors were kept in prison (although Rodríguez was
allowed out on parole and did some carpentry) until 1604, when
he was repatriated (via Seville) as part of a general exchange of
prisoners-of-war. Rodríguez found conditions more attractive in
the New World, however, and as soon as the Twelve Years' Truce
was signed he set sail from the Netherlands for Callao again.

It may well be that from this point onwards Rodríguez was
acting as a spy, a 'sleeper' in the best spy-story tradition, waiting
for the day when he could be useful. Certainly when in May 1624
the fleet of Jacques L'Hermite arrived off Callao, they had with
them full reports of the garrisons, batteries and treasure in the
port provided by Rodríguez. Moreover, when Rodríguez's room
was searched, letters to him from Prince Maurice were found,
while under torture he revealed detailed knowledge of the composition and movements of the Dutch fleet.

However, Rodríguez may only have been recruited for Dutch
espionage in 1623, since two more spies arrived in Lima in that
year direct from Holland. In matters of espionage, where complete
secrecy is essential, it is often almost impossible to establish the
truth. Rodríguez was only discovered (and thus granted a sort of
immortality) because some Spaniards from Callao were captured
by the L'Hermite fleet and later released; when they got back to

Callao, they denounced Rodríguez – presumably because they had heard his name mentioned on the Dutch fleet. They also testified to the impressive organization and preparation that had gone into the operation against Callao; they knew that the Dutch had intended to free the Negro slaves in Peru and arm them with the special weapons brought from Holland for the purpose. Only an unexpectedly swift reaction by the Spanish viceroy cheated L'Hermite of his prize.

Cf. W. Voorbeijtel Cannenburg, *De Reis om de Wereld van de Nassausche Vloot, 1623–26* (Den Haag, 1964), pp. cxv–cxvi, and G. Lohmann Villena, *Las Defensas Militares de Lima y Callao* (Seville, 1964), p. 50. Neither author knew of the other's work. Lohmann Villena cites the two crucial documents: Archivo Histórico Nacional (Madrid), *Inquisición legajo* 1647, no. 7, the confession of Rodríquez, and *libro* 1030/296–303, a report on his case. Both documents deserve to be published.

For further evidence of Jewish–Dutch collusion, cf. Lohmann Villena, 'Una incognita despejada; la identidad del judio portugues, autor de la "Descricion general del Piru" ' in: *Revista de Indias.* 119–122. (1970) 315–87 (e.g. pp. 317–54, (–6); J. A. Gonsalves da Mello, *Tempos dos Flamengos. Influência da Ocupação Holandesa na Vida e na Cultura do Norte do Brasil* (Rio de Janeiro, 1947), pp. 290–311.

For the Jews in Spanish America and the risk they constituted, see: A. Dominguez Ortiz, *Los Judeoconversos en España y América* (Madrid, 1971), pp. 250–3 and J. I. Israel, 'The Portuguese in seventeenth-century Mexico', *Jahrbuch für Geschichte Latein Amerikas*, XI (1974), pp. 12–32.

Notes

1 G. N. Clark, *The Seventeenth Century* (London, 1929); 2nd edn (London, 1945), p. 98.
2 H. J. C. von Grimmelshausen, *Der Abenteurliche Simplicissimus Teutsch* (1669), ed. A. von Keller (Stuttgart, 1862–3), I, 3, Chs 4 and 5: 'Von dem Teutschen Helden, der die gantze Welt bezwingen und zwischen allen Völkern Fried stifften werden' and 'Wie er die Religionen miteinander vereinigen und in einen Model glessen wird'.
3 Report of Gaspar van Vosbergen to the States-General in 1625, quoted in G. W. Vreede, *Inleiding tot eene Geschiedenis der Nederlandsche Diplomatie*, I (Utrecht, 1856), p. 1. See also the

view of Christopher Hill, *Puritanism and Revolution* (London, 1958), p. 127: 'The Dutch Revolt played a similar part in the politics and thought of the early seventeenth century to that of the Spanish Civil War in the 1930s, only for a longer period.'

4 J. Meerman, quoted Vreede, op. cit. For a more extended analysis of why the Dutch revolt succeeded cf. G. Parker, 'Why did the Dutch Revolt last so long?' in *Transactions of the Royal Historical Society*, XXVI (1976), pp. 53–72.

5 G. Groen van Prinsterer, *Archives ou correspondance de la maison d'Orange-Nassau*, 1ère série II (Leiden, 1835), p. 397; Brederode to Count Louis, 11 August 1565. For a fuller discussion of the connection between the Dutch Revolt and the Ottoman naval offensive in the Mediterranean cf. G. Parker, *The Dutch Revolt* (London, 1977), p. 286 n. 46.

6 Cf. Parker, op. cit., p. 290 n. 19.

7 Information from W. Hahlweg, *Der Augsburger Reichstag von 1566* (Neukirchen, 1964), pp. 197–209; J. V. Polišenský, *Nizozemská Politika a Bílá Hora* (The Bohemian War and Dutch Policy, 1618–20) (Prague, 1958), pp. 94–6; N. Mout, *Bohemen en de Nederlanden in de 16e eeuw* (Leiden, 1975), pp. 28–9; B. Chudoba, *Spain and the Empire, 1519–1643* (Chicago, 1952), pp. 134–8.

8 The early contacts between Protestantism and the Turks were noted by Ranke. For more recent surveys cf. S. Fischer-Galati, *Ottoman Imperialism and German Protestantism, 1521–55* (Oxford, 1959), *passim*, and K. M. Setton, 'Lutheranism and the Turkish peril' in *Journal of Balkan Studies*, III (1962), 133–68. Cf. the letters of the Landgrave of Hesse to William of Orange in Groen van Prinsterer, *Archives* (cf., for example, II, pp. 70–3).

9 F. Strada, *De la Guerre Civile de Flandre*, II (Brussels, 1712), p. 343. Although Strada *may* have fabricated the story, the evidence points towards authenticity. The Duke of Naxos certainly possessed direct contact with Antwerp, where he had lived for about nine years as a junior partner in one of the city's Portuguese banks. Since several 'Marranos' were prominent in the Antwerp consistory in 1566, and since they would have been known to Miques personally, the additional information provided by Strada (possibly from documents destroyed at Naples in 1943) must be taken seriously. Cf. on the Duke of Naxos: C. Roth, *The House of Nasi: the Duke of Naxos* (Philadelphia, 1948), pp. 58–62; and P. Grunebaum-Ballin, *Joseph Naci, Duc de Naxos* (Paris, 1968), p. 140 (the Duke was probably taken by Christopher Marlowe as the model for his *Jew of Malta*). On the Antwerp Marranos, the latest word is by B. A. Vermaseren, 'De Antwerpse koopman Martin Lopez en zijn familie' in *Bijdragen tot de Geschiedenis*, LVI (1973), pp. 3–79.

10 E. Charrière, *Négociations de la France dans le Levant*, III (Paris, 1853), p. 61 ('L'homme du prince d'Orange qui est chez Micques . . .'), and Grunebaum-Ballin, op. cit., p. 61 (quoting Charrière and a Venetian source).

11 H. Inalcik, 'The origin of the Ottoman–Russian rivalry and the
    Don-Volga canal (1569)' in *Annales de l'Université d'Ankara*, I
    (1946–7), pp. 47–110; A. C. Hess, 'The Moriscos: an Ottoman
    Fifth Column in sixteenth-century Spain' in *American Historical
    Review*, LXXIV (1968), pp. 1–25 (especially pp. 14–16); on the
    ways in which the Ottomans gained information about Spanish
    affairs, see N. H. Biegman, *The Turco-Ragusan Relationship
    According to the Firmāns of Murad III (1575–95)* (Paris–The Hague,
    1967), Ch. 6, and Biegman, 'Ragusan spying for the Ottoman
    empire', *Türk Tarih Kurumu Belleten*, XXVII (1963), pp. 237–49.

12 N. M. Sutherland, *The Massacre of St Bartholomew and the
    European Conflict 1559–72* (London, 1973), p. 133 onwards; plus
    two older studies apparently not consulted by Dr Sutherland:
    P. J. van Herwerden, *Het Verblijf van Lodewijk van Nassau in
    Frankrijk* (Assen, 1932), Ch. 5, and J. C. Devos, 'Un projet
    de cession d'Alger à la France en 1572' in *Bulletin philosophique et
    historique*, LXXVIII (1953–4), pp. 339–48.

13 Groen van Prinsterer, *Archives*, IV, p. 396, Orange to Count John
    of Nassau, 7 May 1574. The letter continued: 'And if the poor
    inhabitants of this country, abandoned by the whole world, still
    wish to persevere in their struggle . . . it will cost the Spaniards a
    good half of Spain, both in men and in goods, before they
    manage to make an end of us.' Orange was right.

14 Charrière, *Négociations de la France*, III, pp. 477–82; G. Parker,
    'Spain, her enemies and the revolt of the Netherlands, 1559–1628'
    in *Past and Present*, XLIX (1970), p. 85; Stephen Gerlach, *Tage-
    Buch* (Frankfurt, 1674), p. 51 (on contact between the Porte and
    Beza in March 1574; Gerlach was the chaplain of the Imperial
    ambassador at Constantinople).

15 Hess, 'The moriscos', pp. 19–21 (a passage of critical importance
    because it draws on Ottoman sources).

16 L. Didier, *Lettres et négociations de Claude de Mondoucet, resident
    de France aux Pays-Bas (1571–74)*, II (Paris, 1892), pp. 338–9,
    letter of 23 October 1574: 'On account of this disaster which has
    occurred at Tunis', Mondoucet argued, Philip II would seek a
    settlement in the Netherlands, 'in order to be able to turn all his
    resources and troops against the Turks and offer a more spirited
    resistance there, since the war in the Mediterranean is more
    important to Spain.' On 13 November 1574 the provincial
    government in North Holland was informed of the fall of Tunis
    which would mean, they surmised, 'that the pressure of Spain
    on these provinces will be diminished' (Rijksarchief, Noord
    Holland, *Archief van Gecommitteerde Raden*, 131 fo. 84; reference
    kindly communicated by Mr A. C. Duke).

17 C. Roth, *The House of Naxos*, p. 61; Gerlach, *Tage-Buch*,
    pp. 327–8; J. A. Goris, 'Turksche kooplieden te Antwerpen in de
    XVIe eeuw' in *Bijdragen tot de Geschiedenis*, XIV (1922), pp. 30–8.
    The first Dutch ambassador to the Porte only arrived in 1612;
    D. M. Vaughan, *Europe and the Turk* (Liverpool, 1954), pp. 145–6.

18 *Calendar of State Papers Foreign in the Reign of Elizabeth, 1586-88,*
pp. 508-9: petition to the Sultan by Ambassador William
Harborne, 9 November 1587. Cf. also H. G. Rawlinson, 'The
embassy of William Harborne to Constantinople, 1583-88' in
Transactions of the Royal Historical Society, 4th series, V (1922),
pp. 1-27.

19 *The Somers Collection of Tracts,* ed. W. Scott, I (London, 1809),
pp. 164-70: 'Advice' of Lord Burghley. On the negotiations which
led up to the treaty between England and the Dutch cf. C. H.
Wilson, *Queen Elizabeth and the Revolt of the Netherlands*
(London, 1970), pp. 79-85.

20 Archive du Ministère des Affaires Etrangères, Paris, *Correspondance
de Hollande,* IV, fos. 177-178v, 'Maladies de l'estat de Hollande'
(August 1587: part of the papers of the Earl of Leicester). The
anti-Dutch alliance of Philip II even extended to the Baltic where
King Stephen Bathory of Poland threatened to cut off Dutch
trade with Danzig unless they made peace with Spain: L.
Boratynski, 'Esteban Batory, La Hansa, y la sublevación de los
Paises Bajos' in *Boletín de la Real Academia de la Historia,* CXXVIII
(1951), pp. 451-500. For an assessment of the feasibility of the
Armada campaign, see G. Parker, 'If the Armada had landed',
History, LXI (1976), pp. 358-68.

21 Details on the Spanish payments from Parker, *The Dutch Revolt,*
pp. 226-7; details on the papal assistance from I. Cloulas,
'L'armée pontificale . . . pendant la seconde campagne en France de
Alexandre Farnèse (1591-2)' in *Bulletin de la Commission royale
d'histoire,* CXXVI (1960), pp. 83-102; and A. de Mosto.
'Ordinamenti militari delle soldatesche dello stato romano nel
secolo xvi' in *Quellen und Forschungen aus Italienische Archiven und
Bibliotheken,* VI (1904), pp. 72-133 (cf. p. 102).

22 Details on German aid in B. Vogler, 'Le rôle des Electeurs
palatins dans les guerres de religion en France, 1559-92' in
Cahiers d'Histoire, X (1965), pp. 51-85, and C. P. Clasen, *The
Palatinate in European History, 1555-1618* (Oxford, 1966),
pp. 5-19. England's aid during these years is described by H. A.
Lloyd, *The Rouen Campaign, 1590-92* (Oxford, 1973), pp. 81-103,
and C. G. Cruickshank, *Elizabeth's Army* (Oxford, 1966), pp.
236-51.

23 On the Emden occupation (which was made permanent in 1599),
cf. J. den Tex, *Oldenbarnevelt, II: Oorlog 1588-1609* (Haarlem,
1962), pp. 437-41; on the Dutch subsidies to Henry IV, cf. ibid.,
pp. 63-99.

24 J. H. H. Siccama, *Schets van de Diplomatieke Betrekkingen
Tusschen Nederland en Brandenburg, 1596-1678* (Utrecht, 1867),
pp. 12-13.

25 F. Boersma, 'De diplomatieke reis van Daniel van der Meulen
en Nicholaes Bruyninck naar het Duitse leger bij Emmerik,
Augustus 1599' in *Bijdragen en Mededelingen Betreffende de
Geschiedenis der Nederlanden,* LXXXIV (1969), pp. 24-66.

26 Siccama, op. cit., p. 40.

27 D. Buisseret, *Sully* (London, 1968), p. 82, gives the annual
    subsidies, which averaged 2 million livres. This sum represented
    about 10 per cent of Henry IV's total income – a generous effort.
    On Dutch efforts to prevent the peace of Vervins and to expedite
    regular payment of the subsidy, cf. S. Barendrecht, *François van
    Aerssen, Diplomaat aan het Franse Hof (1598–1613)* (Leiden,
    1965), Chs 3 and 8–10. On the significance of Philip II's
    preoccupation with France, cf. Parker, *The Dutch Revolt*, Ch. 6.

28 J. Heringa, *De Eer en Hoogheid van de Staat. Over de Plaats der
    Verenigde Nederlanden in het Diplomatieke Leven van de 17e eeuw*
    (Groningen, 1961), pp. 252–3. The Dutch consulates that were
    opened in the Mediterranean during the seventeenth century are
    listed in H. Waetjen, *Die Niederländen im Mittelmeergebiet zur
    Zeit ihrer höchsten Machtstellung* (Berlin, 1909), pp. 111–13.

29 E. van Reyd, *Historie der Nederlandtscher Oorlogen . . . tot den
    jare 1601* (Leeuwarden, 1650), p. iii.

30 L. van Aitzema, *Saken van Staet ende Oorlog*, I (Amsterdam,
    1669), p. 1103. Texts for most of the treaties are printed in this
    work and may be conveniently found by consulting the index of
    each volume under 'Accoord' and 'Tractaet', or under the name of
    each country.

31 van Aitzema, op. cit., I, p. 146: treaty with the King of Algiers,
    July 1622.

32 Francis Bacon, *Certaine Miscellany Works* (London, 1629), p. 32.

33 330,551 florins of 60 *kreizers* (or 33.3 *pattards*; the Dutch florin
    was worth 20 pattards) were paid for the war in Friuli by the
    Spanish ambassador to the Imperial Court, Don Balthasar de
    Zúñiga, between March 1616 and January 1617. In all, between
    July 1608 and February 1617 Zúñiga spent 1,482,392 florins of 60
    kreizers, much of it in pensions and bribes (51,478 florins to the
    Cardinal-Elector of Cologne, 22,500 to Cardinal Khlesl, chief
    adviser of the Emperor Matthias, and so on); cf. Archivo General
    de Simancas (Spain), *Contaduría Mayor de Cuentas 3a época*, no.
    669, audited accounts of Zúñiga; Zúñiga's predecessor, Don
    Guillén de San Clemente, spent a further 600,000 florins during his
    embassy between 1599 and 1608; more still was sent from Spain to
    finance a detachment of Spanish troops fighting at Philip III's
    expense in Hungary: cf. Marques de Ayerbe, *Correspondencia
    Inédita de Don Guillén de San Clemente* (Zaragoza, 1892), pp. 315–99.

34 Chudoba, *Spain and the Empire*, pp. 225–48. There is much new
    material in P. Brightwell, 'Spain and the Origins of the Thirty
    Years' War' (unpublished Cambridge University Ph.D. thesis, 1967).

35 Figures from D. Albrecht, *Die Deutsche Politik Papst Gregors XV*,
    (Schriftenreihe zur bayerischen Landesgeschichte no. 53), p. 13
    n. 28. The total cost of papal aid to the Catholic cause in 1618–23
    (763,000 *scudi*) should be compared with the total cost of papal
    aid to the Emperor in 1595–6 during the war in Hungary
    (600,000 *scudi*: cf. de Mosto, op. cit.).

36 Detailed figures in D. Albrecht, 'Zur Finanzierung des Dreissigjährigen Krieges. Die Subsidien der Kurie für Kaiser und Liga, 1618–35' in *Zeitschrift für Bayerischen Landesgeschichte*, XIX (1956), pp. 534–67, and *Die Auswortige Politik Maximilians von Bayern, 1618–35* (Göttingen, 1962), pp. 37–42 and 198–200.

37 Archivo General de Simancas, *Contaduría Mayor de Cuentas 3a época*, no. 949, audited accounts of Nicolas Vizente Escorza, *Pagador General de Alemaña* (in florins of 60 kreizers or 33.3 pattards):

April 1635 – April 1637 803,564
April 1637 – September 1640 (sic) 2,673,382
March 1640 – August 1641 865,944
August 1641 – March 1643 997,094

Unfortunately I have not yet been able to find any further accounts of the 'Spanish treasury in Germany'.

38 The existence of an 'international' was suggested (and christened) by the Dutch historian A. A. van Schelven, 'Der Generalstab des politischen Calvinismus in Zentraleuropa zu Beginn des Dreissigjährigen Krieges' in *Archiv für Reformationsgeschichte*, XXXVI (1939), pp. 117–41. Two important members of the 'General Staff' have been the subject of major biographies since van Schelven: H. Sturmberger, *Georg Erasmus Tschernembl: Religion, Libertät und Widerstand* (Linz, 1953); F. H. Schubert, *Ludwig Camerarius (1573–1651). Eine Biographie* (Kallmünz, 1955). For some perceptive remarks on the central European members of the 'international' (and much more besides), cf. R. J. W. Evans, *Rudolf II and his World* (Oxford, 1973), pp. 5–42. See also R. Kleinman, 'Charles Emanuel I of Savoy and the Bohemian election of 1619' in *European Studies Review*, 5 (1975), pp. 3–29.

39 E. Wrangel, *De Betrekkingen Tusschen Zweden en de Nederlanden . . . Voornamelijk Gedurende de 17e eeuw* (Leiden, 1901), Ch. 1; P. Geyl, *Christofforo Suriano. Resident van de Serenissime Republiek van Venetië in den Haag, 1616–23* (Den Haag, 1913), Chs 1–3; J. G. Smit, ed., *Resolutien der Staten-Generaal*, n.r. III (R.G.P. grote serie 152, Den Haag, 1975) resolutions 816, 817, 1000. News of the proposal to send Dutch troops to Savoy reached Spain and provoked the Council of War to declare that the Twelve Years' Truce would be broken if any aid was sent (Archivo General de Simancas, *Guerra Antigua* no. 808, unfol., *consultas* of 16,26 and 28 December 1616). In the end, no aid was sent. Cf. also L. Pearsall Smith, *The Life and Letters of Sir Henry Wotton*, 2 vols (Oxford, 1907), pp. 111–12, 152–6, 180–3.

40 J. V. Polišenský, *Nizozemska Politika a Bílá Hora* (Prague, 1958): this study reveals how little *political* contact there was between Bohemia and the States-General before 1618; J. V. Polisenskij, *Anglie a Bílá Hora* (The Bohemian War and British policy) (Prague, 1949). Both these books have useful English summaries. See also F. A. Yates, *The Rosicrucian Enlightenment* (London, 1972), *passim* (e.g. p. 90).

41 The quotation comes from S. R. Gardiner, *Letters and Other Documents Illustrating the Relations between England and Germany*, II (London, 1868), p. 7 (Dudley Carleton to Secretary of State Naughton 13 September 1619 new Style); figures for Dutch aid from Polišenský, *Nizozemska Politiká*, p. 335. The States-General's Staat van Oorlog, however, voted to send over 1,000,000 florins to Bohemia (cf. Algemeen Rijksarchief, Den Haag, *Raad van State*, nos. 1499 and 1500, *Sub annis*, 1618–21).

42 Quotation in A. Soman (ed.), *The Massacre of St. Bartholomew; Reappraisals and Documents* (Den Haag, 1974), p. 254. The tentacles extended further at times, even to Moscow and Constantinople. See F. L. Baumer, 'England, the Turk and the common corps of Christendom', in: *American Historical Review*, L (1944–45), pp. 26–48. In the 1630s the Orthodox church leaders tried to establish a rapport with the Calvinists at Geneva and Leiden. See B. F. Porshnev, 'Les rapports politiques de l'Europe occidentale et de l'Europe orientale à l'époque de la guerre de trente ans' in: *Rapports du XIe Congrès des Sciences Historiques*, IV (Stockholm, 1960), pp. 136–63 and P. G. Westin, *Negotiations about Church Unity, 1628–34: John Durie, Gustavus Adolphus, Axel Oxenstierna* (Uppsala, 1932), pp. 57–60.

43 Although the distinguished Czech historian J. V. Polišenský referred to the years 1621–5 as the 'Dutch period' of the Thirty Years' War (*The Thirty Years' War* (London, 1971) Ch. 5), the German historian F. H. Schubert has made out a convincing case for regarding the Calvinist exiles from the Palatinate as the driving force in the polarization of European politics during the 1620s: cf. his biography of Camerarius (n. 38 above), and his articles 'Die pfälzische Exilregierung im Dressigjährigen Krieg. Ein Beitrag zur Geschichte des politischen Protestantismus' in: *Zeitschrift für Geschichte des Oberrheins*, CII (1954), pp. 575–680, and 'Die Niederlande zur Zeit des Dreissigjährigen Krieges im Urteil des Diplomatischen Korps im Haag' in: *Historisches Jahrbuch*, LXXIV (1955), pp. 252–64. In his latest book, Polišenský appears to accept this view: *Documenta Bohemica Bellum Tricennale Illustrantia, 1. Der Krieg und die Gesellschaft in Europa, 1618–48* (Prague, 1971), pp. 109–15.

44 On the limitations of the Dutch diplomatic service, cf. M. A. M. Franken, 'The general tendencies and structural aspects of the foreign policy and diplomacy of the Dutch Republic in the latter half of the seventeenth century' in: *Acta Historiae Neerlandicae*, III (1968), pp. 1–42.

45 The *Staten van Oorlog* are to be found in ARA *Raad van State*, 1499 and 1500; the Portuguese intervention is described by M. de Jong, 'Holland en de Portuguese restauratie van 1640', in *Tijdschrift voor Geschiedenis*, LV (1940), pp. 225–53, and C. van de Haar, *De Diplomatieke Betrekkingen Tussen de Republiek en Portugal, 1640–61* (Groningen, 1961), Ch. 3; the abortive efforts to send aid to the 'revolutie in Catalogne' are chronicled in van Aitzema, *Saken van*

Staet ende Oorlog, II, p. 729. Cf. also J. H. Elliott, *The Revolt of the Catalans* (Cambridge, 1963), p. 538. On the nature of Dutch foreign policy at this time, cf. the perceptive analysis of E. H. Kossmann, *In Praise of the Dutch Republic; Some Seventeenth-century Attitudes* (London, 1963), pp. 3–8.

46 van Aitzema, *Saken*, I, p. 905.

47 R. Hackluyt, 'Discourse of Western Planting' (1584), in E. G. R. Taylor (ed.), *The Original Writings and Correspondence of the Two Richard Hackluyts* (London, 1935), p. 249. For the nature of the maritime conflict between England and Spain, cf. K. R. Andrews, *Elizabethan Privateering. English Privateering during the Spanish War, 1585–1603* (Cambridge, 1964).

48 J. de Laet, *Iaerlyck Verhael van de Verrichtingen der Geoctroyeerde West-Indische Compagnie* (1644), ed. S. P. L'Honoré Naber and J. C. M. Warnsinck, I (Den Haag, 1931), p. 2.

49 B. Keen, 'The Black Legend revisted', in *Hispanic-American Historical Review*, XLIV (1969), pp. 703–19; J. G. van Dillen, 'De West-Indische Compagnie, het Calvinisme en de politiek', in *Tijdschrift voor Geschiedenis*, LXXIV (1961), pp. 145–71.

50 W. Voorbeijtel Cannenburg (ed.), *De Reis om de Wereld van de Nassausche Vloot, 1623–6* (Den Haag, 1964), p. xx. The fleet was instructed to continue the contacts made by Spilsbergen with the Indians of Chile (ibid., p. xix).

51 Dierick Ruiters, *Toortse de Zee-vaert* (Flushing, 1623), ed. S. P. L'Honoré Naber (Den Haag, 1909), p. 35. On the Jews in Spanish America, cf. L. Garcia de Proodian, *Los Judios en América. Sus Actividades en los Virreinatos de Nueva Castilla y Nueva Grenada en el SigloXVII* (Madrid, 1966), pp. 93–4; and J. A. Gonsalves da Mello, *Tempo dos Flamengos. Influencia da Ocupacao Holandesa na Vida e na Cultura do Norte do Brasil* (Rio de Janeiro, 1947), pp. 268–70 and 290–311 (from 1636 the Dutch authorities permitted a synagogue, rabbi and Jewish printing press in Recife).

52 As with all matters of espionage, a charge like this is hard to substantiate. Evidence against one 'marrano spy' is therefore included in the Appendix on p. 73.

53 The standard account of the Dutch assaults on Brazil is C. R. Boxer, *The Dutch in Brazil, 1624–54* (Oxford, 1954). On Bahía itself, cf. T. de Azevedo, *Povoamento da Cidade do Salvador* (Bahía, 1969): the city had a white population of around 8,000 in 1624 (p. 156). Cf. also J. Pérez de Tudela, *Sobre la Defensa Hispana del Brasil contra los Holandeses, 1624–50* (Madrid, 1974). On the Dutch attack on Peru, cf. G. Lohmann Villena, *Las Defensas Militares de Lima y Callao* (Seville, 1964), Part I, Ch. 2.

54 Cf. Boxer, op. cit., and *Salvador de Sá and the Struggle for Brazil and Angola, 1602–86* (London, 1952). A perceptive short study is also to be recommended: E. Sluiter, 'Dutch maritime power and the colonial status quo, 1585–1641', in *Pacific Historical Review*, XI (1942), pp. 29–41.

55 Lohmann Villena, op. cit., p. 93. On the Dutch and Peru in general cf. P. Gerhard, *Pirates on the West Coast of New Spain, 1575–1642* (Glendale, Ill., 1960), Ch. 3. The Spaniards had always feared an alliance between the Dutch and the Araucanian Indians. One of the best reflections of this fear was written by the great luminary of the Golden Age, Quevedo, in 1635–36: D. A. Fernández-Guerra y Orbe (ed.), *Obras de Don Francisco de Quevedo Villegas*, I (Madrid, 1946), pp. 407ff. (*La Hora de Todos*, no. 36, 'Los de Chile y los Holandeses', and 39, 'La isla de los monopantos').

56 N. Steensgaard, *The Asian Trade Revolution of the Seventeenth Century* (Chicago, 1974), pp. 131–41. Steensgaard effectively refutes the rival theory of M. A. P. Meilink-Roelofsz, 'Aspects of Dutch colonial development in Asia in the seventeenth century', in J. S. Bromley and E. H. Kossmann (eds), *Britain and the Netherlands in Europe and Asia* (London, 1968), pp. 56–82 (cf. pp. 70–1).

57 K. W. Goonewardena, *The Foundation of Dutch Power in Ceylon, 1638–58* (Amsterdam, 1959), pp. 6–22.

58 T. Raychaudhuri, *Jan Company in Coromandel, 1605–1690* (Den Haag, 1962), pp. 15, 22–5; Chang T'ien Tsê, *Sino-Portuguese Trade from 1514 to 1644* (Leiden, 1934), p. 118.

59 A special Japanese word was coined for Dutch studies (*rangaku*), and it came as a sad shock when the *rangaku* scholars discovered in 1853 that Dutch, the only European language that they knew, was not spoken by the entire world outside Japan. Cf. G. K. Goodman, *The Dutch Impact on the Japanese, 1640–1853* (Leiden, 1967), pp. 1–25; A. Hyma, *The Dutch in the Far East, A History of the Dutch Commercial and Colonial Empire* (Ann Arbor, 1942), Ch. 6; and C. R. Boxer, *The Christian Century in Japan, 1549–1650* (Berkeley, 1951).

60 Cf. the quotation, in K. Ratelband (ed.), *De Westafrikaanse Reis van Piet Heyn, 1624–1625* (Den Haag, 1959), pp. xxxiii–xxxix (from Spranckhuysen's funeral oration of 1629).

61 Adriaen Valerius, *Nederlandtsche Gedenck-Clanck* (Haarlem, 1626; re-edited Amsterdam, 1942), p. 176.

62 C. P. Hooft, *Memorien en Adviezen van Cornelis Pieterszoon Hooft*, I (Utrecht, 1871), p. 182.

63 J. W. Smit, 'The Netherlands and Europe in the seventeenth and eighteenth centuries', in J. S. Bromley and E. H. Kossmann, op. cit., p. 16.

64 J. L. Motley, *The Rise of the Dutch Republic* (London, 1856), p. i.: these words are, in fact, the first of Motley's epic narrative.

Chapter four

Did Holland's Golden Age Coincide with a Period of Crisis?*

Ivo Schöffer

It sometimes seems as if the seventeenth century, wedged between the sixteenth and eighteenth centuries, has no features of its own. With Renaissance and Reformation on the one side, Enlightenment and Revolution on the other, for the century in between we are left with but vague terms like 'transition' and 'change'. To trace the titles of history textbooks dealing with the seventeenth century is often amusing. They frequently illuminate only one aspect, occasionally not very typical, of that century. Sometimes a re-shuffling of the international cards is considered most significant: 'From Spanish to French Ascendancy'; or emphasis is placed on the rise of monarchical power: 'The Age of Absolutism'. The same incertitude prevails in economic history: the sixteenth century is grouped round the international phenomenon of the price revolution, the eighteenth century is interpreted in the light of the Industrial Revolution; for the seventeenth century, however, we read only fragmentary treatment, country by country, with mercantilism brought forward as the only common international politico-economic trend.

Now it can be objected that such observations merely strengthen the case against typifying any century at all; indeed, it may appear as a positive advantage when a century for once does not bear an indelible stamp. It is perhaps not justifiable to plot historic development in separate centuries. We have to go back as far as the year AD 1000 to find a turn of the century that was actually realized by its contemporaries as a turning point, and the very disappointment or relief at finding that that year brought no change should warn us against being too hasty in handling full

* Lecture held at the General Meeting of the Historisch Genootschap at Utrecht, November 1963; published in *Bijdragen en Mededelingen van het Historisch Genootschap*, LXXVIII (1964), pp. 45–72, and reprinted in *Acta Historiae Neerlandica*, I (1966), pp. 82–107. It appears here by permission of the publishers of the *Acta*, E. J. Brill.

centuries as periods. Trends and developments do not in fact take 31 December or 1 January into account, and pass unnoticed from the year 99 to 100. But in spite of these rational objections, the desire to treat a century as an era does not seem to die down. For example when a German textbook allows the Reformation and Counter Reformation to run on till 1660 and from that point lets a period of Absolutism continue till 1789, our traditional feelings rise in protest whether we wish it or not.[1] Has there never been a seventeenth century, we wonder. Did not that age possess any typical features and peculiarities; was there really no place for such a period in the general development of European civilization? It may be traditionalism, against our better judgement, but we just simply have to give the seventeenth century a place of its own. Our imagination needs it.

This desire to conceive and depict a period in the history of a greater area than a state, region or city has increased of late. Now that national confines are being felt as oppressive and the wider international coherence of modern nations and states is in any case being admitted, this has also its consequences for our understanding of the past. Attempts to grasp the complete history of mankind straightaway as one whole may have been slightly forced. Contacts between the various parts of the world and the different great civilizations were often quite superficial in the past, and because of this we are once again obliged to take Europe as the focal point. But for regions and countries close to each other in culture and geography attempts to understand a certain period comprehensively makes good sense. This, too, can lead to a dangerous myth formation – such as the magnifying of historic figures like Charlemagne or Charles V into 'European' heroes – and a firm stand should be taken against such anachronisms. But to raise historical writing above politico-national frontiers, to examine experiences common to several European countries, is generally to be applauded, although one need not insist upon such an approach to the exclusion of more traditional historical investigations. For this reason, I should like to discuss seriously and appreciatively the efforts made since the last war to give the seventeenth century an image of its own.

I shall certainly not detract from any other effort in this direction if I pay most attention to Roland Mousnier's impressive and enthralling book on *Les XVIe et XVIIe Siècles*, published in the 'Histoire Générale des Civilisations' series, vol. IV in 1954.[2]

Mousnier, an expert in seventeenth-century French history, gives us in this book, among other things, a comprehensive study of the development of Europe in 'his' century. Within the narrow limits of 200 pages he succeeds in summarizing and describing in close interrelationship the political, economic, social and cultural material – seemingly so disparate and so difficult to survey – of more than one century, i.e. from 1590 to 1715. He achieves this by characterizing the seventeenth century as a *century of crisis*. He announces this theme in his preface:

The seventeenth century was a time of crisis which affected all Mankind. . . . The crisis was permanent with, so to say, violent shifts in intensity. The contradictory tendencies had coexisted for a long time, entangled with each other, by turns amalgamating and combating, and there is no easy way of discerning their limits nor the date at which their relationship changed. Not only did these tendencies coexist at the same time throughout Europe, but even in the same social group, even in the same man, they were present and divisive. The state, the social group and the individual were all struggling ceaselessly to restore in their environment and in themselves order and unity.[3]

For Mousnier seventeenth-century Europe is in a phase of economic decline, intensified into a constant crisis by violent price fluctuations and fierce wars. On the social plane the contrasts become acute: nobility and bourgeoisie fly at each other's throats to preserve their own existence; the rising power of the sovereign steers a middle course through this conflict, confusing and extending it. The broad substratum of the population tries in vain to shake off their lot of hunger and misery by revolt and resistance. Internationally Europe is experiencing the decline of the supra-national power of the Pope and of Habsburg, the rise of an expansionist France with all its consequent wars. In matters of culture, Church and science are in a state of uncertainty and confusion, art flares up in the uncontrolled tragic baroque form. The struggle against this general crisis fails: all sober forms of government organization, of systems of thought such as Cartesianism or of soberness of style as in Classicism, of international ideas regarding balance of power and international law were unable to check the crisis. This period therefore also ends in crisis: economic depression, lengthy, expensive wars, new uncertainty in thought and faith.

Since Mousnier's book this crisis in the seventeenth century has become a familiar concept. Apart from Mousnier's gripping, concise exposition, the word 'crisis' itself struck a spark that turned the dullness of the seventeenth century into colour and brightness. All kinds of seemingly unrelated events and trends that made no contact fell into place in a greater whole. The profound tragedy of the seventeenth century suddenly became apparent. The whole baroque style of art, often so difficult for us to understand and appreciate, received from it a new dimension; its dramatic quality and suspense could be understood as fundamental. The idea of crisis therefore found great favour. Historians who from the history-of-culture point of view were familiar with the baroque concept in more general terms than the strictly stylistic–aesthetic definition seized upon the idea. The idea of crisis appealed strongly to English scholars who, by placing the English 1640–60 revolution within the larger context of European developments, sought to free England from insular isolation. Already before the war in 1938 the American historian Merriman pointed out that there had been 'six contemporaneous revolutions' which could be studied in their interrelationship: beside the English revolution he mentioned the Fronde in France, the rebellion in Catalonia, Naples and Portugal and Stadtholder William II's attack on Amsterdam. But Merriman's working out of the ascertained contemporaneousness did not extend beyond a land-by-land description of the points of cross-contact for the various parties in two revolutions at a time. These points of contact were mostly on the diplomatic plane or had led sometimes to one being ideologically influenced by another.[4]

But with the concept of a general European crisis that contemporaneousness acquired a new depth: the six revolutions were as many expressions of the general European tensions, and their contemporaneity proved once more that about 1650 the crisis just *had* to come to a head. When looked for, even more contemporaneous disturbances were discovered: a revolt in Sicily in 1647, in the Ukraine in 1648, not to speak of local peasant revolts in Austria, Poland, Sweden and Switzerland and a palace revolution in Turkey. The economic historian Hobsbawm elaborated still further the idea of a seventeenth-century economic crisis in a circumstantial article in which he used the Marxist theory of social evolution as a basis.[5] Trevor-Roper took up the idea with a theory entirely his own in which he attempted to show that the crisis was one that had been caused by the abnormal rise in the cost of state organization – court, Church, army and bureaucracy – which, too, had raised so much opposition by their waste and corruption that reforms or revolutions were inevitable.[6] Elsewhere in Spain and Italy, and I imagine also in Germany, the crisis theory was gratefully welcomed offering as it did an explanation of the decay of these very countries in that century.

In the chorus of delight Dutch voices have been practically silent.[7] This is to be understood, for how can this general crisis be made to square with the Dutch Golden Age? A glance around will show others who did not join in the chorus too gratefully: the Belgians, the Swedes, the Portuguese.[8] For their countries, too, enjoyed in this period at least a reasonable measure of prosperity, even to the extent of flourishing. No, it remains difficult to fit in Holland's period of prosperity and the well-being of other countries with the seventeenth-century crisis. Were they, and the Dutch Republic in particular, only exceptions to the rule? Or, a more searching question, is the crisis maybe a not quite satisfactory characterization of the general condition of Europe? In any case it is perhaps as well that a word of criticism be heard from the Netherlands themselves. It is a temporary dissonance in the cantata but it may in the long run lead to a better performance.

Every term that passes through many hands gets thumbed, declines in value and becomes worn out. Even in Mousnier, the term 'crisis' is fairly vague. He had to do justice to historical reality by finding a counterpart to his crisis: 'la lutte contre la crise' and only with the aid of this *pair* of concepts did he succeed at last in catching his century. Can the word 'crisis' really encompass a whole century? Is the term not more appropriate when referring to a condition of short duration, or even a decisive moment of great tension? With other historians, in fact, the 'crisis' began to change and shift in meaning owing to a desire to make it cover their point of view. With Mousnier 'crisis' still had the widest meaning. The *Shorter Oxford Dictionary* calls it 'a state of affairs in which a decisive change for better or worse is imminent'. Among Italians and Spaniards 'crisis' must have acquired rather the meaning of a 'temporary decline in prosperity'. Many English historians attach to it the meaning of 'turning point'. Baroque adherents see it as a category of general civilization: 'disturbance', 'tension'. I readily admit that all these meanings lie very close together and are related to each other. But there remain differences in meaning and when applied the word may confuse and cause discrepancies.[9]

Moreover, could not the 'crisis' be used for any period? If we consider the points brought up by Mousnier in regard to the sixteenth century we again find the term scattered about in his general characterization of the century of 'Renaissance'. For example, there is in the sixteenth century according to Mousnier 'une crise de la scolastique' and 'une crise du capitalisme' and, still more serious, even a 'crise de la Renaissance' itself. In fact, mankind proceeds from crisis to crisis. But it was surely not just this common piece of human wisdom that Mousnier wished to proclaim? Hobsbawm does, as a matter of fact, go a step further. For him the general crisis of the seventeenth century is a part of a long series of crises said to cover the whole period of transition from feudalism to capitalism, actually beginning in the thirteenth century and only ending in the nineteenth.[10] The seventeenth-century crisis is thus a crisis within a crisis, like a Chinese puzzle. Hobsbawm finds in the seventeenth century *the* crisis *par excellence* because in his opinion society only then fundamentally changed. In that very century capitalism at last burst through the chrysalis of the old feudal order.

I would think it fruitless to ponder much about the tendency to characterize the seventeenth century crisis as 'the' crisis. Trevor-Roper goes very far in this direction when he belittles the sixteenth-century changes and esteems them negligible compared with what happened in the seventeenth century.

> Speaking generally, we can say that for all the violence of its religious convulsions, the sixteenth century succeeded in absorbing its strains, its thinkers in swallowing their doubts, and at the end of it, kings and philosophers felt satisfied with the best of possible worlds.[11]

Nor could he keep this up long, for he mentions even in his own article that the Dutch Revolt in the sixteenth century already removed in the northern Netherlands what was to be elsewhere the cause of the seventeenth-century crisis, i.e. the top heavy royal court.[12] Perhaps we should award each century its own crisis, and to my mind also its own contemporaneous revolutions. It is indeed surprising that between 1640 and 1660 we can point to no less than eight such revolts and disturbances, and the supposition that there was some sort of interrelationship must have some base. But let us just see what other important contemporaneous revolutions exist in other times. I for my part found for the years round 1566, which marks the beginning of the Dutch Revolt, no less than six upheavals, and around the rebellion of Bohemia in 1618 yet another eight (see also pp. 112–13 and 128 below).

But what in my opinion is useful in this discussion of the general crisis of Europe in the seventeenth century, and deserving of further study and continuing discussion, is the question whether in this crisis any permanent strains and problems played a role that was not only typical of that century alone but was intrinsically linked up with the structure of society. That *ancien régime* possessed on the one hand a vulnerability, an instability, that is now no longer to be found in Europe, but on the other hand also a constancy, a stability that has also been lost to us. Taking these permanent characteristics as our starting point we can perhaps trace what specific influences in the seventeenth century played a part and to what extent there was then actually any question of crisis or of anything else. We shall then incidentally have to keep referring to the Dutch Republic and its possibly special character in order to obtain an impression of the place of this Republic in the general pattern of developments in Europe.

Meanwhile, one aspect of the discussion about the seventeenth-century crisis I prefer to avoid, even though I feel obliged to offer some explanation. One adherent of the seventeenth-century crisis theory, Robert Mandrou, has given much time and labour to the cultural phenomena, which, in his opinion, are a clear proof of the crisis.[13] The fact that Mandrou turned his special attention to Spanish cultural expressions weakens his article considerably, for there was in Spain an evident depression which need not directly indicate a general European crisis. Be that as it may, Mandrou points to the pathetic and passionate baroque, if you would call it so, in the Spanish folk literature of that century, lamenting the shocking, heart-rending, bitter sufferings of its own civilization in a kind of 'romantic agony'. But even if we should find exactly the same thing in other literatures and in the visual arts, I doubt if this is a proof of a state of crisis. In art all kinds of elements are so intertwined that we nod our heads to every new explanation that throws light on one aspect. Thus, for example, it was once the vogue to see in baroque something triumphantly grand, a defiant *joie de vivre*; now in contrast we discern something violently moving and a pathetic protest. On both occasions we muttered 'yes indeed'. But are these not simply continually recurrent expressions in some form or other of the eternal strains in life and society, always more acutely felt by the artist than by the man in the street? Could we not call the artist an oscillating needle of the seismography of life rather than of a particular period? How individualistically and distinctively artists react to problems of their life and times! We need only contrast the serenity and harmony in Vermeer's or De Hoogh's art with the tensely grave scenes of Rembrandt and Ruysdael to feel this. Of course we can – and must – time and again make every effort to discover in works of art what was going on in a certain era in certain circles, and we must study style, imagination, traditional forms of expression and technical possibilities to get to know in what manner the artist was at once inspired and directed. Nor do I object to the history of art being involved in general historical research – on the contrary, we 'ordinary' historians do this far too little – but I would like to utter a warning against the many snags and pitfalls to be encountered here. How often do we not find reality filtered through style-standards and tradition, diluted by the personality and the special position of the artist? Thus at this stage I should at the most dare to use the cultural expressions of the seventeenth century as illustrative or inter-pretative material, not as evidence.

Turning to economic, social and political developments in the seventeenth century we find ourselves on seemingly firmer ground. But even this is a bog of detail and uncertainty. Let us try to make our way through it with the jumping-pole of generalization. To understand the socioeconomic reality of the seventeenth century we should keep our eye fixed on the permanent, sometimes latent, structural phenomena. Above all the continuous tension between food production and food distribution on the one hand and the population's food requirements on the other created a situation where malnutrition was endemic, hunger often epidemic. This tension remained from the time the population had recovered from the disasters of the fourteenth century until far into the eighteenth century. Malnutrition was so general that even the wealthiest suffered from it, in their case due to ignorance and heedlessness. It is probable that only a relatively small part of the poorest population was permanently hungry, perhaps some 10 per cent of the total: especially town proletariat and vagrant beggars. But hunger could spread like wildfire in unfavourable times of crop failure, high prices or transport difficulties. It is possible that some 40 per cent of the population of Europe may have lived on the verge of starvation due to a one-sided distribution of prosperity and a local scarcity of food production while a seemingly very small cause might precipitate it into the abyss of famine.[14] There is no ignoring the fact – we say from the pinnacle of our achievements – that there was a great lack of organization, of skill and imagination, of economic and technical possibilities that could help to relieve or break this permanent tension, ready at any moment to discharge itself. The fact that society in those days was still preponderantly agrarian, however, tended strongly to reduce this latent tension. In most districts more than 70 to 80 per cent of the people were engaged in agriculture. Famines primarily affected the urban population and only secondarily the rural inhabitants, though, if crops failed, these too could suffer great want. In itself this preponderantly agrarian structure had also a socially stabilizing influence: the peasants lived mostly at a distance from each other and had their own traditional bonds with their landowners, while unrest plagued people living packed together in cities, where emotional relationships with the upper classes were much weaker. Here riots were more frequent than in the country, but when rural unrest did explode it was at least equally violent and atrocious.

So, partly as a result of the permanent, latent tensions, in the seventeenth century also, one insurgency, peasant revolt or civil war followed another. We need only think of the terrible peasant risings that broke out all over France between 1623 and 1648, sometimes true *jacqueries*, disrupting the whole of society and displaying in themselves all the elements of crisis.[15] There were violent epidemics, paralysing crop failures, horrific wars. We need only read Simplicissimus Deutsch or look at Callot's etchings *Les misères de la guerre* to get an impression of the ravages caused by the soldatesque, especially during the Thirty Years' War.

But were these phenomena more frequent and more serious than in previous ages? Or were they only the almost inevitable accompaniments of the old structure of society? Now, generally speaking, it is extremely difficult to plot and compare all the factors properly. We know, for instance, too little about the weather – nor shall we ever get to know enough of this to be able to say whether crop failures were then exceptionally frequent or severe.[16] We also happen to know more of the seventeenth century than we do of preceding centuries because more archive material of a time closer to us has been preserved and because bureaucratic governments began more intensively than before to record administratively and statistically the fortunes of the population. We are well informed about the plague epidemics of the seventeenth century, but it has been rightly remarked that the reason the Great Plague of London in 1665 remained so long in historical memory was that it was the last violent outbreak of such an epidemic in England. If we count the total number of epidemics in that century and compare it with that of the sixteenth century we are immediately struck by their great frequency in the sixteenth century also, and are more and more confronted with the riddle of why exactly in the eighteenth century these epidemics fell off in frequency and violence. The seventeenth century was not a particularly unfavourable exception, while on the other hand a turn for the better took place only in the eighteenth century.[17] If we then point to the serious consequences of the Thirty Years' War for great parts of Germany it is as well to remember that the French religious wars of the sixteenth century were so destructive that a part of the unrest and misery that followed must be attributed to this period of devastation.

It is odd that the Dutch Republic in the seventeenth century enjoyed comparatively great internal tranquillity. Perhaps nine-teenth-century historians saw this in too rose-coloured a light, while, in that respect, *we* have become more sensitive to the tensions in the Republic also. It would be foolish to ignore the frequently recurring urban excise riots or the acute labour conflicts in the industrial towns of Holland. But even admitting this, it does remain odd that the Republic was so peaceful as compared with other countries. Only towards the end of the century is there question of a real riot, i.e. in 1672, and also in 1696 on the occasion of the Undertakers' Riot in Amsterdam. This is all the more remarkable when we recall that the province of Holland was not preponderantly agrarian, for here more than 50 per cent of the population was urban. Moreover, as is well known, Holland was densely populated and therefore especially vulnerable to any disturbance in food production and distribution. The Republic's relatively favourable position was due largely to the economic prosperity enjoyed by the United Provinces; a prosperity so elastic that even the poorest people did not suffer real famine despite low wages and permanent malnutrition, which, for instance, became at once manifest in the outbreak of scurvy on voyages lasting more than a fortnight. The favourable circumstances of the Republic were also partly due to good diet. Thanks to cattle-breeding and the finishing industry, people got more protein in their food. Finally, food distribution was decidedly better organized than elsewhere owing to the regular import of grain from the Baltic and a well-functioning regular inland shipping.[18]

Therefore, when the pattern of unrest in seventeenth-century Europe is examined, no sufficient reason can be found for saying that this century was in an exceptional situation of crisis. Compared with the complete data of other periods we cannot say that people suffered more economic dislocation than in other periods. And from a regional point of view, the Dutch Republic, more than any other, stands out like a spot of light on the black canvas of permanent tension and misery.

Economic imbalances and a relative inflexibility, an inadequacy of response, made the economy of the *ancien régime* especially fragile. One line of business or one special product could expand economic activity in a district or country so as to make it top-heavy and susceptible therefore to unexpected collapse. Foreign competition, trade or transport disturbances or internal difficulties might suddenly wither this branch of industry. Also, speaking generally, the purchasing power of a great majority of the population was so low that prosperity in some aspect of trade or industry, agriculture or fishery depended entirely on the needs of a small élite, thus intensifying the fragile character of such prosperity. When this precarious demand failed the whole economy was temporarily shaken, since the rapid development of one activity had involved and distorted the whole internal economy. Catalonia's one-sided trade-mindedness brought terrible repercussions with the decline of Mediterranean trade at the end of the fourteenth century. Not even by the sixteenth century had the country recovered from the blow.[19] Similarly, all of Bohemia had great difficulty adjusting to the interruption of silver production in 1540.[20] Castile at the end of the sixteenth century lost the advantageous market for agricultural products in America, which was a blow struck at the heart of the Spanish empire, already staggering under other difficulties.[21]

Just as the seventeenth century had its unexpected economic collapses, so it also had its sudden developments. What happened in this century can best be described as demarcation on the one hand and on the other redistribution within these demarcated lines. The limits of the possibilities of continuing expansion were made perceptible and demonstrated by the collapse – it cannot be called otherwise – of the Spanish economic exploitation of America. The horizon of that strange, remote paradise had seemed in the sixteenth century to be eternally expanding. New estates, new mines, new masses of Indians had made a repeated shifting of the sites of exploration and exploitation possible. But now in the seventeenth century that territory, at least as far as Europe was concerned, had seemingly reached its limits: in Chile the Spanish troops had met with a bloody repulse; the native population (especially in the Caribbean area and Mexico, less so in Peru), literally decimated by disease and physical debility, could no longer be fully exploited; the mines seem to have become exhausted and the Creoles began to look after themselves and became true Americans, bothering little about their shrinking imports of wine, grain and olives from Spain.[22] Only with difficulty could new riches be amassed by the import of 'black ivory' from Africa and the cultivation of sugar and tobacco: English and Portuguese, Danes, French and Dutch would at the end of the seventeenth century in this way find new prosperity. And the same happened in Asia, though in a less obvious manner. Here the Dutch drove out the Portuguese, but the East India Company had great trouble in actually taking over what the Portuguese had given up. Moreover, the available amount of gold and silver needed for the proper functioning of Asiatic trade also imposed limits on any new English, French or Dutch initiative. Much later, the Dutch East India Company itself was to start the cultivation of plantations which opened new economic prospects for the Asiatic trade. Thus the hopes cherished for a continuing extension and expansion were extinguished: the overseas expansion of the seventeenth century was stopped by the limits of its own possibilities.

Such limitation can also be deduced from data regarding prices, monetary supplies and population. Mousnier prefers to interpret this as depression and crisis. Especially owing to the great progress made in the historical field of price research, we have many price statistics for the seventeenth century. Mousnier did indeed explicitly include them in his treatise and the whole study and discussion of these has now become the centre of interest for French historians. From these price statistics Mousnier conjures up a serious economic depression for the whole of Europe, with price fluctuations much worse than those of the sixteenth century. Whether it is correct to plot the value of precious metal in graphs, as Mousnier does, so that the picture shows a very unfavourable depression, I venture to doubt.[23] But even if we waive this, it seems unmistakable that the general trend of nominal prices, at least in the latter half of the seventeenth century, tended towards a slump.

Mousnier, and many historians with him, therefore share the ideas of the French economist Simiand who speaks of phase A for the sixteenth century, which is seriously retarded in the seventeenth century and finally turns into phase B about 1650, in which a regular slump becomes visible. And I certainly believe that there is actually such a phase B, a certain economic, and especially an agrarian, regression or depression after 1650.[24] But I mention this with every reserve, and I would not like to speak of a general economic *crisis* on the grounds of a phase B ascertained from price statistics, even if this phase did begin round about 1650. For I should like to issue a few notes of warning here. Firstly, seventeenth-century slumps are too often judged against the background of a really spectacular boom at the end of the sixteenth century. This was not a normal expansion but something exceptional even for those times of violent fluctuation. Second, I doubt whether so much faith and reliance on price statistics themselves is justified. They reflect after all only a restricted aspect of economic activity, and there is a tendency to attach disproportionate value to them because they are actually the only statistic data we possess for many countries over an extensive period in past centuries. To what extent price statistics taken alone can even mislead was recently shown by Baehrel's investigation into the economic development of the Basse Provence in the seventeenth and eighteenth centuries. He found for his district in the seventeenth century, in spite of a slump in price statistics, a surprising economic growth. He was able, in fact, to make statistics of the proceeds and value of land, and in both there appeared in the course of the seventeenth century to be even a favourable rise, indicating expansion, reclamation and soil improvement, in short an advantageous increase of production.[25] Third, national and regional variations, even in price statistics, are much greater than some historians are willing to admit. Not only does the so-called descending line start in every country at different periods – for southern Europe about 1620, for western Europe about 1650, for the Dutch Republic about 1660 – but, besides this, there are intercyclic waves which deviate strongly from one another and confuse the general trend picture. In times of general slump years of recovery and improvement can still be very important. As we are inclined, speaking generally, to shorten time in our imagination, the internal fluctuations within a great trend seem of little importance. For the contemporary living in a period in which he might, for instance, experience a recovery three times, intermediary fluctuations were however of very great significance as he could not see or even suspect the existence of a general trend.

Mousnier also lays great emphasis on the severe fluctuations from year to year, showing sharper rises and falls than in the sixteenth century. This comparison also requires caution: currency value had fallen considerably and fluctuations on the graph show sharper ups and downs. But in any case there *were* many fluctuations and they had, as we have already mentioned, serious consequences and reflected severe drops in prosperity and social order. But over against these sharp fluctuations stands the fact that in general the price *average* remained at the same level. As compared with the price revolution of the sixteenth century, of which there were offshoots right into the first decades of the seventeenth century, the time that followed shows up very favourably. There is a certain global stabilization that must have had favourable influence on wages. Thus, unlike Mousnier, I should prefer to qualify the fall in the import of silver from Spanish America as a stabilizing factor for economy, which had been ravaged by an all-too-extravagant inflation. I admit at once that the circulation of money was here and there probably slowed down, hampering economic growth, but it seems to me wrong to jump to the conclusion that the total supply of currency was reduced to a minimum. Hoarding and export of precious metals, the latter especially to Asia, did indeed drain money from circulation, but there was always a new supply, especially later on in the seventeenth century, e.g. gold from Brazil; and in the meantime copper met the emergency. Now if we consider conditions in France in the seventeenth century and then calculate the supply of gold and silver (in coinage) together with that century's imports, we shall probably find more money in circulation than in the sixteenth century.[26] Finally, I think we meet the same picture in the general situation of the population. I admit we know very little about seventeenth-century population growth, but from existing data I get the impression of a slight rise rather than of a spectacular drop. The great disasters like plague epidemics (for example the 1694-5 crisis in France) should not be allowed to confuse this general picture. Such disasters – mostly local – probably kept the people below a maximum of over-population but were very likely less sweeping as regards the general level than was once thought.[27]

Thrust back from the path of seemingly never-ending expansion and with a stabilizing tendency as regards prices, monetary circulation and population seventeenth-century Europe looked quite different to its contemporaries from that of the turbulent, expansive sixteenth century. How very greatly people were aware of this can be gathered from the many economic treatises on trade and navigation published in the seventeenth century, which are often lumped together as expressions of the economic theory of mercantilism. For here we find the results of the demarcation lines in Europe and of their stabilization: the bounds of the economic possibilities were seen so well that people were convinced, and published their conviction that prosperity would be possible *at the expense* only of other countries.[28] Was it not happening under their very noses? At the expense of the Mediterranean world, at the expense of central Europe, the Atlantic powers were rising; at the expense of the Spanish–American colonies the English were beginning their exploitation of Jamaica, the Portuguese their full exploitation of Brazil. Was there not also a bitter struggle among the naval powers? The Dutch Republic strove first against Portugal and later against England and France. Instead of economic growth they saw the marking off of economic boundaries: a fixed trough of economic welfare for all the European pigs to feed from.

Certainly an enormous shift took place in seventeenth-century Europe within the lines of demarcation. The whole weight of commerce and industry moved away from the countries round the Mediterranean, especially Italy and Spain, to the Atlantic coast, to western France, England and the Low Countries in particular. At the same time the balance, assisted partly by the destructive Thirty Years' War, shifted from south and central Germany to the North Sea ports of Hamburg and Bremen and from Poland and the Baltic coast to Scandinavia.[29] The most spectacular fact in this shift was of course the complete collapse of Italy as an important industrial and commercial leading country, and of the Spanish Empire, which had actually only a century before risen to great prosperity and power. It is a tragically engrossing tale to tell how the ancient, proud cities of Genoa and Venice, Leghorn or Pisa fell into decay, while the whole perished glory of Spain assumed a pathetic glamour when one saw pot-bellied galleons of the one-time Spanish merchant marine rotting to pieces in the roads of Cadiz after 1630.

But over against this there are other stories. They are all too well known to the Dutch: Spanish silver that found its way to the Amsterdam exchange bank, even without that famous privateer hero Piet Heyn; the proud palace that rose in Amsterdam and – *mirabile dictu* – was not a palace at all but a city hall; the impressive setting up of trading stations round the whole globe. How vague the term 'crisis' is when used here appears exactly in the interpretation that Hobsbawn gives to it in this respect. For him crisis is also a new birth, which he describes with particular reference to England. The American historian Nef had already spoken of a first industrial revolution in England before 1640.[30] Hobsbawn now expatiates on the increasing concentration of capital, refinement of monetary economy, agrarian changes, all of which laid the foundation for the later, so no longer 'only genuine', Industrial Revolution.[31] Portugal, whom one would have expected to share the Spanish decline, progressed towards new prosperity, first that of Brazilian sugar and later on of gold.[32] Sweden, revived by copper and iron production, transformed itself within one generation into a – for those days – modern industrial state.[33] Finally, the South Netherlands were really not steeped in such misery as was once thought; trade and industry were developing there in a reasonably favourable way.[34] If this shift is to be called a 'crisis', I have no objection, but it is not unrelieved gloom. Within a process of general stabilization there was a shifting of gravity which brought new countries new profits.

It is clear that of all these countries the Dutch Republic had advanced in probably the most surprising way. Leaning on its old staff of trade and navigation, Holland (including Zeeland and Friesland) had pushed to the fore. Undoubtedly in this the Republic had profited by the decline of others. I have already made some slight mention of the fierce attacks on the Portuguese in the Asiatic trading area. We can also call to mind the famous voyage of Dutch skippers to Italy with grain from the Baltic, when overpopulated Italy was in the grip of famine. From that year, 1592, onwards, the Dutch Republic began to make a niche for itself in Mediterranean trade from which Italian and Catalan competition seemed to melt away.[35] In the Baltic area the German and Polish landowning nobility became important connections who, without consulting the ports, could ask low prices for the grain which they were able to produce cheaply by means of increased serfdom.[36] Wherever openings appeared, the Hollanders and the Zeelanders rushed in. To a certain degree, we can call the economic prosperity of the Dutch Republic parasitical, but yet it was also profiting by the general economic shift which was busy moving the centre of gravity to our particular corner of Europe.

Certainly the Republic was bound to Europe in all its fibres. The very one-sided stress laid on trade and navigation necessitated this. Hence Holland's and Zeeland's great prosperity is, it would seem, explicable only by the fact that it took place – in the initial phase, the sociologists say – during the time of a general European boom. It was the fascinating Ten Years (1588–98) that the historian Fruin with such insight and intuition has pointed to as crucial for the Republic. It is not without irony, for example, that Spain was then enjoying the same prosperity, only for Spain it was the end and for Holland the beginning; just then the most bulky silver fleets in the whole of the impressive history of Spanish navigation were sailing from Havanna to Seville.[37] And we need only look up the Sound Toll tables to be struck by the unusually high numbers of ships passing through the Sound at the same time.[38] Undoubtedly the subsequent years of possible European depression also cannot have failed to affect the Republic. On this point we have not yet sufficient information; it would seem a most fruitful area of investigation, for example, to examine the consequences of European depression for the Republic, especially the English experience of 1621, which was probably connected to the Spanish low point in the same year. In any case Holland's prosperity waned after 1660, the Republic was also enmeshed in the B phase of European economic development. When studying the economic decline of the Dutch Republic in the eighteenth century, it might be advisable to keep in mind that this declining trend had its starting point in the second half of the seventeenth century, despite a trade revival in the last decade of that century and the continuing growth of Amsterdam. In some measure Amsterdam's wealth shrouded this decline. The economic suction power of the great city drew, as it were, the strength of the province to itself. The rural districts pined and the smaller cities languished after 1660. To understand these times we should pay more attention to such dwarfs as Enkhuizen or Hoorn in West Friesland, Gouda or Dordrecht in South Holland as well as to the giant Amsterdam. Unlike the experience of England and Portugal, the B phase in the long run became for the Republic, for instance, such a strangulation that it was no longer able to struggle loose. After Catalonia, Bohemia or Castile we also find in the Dutch Republic an example of a decline as striking as it was enigmatic.

While we can speak of a certain stabilization in the economic relationships, in which striking and sometimes dramatic economic shifts occur, it may be worthwhile to see whether a real crisis in the seventeenth century can be found in the social relationships. Trevor-Roper at any rate concentrates wholly on this aspect for his crisis theory, while Mousnier stresses it equally emphatically. The upward-striving bourgeoisie, says Mousnier, ousted the decaying nobility, the nobility resisted and hunger drove the common people towards support of the one class or the other.[39] But here again, we must be extremely cautious. Was the nobility decaying? Was there a strongly upward-striving bourgeoisie in particular during the seventeenth century? One is perhaps best reminded of a remark made by Michael Karpovich: 'The trouble with the middle class is that it is always rising.'[40] Certainly it seems as if each era had had not only its crisis but also its 'rising middle class'.

What is usually overlooked, however, is the very firm position that the nobility continued to hold throughout many centuries on the very topmost rung of the social ladder. And the difficulties the gentry had in maintaining themselves lay not so much in the supposed pressure exerted upon them by a continuously upward-striving middle class, as in the fact that internal problems of this nobility led to the danger of enfeeblement and crumbling away, while the middle class usually helped the nobility to overcome this danger at the cost of its own strength. The rigid conception as to the way in which the aristocracy should maintain itself had an undermining effect on its exclusive position. The nobility were obliged to live in a manner that cost a disproportionate amount of blood and money. Money especially was every nobleman's Achilles heel. His revenues were always diminishing when he was unable to occupy himself with them, since other achievements were required of him than economic activity and intelligent book-keeping. The estates of the nobility were always being split up, the relations between the nobleman and his peasants underwent changes that were mostly unfavourable to him; price fluctuations were usually to his disadvantage; and there was a tendency to neglect the estates as a source of revenue in favour of the use of hunting grounds. Impoverished gentry who were unable to keep up their rank for economic reasons were continually dropping out, while the remainder, if they did not wish to eat into their capital to the same extent, were obliged either to alter their way of life or to tolerate the fact of newcomers intruding upon their station by marriage or ennoblement. The newcomers were of course accepted only if they brought not only new blood but new money, and those that were able to do so were the wealthy citizens and patricians.

For the middle-classes this continuous drain towards the nobility meant a serious blood-letting of their own: again and again the wealthiest and most powerful were transfused to fortify the aristocracy, and only replenishment from below and above kept the middle classes going. The effect was, as it were, one of communicating vessels between the classes; it helped to maintain the social hierarchy, but never without trouble and difficulty. For, on the one hand, the middle classes, enfeebled by desertion, resented the strengthened privileges of aristocracy; on the other hand, the destitute among the aristocracy became a truly festering sore on the body politic of the *ancien régime*.[41] In the various religious wars of the sixteenth century the noble desperadoes sometimes played a leading role. It is to Trevor-Roper's credit that he has pointed to the phenomenon of a 'falling gentry' which might have been one of the causes of the English revolution in the seventeenth century.[42] The resentment and discontent of the middle-class townsman had a long history of siege and revolt, too.

But in the sixteenth century in particular a new confusing factor began to play a part: the growth of state centralization. The intensifying of traffic and trade, the new technical possibilities of administration and planning, the national disruption of the Church, the economic interweaving of towns and areas within the boundaries of the State are part of the picture of the systematization of authority and the growth of larger political units. In such a growing unity of the State it was one of the highest noblemen, mostly a prince or a king, who symbolically, and effectively, assumed power. But everything was not drawn into the new whirlpool. Old social tensions remained alive for a long time and regional or local resistance died a lingering death. The sovereign had to take sides, sometimes in favour of the resentful middle class or the impoverished gentry; more often, however, the Crown supported the obedient and order-loving among both middle class and nobility. It was not that the rich and well-born loved royal centralization for its own sake, but their love of order was mostly a sensible and deliberate self-interested calculation. Citizens and nobles might seek and find their own good in the new and old institutions of centralizing power. In the court, army, counting-house and Church they saw their chance to preserve, or preferably to enhance, their own power and riches. It was easier for a noble-man, if he perceived the opportunity, to enter the bastion of government; especially at court and in the army, aristocracy was more acceptable to the sovereign from a sense of caste. Titles and tradition might add extra glamour to governmental position. On the other hand the middle class was often preferred for high office for the very reason that they were powerless and not too distinguished. So in this new bureaucracy, in this medley of parts of the old classes, of conforming citizens and gentry, the old feudal tradition and aristocratic style might still set the tone.

To other parts of the bourgeoisie and gentry, poor or rich, powerless or mighty, conformity to the growing state was not attractive. Remaining loyal to regional and local ties, feeling menaced in their traditions and customs, these groups provided the source for long-tenacious opposition to centralizing forces. Thus the old motifs of unrest and rebellion, bound up with a previous social hierarchy, continued to play across the new melody of resistance to the systematization of authority, especially in the sixteenth century. In the seventeenth century, however, the cacophony of traditional unrest and new resistance began to die down. The nobility, now at last, economically speaking, safely ensconced in the service of the central power, was obliged for the last time to suffer the pain of replenishment from below by the admission of the *noblesse de robe* and began to close its ranks. The old channels became clogged because the nobility no longer underwent a crumbling process and were able economically to maintain themselves. New and different tensions, however, would in the long run be created by the closing of ranks. For while one vessel's contents remained the same the other began to overflow: for the first time in the eighteenth century appeared the danger of a 'rising middle-class'.

So unrest and the long-continued resistance to centralization of high nobility and cities came to an end in the seventeenth century. The resisting bourgeoisie, always very weak, capitulated sooner than the rebellious groups among the nobility. Class-consciousness and tradition were stronger with the gentry. In the course of the sixteenth century most middle-class resistance had already subsided. Examples may be seen in the futile rising of the Comuneros, Ghent's courageous last stand against Charles V, the final surrender of most of the Hanse cities in the same century. The siege of La Rochelle in 1629 can count as the symbolic end of medieval civic power. New metropolises arose in the place of independent cities. They were often open cities, centres of trade and industry, of political power and political government with an enormous concentration of inhabitants, growing rapidly beyond their walls. First came Seville and Lisbon and later Paris and London, not to forget Amsterdam.[43] The gentry's last resistance was of longer duration, causing great strife and bloodshed, even in the seventeenth century. Finally, in the case of the Fronde the struggle seems to shift from the older, traditional aristocratic opposition to a struggle for the best posts within the central power; and about the same time we see an end to noble resistance in England and in most German states.

Once more the Dutch Republic forms an odd variant. As a result of the revolt against Spain here, unlike in other countries, an end was made to all centralization. And the United Provinces were unique in that the city bourgeoisie of Holland and some other provinces, in contrast to the nobility of most other European republics, was able to concentrate most of the power in itself. Understandably there was some aristocratic opposition: a rudiment may be found in the party struggle where provincial gentry sometimes moved against the bourgeoisie of Holland and Zeeland, and in Holland itself one holder of office remained half an hereditary sovereign and half a powerful nobleman – nor was he willing always to forget his princely position in the subordinate office of stadtholder. But compared with what happened elsewhere, this old-fashioned gentry opposition was of little significance in the Republic. Another remarkable fact in this respect was the continuing independence of the cities which, against the trend of the times, as it were, actually set their stamp on the Republic.

And yet the apparently irrepressible need for state unification had its effects on the Republic, too. Thanks to Holland's leadership a loose federation of states was drawn closer and given more political coherence. Clumsy institutions, often created for other purposes, were adjusted to form a front of provinces and cities united against the outer world and initially for very reasonable co-operation in home affairs – a co-operation that remained satisfactory so long because trade and navigation enjoyed total freedom of action. The fact that something of the real civic independence disappeared in the long run and that Amsterdam, as the metropolis, absorbed much of what other cities had originally possessed of prosperity and therefore power, also pointed to the necessity of government formation and organization. And if a kindred though later process in connection with the general aristocratization is only casually mentioned, this is because I have spoken about it on an earlier occasion and have now said enough.[44] The Dutch patriciate finally became itself an aristocracy with its own privileges and fewer duties, adapting within two or three generations an aristocratic way of life and philosophy. The bureaucratic administration of the federation of states became nursery and bulwark for aristocratization.

I have repeatedly spoken of 'stabilization' and sometimes of 'shift' instead of crisis. To a certain extent the seventeenth century was, as I see it, a period of solidifying and organizing. Inside Europe the prices, currency circulation and the growth of population became more settled and stable. Economic expansion overseas came up against inevitable contemporary setbacks and restrictions. And, while at home there are startling economic shifts, there was in the economic sphere a certain retardation, maybe even regression. The State achieved its growth, and society, convulsed and still being convulsed by wars and uprisings, seemed slowly and with difficulty to be settling down. At home the social process for the first time lost part of its own unrest. I do not deny that great suffering was caused by all these shifts and strife, and if that has to be called 'crisis' I have no objection, but it is then rather the permanent crisis of the *ancien régime* that is seen slightly to diminish precisely during the seventeenth century.

Many inhabitants of Europe found themselves suddenly enclosed like mice in a glass cage. This was for that matter not more so than it used to be, and it would soon appear that there were again sufficient loopholes. But while mice so caged can do nothing except vainly scratch the walls, devour each other or copulate, human beings behaved differently. Naturally even among these there were some who slid round the walls with outspread arms, many devoured each other and most of them behaved as people always do in happiness and distress. But there were some who examined their own cage, surveyed their boundaries of will power and ability, drew up laws and regulations of their own imprisonment and tried to create peace and order in their own society. There were some who occupied themselves with introspection and searchings of the heart. In this process of coming to their senses I would venture to include the Scientific Revolution of the seventeenth century, the growing felt need of understanding microcosms and macrocosms by the aid of Reason; also the new theories regarding the power of the State and shared sovereignty, monarchic power and monarchic absolutism. It is possible that here too lies a basis of explanation for the inner deepening of religious life as found by the Jansenists or the Huguenot fugitives. Probably, too, it was brightened by the gravity and inwardness of baroque as it reveals itself in Dutch painting. For even though our Golden Age does not seem to fit entirely into that period of consolidation, it was consistent with it and shared in it. While here and there attaining to unexpected heights, the Republic was yet every time drawn back to its own place at a junction of waterways, among the great powers, among the civilizations of the West, drawing breath with the rise and fall of the destiny of European nations.

Notes

1 See *Propyläen Weltgeschichte*, V (1930) and VI (1931).
2 R. Mousnier, *Les XVIe et XVIIe Siècles. Les Progrès de la Civilisation Européenne et le Déclin de l'Orient (1492–1715), Histoire Générale des Civilisations,* ed. M. Crouzet, IV (Paris, 1954).

3 ibid., p. 143. Translated by the editors of the present work.

4 R. B. Merriman, *Six Contemporaneous Revolutions* (Oxford, 1938), an elaboration of a David Murray Lecture published under the same title (Glasgow, 1937).

5 E. J. Hobsbawm, 'The general crisis of the European economy in the 17th century', first published in *Past and Present* (1954), now reprinted with a postscript, in Trevor Aston (ed.), *Crisis in Europe 1560–1660 Essays from Past and Present* (London, 1965), pp. 5–59.

6 H. R. Trevor-Roper, 'The general crisis of the 17th century', first published in *Past and Present* (1959), now reprinted in Aston, op. cit., pp. 59–97. See also 'Discussion' of E. H. Kossmann, E. J. Hobsbawm, J. H. Hexter, R. Mousnier, J. H. Elliott, L. Stone with 'Reply' of H. R. Trevor-Roper in *Past and Present*, XVIII (1960), pp. 8–42, only partly reprinted in Aston, op. cit.

7 One exception: B. H. Slicher van Bath, *The Agrarian History of Western Europe A.D. 500–1850* (London, 1963), paid full attention to the crisis (especially pp. 206–21). In agriculture itself, which came for the Republic in the second or third place and was the first to suffer from a depression, a slump was sooner discernible.

8 It should be said, however, in all fairness that on Sweden and Portugal 'crisis' essays have been written: M. Roberts, 'Queen Christina and the general crisis of the seventeenth century', reprinted in Aston, op. cit., pp. 195–223 and P. Chaunu, 'Brésil et Atlantique au XVIIe siècle', in *Annales E.S.C.*, XVI (1961), pp. 1176–1207.

9 These discrepancies can lead to very great divergences even in the dating of the crisis. French historians see the crisis reach its lowest point only after 1650; English historians on the other hand see the end of the crisis already in 1660. Compare for this the title of Aston, op. cit.

10 Hobsbawm, op. cit., p. 5.

11 Trevor-Roper, op. cit., p. 62. Compare also the following sentence on the same page: ' . . . the sixteenth century goes on, a continuous, unitary century and society is much the same at the end of it as at the beginning. Philip II succeeds to Charles V, Granvelle to Granvelle, Queen Elizabeth to Henry VIII, Cecil to Cecil; even in France Henry IV takes up, after a period of disturbance, the mantle of Henry II. Aristocratic, monarchical society is unbroken: it is even confirmed.' This is striking but deceptive rhetoric: between Henry VIII and Elizabeth or Henri II and Henri IV lie worlds of difference. In this way we can just as well paraphrase developments in the seventeenth century: 'Philip IV succeeds to Philip III, Don Luis de Haro to Olivares, Louis XIV to Louis XIII; even in England Charles II takes up, after a period of disturbance, the mantle of Charles I.'

12 Cf. E. H. Kossmann's remarks on this subject, in *Past and Present*, XVIII (1960), p. 10.

13 R. Mandrou, 'Le baroque européen: mentalité pathétique et révolution sociale', in *Annales E.S.C.*, XV (1960), pp. 898–914.

14 All percentages given here are of course very crude estimates, mainly based on urban data, substantially reduced for the more favourable situation on the countryside. Regional differences can be very great.

15 Cf. B. F. Porshnev, *Les Soulèvements populaires en France de 1623 à 1648* (Paris, 1963). This work appeared in Russian in 1948.

16 While hot summers or long winters, violent storms or other exceptional weather phenomena have been recorded and can be treated statistically, there is too much regional difference, in particular in respect to irregularity in the degree of humidity and rainfall, to allow for complete statistical data on harvests and crop failure in connection with weather conditions. The yield ratios also confirm this (cf. B. H. Slicher van Bath, *Yield Ratios 810–1820* (Wageningen, 1963)).

17 For the remark on the London epidemic of 1665, see J. Saltmarsh, 'Plague and economic decline in the latter Middle Ages', in *Cambridge Historical Journal*, VII (1941–3), p. 32 (' . . . is remembered not because it was the greatest but because it was the last London plague'). [For two recent surveys of plague see J. F. D. Shrewsbury, *A History of Bubonic Plague in Britain* (Cambridge, 1970), and J. N. Biraben, *Les Hommes et la peste en France*, 2 vols (Paris, 1975)—eds.]

18 The favourable factors mentioned here are given merely as a working hypothesis, partly due to yet unpublished remarks on this subject by E. Jonxis and B. H. Slicher van Bath. This deserves further elaboration and further studies. [But see the recent list of riots in R. M. Dekker, 'Oproeren in de provincie Holland, 1600–1750', in *Tijdschrift voor Sociale Geschiedenis*, IX (1977), pp. 299–329—eds.]

19 P. Vilar, *La Catalogne dans l'Espagne Moderne*, I (Paris, 1962).

20 J. U. Nef, 'Mining and metallurgy in medieval civilisation', in *Cambridge Economic History*, II (Cambridge, 1952), pp. 469–70.

21 J. H. Elliott, 'The decline of Spain', in Aston, op. cit., pp. 187–95. See also his *Imperial Spain, 1469–1716* (London, 1963), especially pp. 286–95.

22 P. Chaunu, *Séville et l'Atlantique (1504–1650)*, especially VIII, 2 (2 vols) (Paris, 1959). As this gigantic work is difficult to handle, see also the short résumé P. and H. Chaunu, 'Economie atlantique. Economie mondiale (1504–1640)', in *Journal of World History* (1953–4), pp. 91–104, and here especially p. 97.

23 Cf. R. Baehrel, *Une Croissance: La Basse Provenance Rurale (Fin du XVIe Siècle—1789), Essai d'Economie Historique Statistique* (Paris, 1961), especially pp. 12–20. Cf. also my review, in *Tijdschrift voor Geschiedenis*, 77 (1964), pp. 17ff.

24 Slicher van Bath, *Agrarian History*, p. 206, calls this depression one 'of a far milder sort than the serious economic decline of the late Middle Ages. . .'. The depression was especially serious for so-called under-developed areas; while it could work on the other hand in a rationalizing and intensifying direction: spread of cottage

industries, specialization in cattle-breeding, wine-growing, market gardening, etc.

25 Baehrel, op. cit., *passim*.

26 ibid., pp. 33–41 and Planche VI. See also pp. 206–13 below.

27 Regarding the population curve in general and also in the seventeenth century, cf. my 'De demografie van het oude Europa' in *Tijdschrift voor Geschiedenis*, LXXIV (1961), pp. 1–31. As to the possibly slighter consequences of disasters than presumed see Baehrel, op. cit., pp. 231–306, especially pp. 267–9.

28 This is sharply drawn by D. C. Coleman, 'Eli Heckscher and the idea of mercantilism', in *Scandinavian Economic History Review*, V (1957), pp. 3–25, in particular, pp. 18–20.

29 Cf. articles connecting this economic shift with the developments and influence of Reformation and Counter-Reformation: K. Samuelsson, *Religion and Economic Action. A Critique of Max Weber* (New York, 1961), pp. 102–37; H. R. Trevor-Roper, 'Religion, the Reformation and social change', in *Historical Studies*, IV (5th Irish conference of historians) (London, 1963), pp. 18–45 and H. Luethy, 'Once again: Calvinism and Capitalism', in *Encounter*, XXII (1964), pp. 26–39.

30 J. U. Nef, 'The progress of technology and the growth of large-scale industry in Great Britain, 1540–1640', in *Essays in Economic History*, I, ed. E. M. Carus-Wilson (London, 1954), pp. 88–107. The idea is also referred to in other publications by Nef.

31 Hobsbawm, op. cit., pp. 31–41.

32 F. Mauro, *Le Portugal et l'Atlantique au XVIIe Siècle 1570–1670. Etude Economique* (Paris, 1960). Cf. Chaunu's attempts to incorporate the Portuguese boom after 1650 in the crisis theory: P. Chaunu, 'Brésil', esp. pp. 1192–6.

33 E. F. Heckscher, *An Economic History of Sweden* (Cambridge, Mass., 1954), pp. 79–130.

34 J. A. van Houtte, 'Onze zeventiende eeuw "ongelukseeuw"?' (Brussels, 1953) (*Meded. Kon. Vl. Acad. v. Wetensch., Lett. en Sch. Kunsten Kl. der Lett.*, XV, 8).

35 Cf. Z. W. Sneller, 'Het begin van den Noord-Nederlandschen Handel op het Middellandsche-Zeegebied', in *Verslag Prov. Utr. Gen. v. K. en W.*, 1935, pp. 70–93; J. H. Kernkamp, 'Scheepvaart en handelsbetrekkingen met Italie tijdens de opkomst der Republiek', in *Economisch-historische herdrukken* (Den Haag, 1964), pp. 199–234; and F. Braudel, *La Méditerranée et le Monde Méditerranéen à l'Epoque de Philippe*, II (Paris, 1949), pp. 494–503.

36 F. Vollbehr, *Die Holländer und die Deutsche Hanse* (Lübeck, 1930), pp. 20–9.

37 P. Chaunu, *Séville et l'Atlantique*, VII (Paris, 1957), pp. 44–5. It starts about 1580, reaches its summit about 1608. These high tonnages do not, however, reflect fully the actual flourishing of the Spanish–American trade, cf. ibid., VIII, 2, pp. 667–1070.

38 Nina Ellinger Bang (ed.), *Tabeller over Skibsfahrt og Varetransport gennem Oresund, 1497–1660*, I (Skibsfarten) (Kopenhagen-Leipzig,

1906), pp. 86–171. High figures start about 1580 and remain high till after 1620.

39 Mousnier, op. cit., pp. 152–60.

40 Quoted by D. Gerhard, *Alte und Neue Welt in Vergleichender Geschichtsbetrachtung* (Göttingen, 1962), p. 55 (see also *American Historical Review*, 61 (1955–6), p. 912).

41 Here I owe much to J. H. Hexter, *Reappraisals in History* (London, 1961), in particular: 'Factors in modern history' (pp. 26–45) and 'The myth of the middle-class in Tudor England' (pp. 71–117). What I made of it is of course for my account.

42 H. R. Trevor-Roper, *The Gentry 1540–1640* (London, 1953).

43 Kindred ideas to be found with J. P. Cooper, 'Differences between England and continental governments in the early seventeenth century', in *Britain and the Netherlands*, I (London, 1960), pp. 62–91, especially pp. 62–4.

44 Cf. my *Ons Tweede Tijdvak* (Arnhem, 1962).

Chapter five

Revolution and Continuity in Early Modern Europe*

John Elliott

Of all the debates that have agitated historians during the past few years, none has been more lively, or less conclusive, than the great debate surrounding what has come to be known as 'the general crisis of the seventeenth century'. While dissenting voices have been raised here and there,[1] the current fashion is to emphasize the more turbulent characteristics of the age. It was in 1954, which seems in retrospect to have been an unusually crisis-conscious year, that Professor Roland Mousnier published a general history of sixteenth- and seventeenth-century Europe, in which the seventeenth century was depicted as a century of crisis, and especially of intellectual crisis.[2] In the same year, Dr Hobsbawm, in an article that now stands as the classic formulation of the 'general crisis' theory, argued that the seventeenth century was characterized by a crisis of the European economy, which marked a decisive shift from feudal towards capitalist organization.[3] Since then, Professor Trevor-Roper, with one eye on the political revolutions of the 1640s and the other on Dr Hobsbawm, has produced a uniquely personal interpretation of the seventeenth century as an age of crisis for the 'Renaissance State'.[4]

It is, I think, striking that three such distinguished historians, of very different views and persuasions, should have united in depicting the seventeenth century in such dramatic terms. They all represent some aspect of the age – whether economic, intellectual or political – in terms of discontinuity, in the sense either of a change of direction or of a change of pace. The change, too, is a violent one, as the use of the words 'crisis' and 'revolution' suggests. But the crisis of one historian is a chimera to another,

* This paper was first given as an Inaugural Lecture at King's College, London, on 22 October 1968. It was first published in *Past and Present: a Journal of Historical Studies*, XLII (1969), pp. 35–56. It is reprinted here by permission of the author and of the Past and Present Society.

and the consensus collapses as soon as attempts at definition begin.

It is not my intention now to embark on the daunting task of reconciling the irreconcilable. Nor do I intend to examine the evidence for and against an interpretation of the seventeenth century as an age of economic and intellectual crisis. Instead, I have chosen to concentrate on the narrower, but still, I think, important, question of the 'political' revolutions of the middle years of the century – those revolutions that (in Professor Trevor-Roper's words) 'if we look at them together . . . have so many common features that they appear almost as a general revolution'.[5]

The revolts and upheavals that may be held to constitute this 'general revolution' have frequently been listed: the Puritan Revolution in England, flanked by the revolts of Scotland and Ireland; the insurrections in the Spanish monarchy – Catalonia and Portugal in 1640, Naples and Palermo in 1647; the Fronde in France between 1648 and 1653; the bloodless revolution of 1650, which displaced the *stadtholderate* in the Netherlands; the revolt of the Ukraine from 1648 to 1654; and a string of peasant risings across the continent. Nor should we disregard the plea of Professor Michael Roberts that 'if we are really determined to bring the Cossacks and the Ironsides within the scope of a single explanation', we should not 'leave Sweden out of the reckoning'.[6] For did not the year 1650 see a dangerous social and constitutional crisis in the troubled realm of Queen Christina ?

This clustering of revolts was a subject of fascinated concern to contemporaries, who saw them as part of a great cosmic upheaval; and it has frequently been commented upon by historians. It is thirty years now since Professor R. B. Merriman published his *Six Contemporaneous Revolutions*. But for Merriman the six revolutions afforded 'an admirable example of the infinite variety of history'.[7] Since the 1950s, however, the tendency has been to emphasize their similarities rather than their differences; and the concept of a 'general revolution' of the 1640s has effectively come to influence the history of seventeenth-century Europe only in our own generation.

Not the least of the attractions of a 'crisis' interpretation of the seventeenth century to our own age is that it offers the possibility of a unified conceptual approach to a complex period. It has, too, the additional advantage of plausibility, with that dramatic decade of the 1640s to bear witness to the turbulence of the times.

Opinions may vary about the long-term consequences of the revolutions. Not everyone, for instance, would agree with Professor Trevor-Roper[8] that the seventeenth century 'is broken in the middle, irreparably broken, and at the end of it, after the revolutions, men can hardly recognize the beginning'. But there would probably be a fairly general measure of agreement with his view that 'the universality' of revolution in the seventeenth century pointed to 'serious structural weaknesses' in the European monarchies – weaknesses that gave rise to revolutionary situations.

Whether these weaknesses were more or less serious at this moment than in preceding generations need not at present concern us. All I wish to do for the time being is to draw attention to the way in which the argument is couched. It is the 'universality' of seventeenth-century revolution that points to structural weakness. This argument from universality underlies most of the theories about the 'general crisis' of the seventeenth century. Six contemporaneous revolutions (at a minimum count) – does not the very number and pervasiveness of revolutionary movements suggest a moment of unique gravity, and a crisis of unique proportions, in the history of Early Modern Europe?

But supposing this unprecedented epidemic of revolutions was not, after all, unprecedented. Let us look back for a moment to the sixteenth century, and in particular to the decade of the 1560s: 1559–60, revolt in Scotland, culminating in the abdication of Mary Queen of Scots in 1567; 1560, revolt of the Vaudois against Emmanuel Philibert, Duke of Savoy; 1562, outbreak of the French civil wars; 1564, revolt of the Corsicans against Genoa; 1566, the beginning of the revolt of the Netherlands; 1568, revolt of the *moriscos* of Granada; 1569, the Northern Rebellion in England. Seven 'contemporaneous revolutions'; and perhaps I may be allowed to anticipate Professor Roberts and plead that the rising of the Swedish dukes against Eric XIV in 1568, and his subsequent deposition, should not be overlooked.

This sudden rash of revolts would hardly have come as a surprise to that doughty professional rebel John Knox, who was able to announce reassuringly to Mary Queen of Scots in 1561: 'Madam, your realm is in no other case at this day, than all other realms of Christendom are.'[9] But while contemporaries seem to have felt that they were witnessing the beginnings of a general conflagration, or what Calvin called 'Europae concussio',[10] I am not aware that any historian has grouped them together under the title of 'the general revolution of the 1560s', or has used them as evidence for a 'general crisis of the sixteenth century'.[11]

Perhaps it is not unreasonable to speculate for a moment on the possible reasons for this apparent discrimination in the treatment accorded the seventeenth century. Merriman seems to have been led to his six contemporaneous revolutions partly by his study of seventeenth-century political histories, and partly by the pre-occupation of the 1930s with the possibility of a coming 'world revolution'. He was also influenced by the example of 1848, which gave him the opportunity to draw parallels and comparisons. His principal concern was to consider the relationship of the various revolutions to each other, and his principal conclusion from a study of the 1640s and the 1840s was that 'national rivalries proved stronger than the virus of revolution' – an encouraging conclusion, no doubt, in the circumstances of the 1930s.[12]

Merriman's approach to the seventeenth-century revolutions by way of diplomatic history was of little interest to historians of the postwar generation. But he had bequeathed them a magnificent subject, ready for exploitation. In the context of the postwar historiography of Early Modern Europe, exploitation proved easy enough. The French economist Simiand had taught Early Modern historians to see the sixteenth century as an age of economic expansion, and the seventeenth as a century in which expansion was first halted, and then, around 1650, succeeded by a slump. Given the existence of a major reversal of economic trends in the middle years of the century, Merriman's contemporaneous revolutions seemed both relevant and suggestive. Here, surely, were the social and political manifestations of a crisis affecting the entire European economy. Had his revolutions been those of the 1560s rather than those of the 1640s – the products of an age of expansion rather than of an age of contraction – they might have attracted less attention. Yet even assuming that we can legitimately speak of a general crisis of the European economy in the mid-seventeenth century – and the evidence, though impressive, is not conclusive – it seems odd that the assumed relationship between economic crisis and political revolution has gone unquestioned. Why should we ignore for the seventeenth century de Tocqueville's perception that revolution tends to come with an improvement rather than with a deterioration of economic conditions?

But the decisive element in the concentration of interest on the revolutions of the 1640s is clearly the supreme importance attributed to the Puritan Revolution in England, as the event that precipitates the collapse of Europe's feudal structure and the emergence of a capitalist society. If the Puritan Revolution is seen as the essential prelude to the Industrial Revolution, it is obvious that a constellation of revolutions benefiting from its reflected glory is likely to outshine any other in the revolutionary firmament. This, at least, seems to be the attitude of the Soviet historian, Boris Porshnev. His Fronde is a bourgeois revolution *manquée*. 'It was', he writes, 'a French variant of the English bourgeois revolution which was breaking out on the other side of the Channel, and a distant prologue of the French Revolution of the eighteenth century.' He presents the sixteenth-century civil wars, on the other hand, as a combination of feudal quarrels and popular insurrections.[13] Yet, given the upsurge of revolt in the towns of the Ligue in 1588, it is not easy to see any intrinsic reason why the French civil wars should not also be categorized as a bourgeois revolution *manquée*. But perhaps the Ligueurs lacked a progressive ideology.

A contest in the revolution stakes between the 1560s and the 1640s does not seem in itself a particularly profitable enterprise. But it does give rise to a larger and more important question – the question of our general conception of revolution, and its applicability to the study of Early Modern Europe. Here the distinction between Marxist and non-Marxist historian dwindles in importance. The language of our age is pervasive – so pervasive that Professor Mousnier, after cogently criticizing Professor Porshnev for his interpretation of the Fronde in terms of class conflict, can refer to the English civil war, in his most recent book, as 'perhaps the first great bourgeois revolution of modern times'.[14]

Coming from the pen of a historian whose approach to the history of his own country is as staunchly anti-Marxist as that of Professor Mousnier, these words hint at the existence of what seems to be a central problem in the history of Early Modern European insurrections. We are all of us the children of our age, but in this particular field of historical writing, the tricks of time have proved to be more than usually deceptive. Between us and Early Modern Europe lies the late eighteenth century, dominated for us by two events that seem to have done more than anything else to shape our own civilization – the French Revolution, and the Industrial Revolution in England. During the nineteenth century, each of these became a paradigm – an exemplar, in one instance, for political and social development, and in the other for economic development. The twentieth century has appropriated these paradigms from its predecessor, and continues to make use of them as best it can.

How far the current paradigm of the French Revolution actually corresponds to what occurred in the course of that Revolution has been a matter for fierce debate. But the paradigm has not been confined to the French Revolution and the insurrections that have succeeded it. Consciously or unconsciously, nineteenth- and twentieth-century historians have looked at revolts in Early Modern Europe in the light of the late eighteenth-century revolutions, and of their assessment of them. This has frequently provided them with valuable insights into the origins of great events; but the very fact that they applied to many of these Early Modern revolts the word 'revolution' suggests the possibility of unconscious distortions, which may itself give us some cause for unease.

It is true that 'revolution' was by no means an unknown word in sixteenth- and seventeenth-century Europe, as applied to upheavals in states. A Spaniard looking back in 1525 on the revolt of the Comuneros expressed his fear of a 'revolution of the people';[15] and in 1647 and 1648 two Italians, Giraffi and Assarino, published accounts of recent insurrections, which they entitled 'The Revolutions' of Naples and Catalonia.[16] But a close study of the concept of 'revolution' by Professor Karl Griewank has shown how slowly, and with what uncertainty, the idea of revolution was brought down from the heavens of Copernicus and applied with any precision to the mutations of states.[17] Sedition, rebellion, *Aufstand*, mutation, revolt, revoltment (John Knox)[18] – these are the words most commonly employed in sixteenth-century Europe. Gardiner's Puritan Revolution was Clarendon's Great Rebellion. Only towards the end of the eighteenth century, under the impact of events in America and France, did 'revolution' effectively establish itself in the European political vocabulary, and acquire those connotations by which we recognize it today.

These include the idea of a violent, irresistible and permanent change of the political and constitutional structure; a powerful social content, through the participation of distinctive social groups and broad masses of the people; and the urge to break sharply with the past and construct a new order in accordance with an ideological programme.[19] Modern historians, accustomed to expect these ingredients of a revolution, have instinctively sought to detect them in Early Modern revolts. Presuming the existence of social protest and class conflict, they have duly found them in the uprisings of the populace. Conditioned to look for minority parties scheming to subvert the State by violence, they have anatomized with great skill the techniques of revolutionary organization. Expecting of a revolution that it should have an innovating ideology, they have effectively isolated and explored the aspirations of those who sought to establish a new order on earth. The work which has been done along these lines has proved immensely fruitful. It has made us aware of motives and forces behind the movements of unrest which were largely veiled from the participants. It has told us things which we could never have known, or could have glimpsed only obscurely, about the patterns of political and social cohesion and the underlying causes of failure or success.

But it would be foolish to ignore the possibility that, in using a concept of revolution that is relatively recent in origin, we may unconsciously be introducing anachronisms, or focusing on certain problems that accord with our own preoccupations, at the expense of others, which have been played down or overlooked. Some recognition of this is implied in recent discussions and debates, particularly on the question of the applicability of the idea of class conflict to Early Modern European society.[20] Although Professor Mousnier has insisted against Professor Porshnev that the popular uprisings in Richelieu's France were fomented by the upper classes and testified to the closeness of the relationship between the peasants and their lords, it would be unwise to disregard the evidence for the existence of fierce social antagonisms in Early Modern Europe. These found expression at moments of unbearable tension – whether in the fury of the Neapolitan mobs in 1585,[21] or in the assault of the Catalan peasants and populace on the nobles and the rich in the summer of 1640.[22]

But it is one thing to establish the existence of social antag-onisms, and another to assume that they are the principal cause of conflict. The Catalan rebels first attack royal officials and royal troops; and it is only after disposing of them that they turn on their own ruling class. A revolt may frequently have started, as in Catalonia, against the agents of the State, and then have been transformed into a war on the rich. But the parallels between this and a modern class conflict cannot automatically be taken for granted, if only because the ordering of society in Early Modern Europe tended to militate against class solidarity. A society grouped into corporations, divided into orders, and linked vertically by powerful ties of kinship and clientage cannot be expected to behave in the same way as a society divided into classes. Intense rivalries between guildsmen and non-guildsmen, and between the guilds themselves, helped to disrupt community action in urban revolts;[23] and it hardly seems a coincidence that one of the rare examples of a fair degree of urban solidarity is provided by the Comuneros of Castile, where guild organization was weak.

The applicability of the modern notion of ideology to Early Modern revolts seems equally open to question. If by ideology we mean 'a specific set of ideas designed to vindicate or disguise class interest',[24] the uncertainties about 'class' in Early Modern Europe must also be extended to 'ideology'. If we employ it more loosely to mean simply the programme of a particular movement (and this is presumably the way in which it is employed by most Western historians), there still remain large unanswered questions about the extent to which it faithfully represents the character of the movement as a whole. To talk, for instance, of Calvinism as the ideology of the Dutch rebels is to ascribe to the rebellion as a whole a series of ideals and aspirations that we know to be those of only a small minority – and a minority whose importance may well have been inflated, simply because they are the group whose ideals correspond most closely to our notions of what an ideology should be.

Perhaps our principal expectation of a revolutionary ideology is that it should break with the past and aspire to establish a new social order. In a society dominated, as Early Modern European society was dominated, by the idea not of progress, but of a return to a golden age in the past, the best hope of finding an ideology of innovation lies in certain aspects of the Christian tradition. In particular, the chiliastic doctrines of later medieval Europe look forward to the coming of a new age on earth – the age of the Holy Ghost, characterized by a new social and spiritual order. Up to a point, therefore, it is possible to see the Bohemian Taborites of the fifteenth century as belonging to the tradition of revolutionary innovation by means of violent action. It is certainly arguable that the Taborites did in practice establish for themselves a society in which new forms of social and political organization predominated over the old.[25] But, on the other hand, the Taborites did not reject the traditional threefold ordering of society; and although they were attempting to establish a new spiritual order on earth, the character of this order was determined by reference to the past – in this instance to the primitive church.

The same kind of difficulties are likely to bedevil attempts to bring religiously inspired movements of the sixteenth century into the category of ideological innovation. The peasant movements in early sixteenth-century Germany, for all their millenarian and egalitarian aspirations, were still dominated by the desire to return to a past order, which was held to be eternally valid.[26] The same would also seem to be true of the Calvinist ideal of the advancement of the kingdom of God – an advancement that was anyhow to be achieved by the winning of the state authorities to the cause, rather than by the action of the revolutionary masses.[27]

Even if we dignify – or debase – these religious aspirations with the name of 'ideology', it would be misleading to see them as providing a programme of action appealing to the majority of the participants in Early Modern revolts. The Taborites, the Anabaptists and the Calvinists all singularly failed to win anything like universal acceptance of their ideas; and it is not clear why we should regard them as speaking with the true voice of the movements to which they belong, unless it is because they happen to be the most articulate. With our ears straining to catch one particular theme, there is always a danger that, amidst the general uproar, other notes and other voices will go unheard. This danger is not always recognized with such clarity, or expressed with such candour, as it has been by Mr Michael Walzer, in his reference to the English sectaries: 'However important they are to latter-day genealogists, the sects (even, the Levellers) are of very minor importance in seventeenth-century history.'[28]

Doubts of this kind might profitably be extended. A fuller recognition of the degree to which our own thinking about revolutions is affected by preconceptions derived from the nineteenth century might at least enable us to isolate more effectively those points at which distortions are most liable to occur. If we accept this possibility, a number of uncomfortable questions about our method and our approach may suggest themselves. I have already hinted at one such question: how far can historians accustomed to look for *innovation* among revolutionaries enter into the minds of men who themselves were obsessed by *renovation* – by the desire to return to old customs and privileges, and to an old order of society? How far, too, has our preoccupation with violence as an essential ingredient of revolution concentrated attention on the agitators and the organizers, at the expense of the more passive and the less committed? For all the brilliance of Calvinist organization in the Netherlands, it is arguable that the fate of the revolt was determined elsewhere – by the great mass of people whose religious affiliation was lukewarm or indeterminate,[29] and by those stolid burghers of Holland and Zeeland who edged their way with such extreme caution along the precipitous path that divided loyalty from rebellion.

Most of all, it is open to question whether our persistent search for 'underlying social causes' has not led us down blind alleys, and has concealed from us more profitable ways of approach. I speak here, as in so much else, as one of the errant wanderers. Not that I would claim to have received some sudden illumination on the road to Damascus. It is simply that the constant reading of modern accounts of sixteenth- and seventeenth-century insurrections is likely in due course to induce a weariness of the spirit, and to provoke a certain critical questioning. While it is clear that all the major upheavals in Early Modern Europe represent a combination of different revolts, animated by different ideals and reflecting the aspirations of different groups, it is less clear why 'social' revolts should be regarded as in some way more 'fundamental'. Nor is it clear why we should be expected to assume that the outbreak of revolt in itself postulates structural weaknesses in society. Political disagreement may, after all, be no more and no less than political disagreement – a dispute about the control and the exercise of power.

An age as acutely attuned as ours to the distress signals of the poor and the starving may be correspondingly less sensitive to the cries of the more fortunate for freedom from arbitrary power. The innumerable peasant revolts – the *soulèvements populaires* – that are now being analysed in such painstaking detail provide a terrifying revelation of the misery in which most of Europe's population lived. But we should not, I believe, be afraid to ask the apparently brutal question: did they make any difference? Or, indeed, *could* they make any difference, in a world in which technological backwardness had at least as much to do with the condition of the populace as exploitation by an oppressive ruling

class ? And if we conclude that they could and did make a difference, we should then go on to determine the precise areas in which
that difference was made.

If we can recognize that contemporary preconceptions about the
nature of revolution may have helped to shape our treatment of
Early Modern revolts, we are at least in some position to attempt
remedial action. Our priorities, for instance, can be set against
those of contemporaries, in an attempt to discover which of theirs
have receded into the background, or have come to be overlooked.
It is a salutary experience to watch the development of the French
civil wars through the sharp eyes of Estienne Pasquier, whose
evaluation of events is that of an intelligent and well-read sixteenth-
century layman.

> There are three things [he wrote] of which one should be
> infinitely afraid in every principality – huge debts, a royal
> minority, and a disturbance in religion. For there is not one
> of these three which is not sufficient of itself to bring
> mutation to a state.[30]

No doubt Pasquier's analysis is inadequate, even by contemporary standards. His historical analogies were essentially
political, and he set the unfolding drama of conflict in France
into the context of famous faction feuds.

> Two miserable words of faction, Huguenot and Papist,
> have insinuated themselves amongst us [he wrote in 1560];
> and I fear that in the long run they will lead us to the same
> calamities and miseries as the Guelfs and Ghibellines in
> Italy, and the White and the Red Rose in England.[31]

But this was not an unreasonable assessment of events from the
standpoint of 1560; and if he omitted the social and economic
considerations – the discontents of the gentry, the social consequences of rising prices – that loom so large in modern accounts
of the French wars, this does not necessarily mean that he was
unaware of their influence on events. Pasquier and his contemporaries were capable enough of seeing the existence of a
relationship between political and social grievance. It was in the
degree of significance to be accorded to this relationship that a
sixteenth-century approach diverges most sharply from our own.
An age that has devoted itself to meticulous research into the
fortunes of nobles and gentry is likely to find something almost

comically casual about the words that Joachim Hopperus slips
into his account of the origins of the Dutch revolt:

> Several of the principal leaders were at this time very
> heavily burdened with debts. This is sometimes considered a
> source of unrest and attempted innovation, since such people
> hope to take advantage of disturbances in the state to
> re-establish their fortunes.[32]

But it may be that we have been equally casual in our approach
to what contemporaries themselves regarded as important:
Pasquier's 'royal minorities', for instance, and indeed the whole
question of kingship. It is now almost impossible for us to grasp
the degree to which changes in the character of kingship affected
the dispositions of power in the State. In societies where all the
threads of patronage ultimately come to rest in the hands of the
king, any of the accidents and hazards to which hereditary
kingship is prone are likely to have profoundly disturbing consequences. The apparent turbulence of politics in the 1560s may
therefore not be entirely unrelated to a remarkably high mortality
rate among monarchs in the preceding decade, and the accession
of new and inexperienced rulers, some of whom were women or
children. Similarly, if a comparison is to be made between the
histories of France and Castile, it does not seem entirely irrelevant
to consider how far Castile's immunity from rebellion after 1521
is to be ascribed to a high degree of social stability, and how far
to the accident that it escaped royal minorities and the baneful
presence (except for a short period in the reign of Philip IV) of
adult cadet princes.[33]

There is, however, another area, in which most modern
historiography seems to have been even less at home, and with far
more considerable consequences. The search for the causes of
discontent is nowadays more likely to lead to religious or social
grievance than to a sense of national loyalty. Yet the apparent
uncertainty of modern historians when faced with the question
of nationalism in Early Modern Europe stands in marked contrast
to the increasingly confident use in the sixteenth century of the
words *patria* and *patrie*. When the Corsican leader, Sampiero
Corso, turned to Catherine de Medici for help in the early 1560s
to free his native island from Genoese domination, she presented
him with a number of banners bearing the heroic inscription:
pugna pro patria.[34] The rebels of Ghent in 1578 not only spoke of

defending their *patrie*, but also referred to themselves as *patriotes*.[35] The lawyers and judges in the reign of Charles I gained a reputation with parliament of being 'good patriots';[36] and Masaniello, the hero of the Neapolitan revolt of 1647, was hailed as *liberator patriae*.[37]

It is possible that, in approaching these apparent manifestations of patriotic sentiment, we have again been both influenced and inhibited by our nineteenth-century inheritance. 'The Commonwealth', wrote Lord Acton, 'is the second stage on the road of revolution, which started from the Netherlands, and went on to America and France.'[38] For all the qualifications introduced by Acton himself, there was a strong temptation to look at Early Modern revolts through the lens of the French Revolution, interpreted this time in accordance with the liberal–national tradition. The modern reaction against the historiographical excesses of this tradition is natural enough. But the manifestations of some kind of community consciousness in Early Modern revolts are too numerous and too forceful to allow the question of nationalism to be left in a kind of historical limbo.

There are obvious difficulties about attempting to equate these various manifestations with a nationalism of the nineteenth-century variety. All too often a supposed allegiance to a national community turns out, on inspection, to be nothing of the kind. The *patria* itself is at least as likely to be a home town or province as the whole nation,[39] and a revolt, like that of the Dutch, that is represented in nineteenth-century historiography as a nationalist uprising may just as convincingly be depicted as a manifestation of particularist, rather than nationalist, sentiments.[40]

Yet even though *patria* might apply in the first instance to a native city, it could at times be extended, as in the Castile of the Comuneros,[41] to embrace the entire community of the realm. But whether the community was local or national, expressions of allegiance to it assumed the same form: a deep and instinctive antipathy to outsiders. Throughout the Early Modern period, this antipathy was a powerful driving force behind popular revolt. It moved the Corsican peasants in the 1560s to take up arms against the Genoese, and the Catalan peasants in 1640 to take up arms against the Castilians. *Visca la terra* – long live the land! – is the perennial cry of the Catalan populace as it turns out, to the summons of the church bells, to attack the bands of Castilian soldiers making their way to their embarkation point at Barcelona.[42]

This popular nationalism figures prominently in the accounts of revolts written by nineteenth-century historians, who were themselves so often the products of a Romantic culture nurtured on the legends and the songs with which the deeds of the rebels were kept alive in folk memory. But in idealizing it, they helped to discredit it, and oversimplified a complex phenomenon. What was often, at its least attractive, no more than an instinctive hatred of outsiders, was transmuted into a self-conscious identification with a national community, embodying certain specific ideals. But the Romantic historians were not totally mistaken in assuming the existence in Early Modern Europe of some such sense of identification, although they may have expected too often to find it expressed even at the very lowest social levels. For alongside the more obvious manifestations of popular sentiment, there was also to be found another phenomenon, which has yet to receive the attention and the analysis it deserves. This might perhaps best be described as a corporate or national constitutionalism; and while it may have reached down, in some form, to the lower levels of society, it was essentially the preserve of the dominant social and vocational groups in the State – nobles and gentry, urban patriciates, the lawyers, the clergy, the educated.

Perhaps it may be defined as an idealized conception of the various communities to which allegiance was owed; and it embraced, in ever-widening circles, the family and vocational community to which they belonged, the urban or provincial community in which they lived, and, ultimately and sometimes very hazily, the community of the realm. This idealized conception of the community was compounded of various elements. There was first, and most naturally, the sense of kinship and unity with others sharing the same allegiance. But there was also a sense of the corporation or community as a legal and historical entity, which had acquired certain distinctive characteristics with the passage of time, together with certain specific obligations, rights and privileges.

The community was founded on history, law and achievement, on the sharing of certain common experiences and certain common patterns of life and behaviour. As such, it was an ideal – indeed, an idealized – entity, already perfect in itself. It was, though, for ever subject to attacks from enemies, and to erosion at the hands of time. The highest obligation incumbent upon its members was therefore to ensure that in due course it should be transmitted intact to their successors. The plea for the faithful fulfilment of this obligation echoes right through the history of Early Modern Europe, from the Florentine who urged his fellow-citizens in 1368 to 'leave to posterity that which was left to us by our ancestors',[43] to the Catalan canon who begged his brother canons in 1639 not to 'let us lose in our own time what our forbears have so bravely won'.[44]

The sixteenth century seems to have contributed a new sophistication and a new awareness to the sacred task of defending a community whose rights and liberties were embodied in written constitutions and charters and kept alive in the corporate memory. In particular, it engaged with enthusiasm in legal and historical research. The great revival of interest in the customary law – a revival symbolized in France by the names of Bodin and Hotman[45] – not only provided new defences against arbitrary power decked out with the trappings of Roman law, but also helped to establish the idea that each nation had a distinct historical and constitutional identity.[46] By endowing the community with a genuine or fictitious constitution, set firmly into a unique historical context, the sixteenth-century antiquarian movement gave new meaning to the struggle for the preservation of liberties. The corporation, the community, the *patria* all acquired a firmer identity as the historical embodiment of distinctive rights.

The idea of the *patria* was also fostered by the new humanist education. A governing class which had imbibed the history of Greece and Rome from an early age would have no great difficulty in making an identification between its own idealized community and the polities of classical antiquity.[47]

> There were [says Hobbes in the *Behemoth*] an exceeding great number of men of the better sort, that had been so educated, as that in their youth having read the books written by famous men of the ancient Grecian and Roman commonwealths concerning their polity and great actions; in which books the popular government was extolled by the glorious name of liberty, and monarchy disgraced by the name of tyranny; they became thereby in love with their forms of government. And out of these men were chosen the greatest part of the House of Commons.
> The core of rebellion, as you have seen by this, and read of other rebellions, are the Universities. . . .

The *Universities* have been to this nation, as the wooden horse was to the Trojans.[48]

Until a great deal more research has been done on education in Early Modern Europe, it is impossible to determine what degree of importance should be attached to Hobbes's angry denunciations. But the intellectual influences that went to shape the conception of their own community among the governing classes of Europe are obviously a matter of the greatest interest, since it was the idealized community or the *patria* that gave them the frame of reference by which they determined their own actions and assessed those of others. In his recent book on *The Community of Kent and the Great Rebellion*, Professor Everitt has shown how the political behaviour of the dominant groups in Kentish society between 1640 and 1660 can only be understood in the light of their intense devotion to an idealized local community. While the gentry of Kent included convinced royalists and parliamentarians among their number, the principal aim of the majority was to 'stand for the defence of the liberties of their unconquered nation' against assaults from either camp.[49]

This devotion to an idealized community can be paralleled all over Europe, on a local, a regional and a national scale. Everywhere, the instinct of the ruling classes was to preserve a heritage. While in some instances this heritage might become indissolubly bound up with religious loyalties, the preservation of a heritage seems to have outweighed every other cause, including that of religion, in its appeal to the majority of the ruling nation.

> If religion be not persuaded unto you [wrote the Lords of the Congregation to the nobility, burghs and community of Scotland in 1559] yet cast ye not away the care ye ought to have over your commonwealth, which ye see manifestly and violently ruined before your eyes. If this will not move you, remember your dear wives, children and posterity, your ancient heritages and houses.[50]

Eloquent appeals for action in defence of laws and liberties were obviously likely to carry additional conviction when the arbitrary power that threatened them was also an alien power. In Scotland, Corsica and the Netherlands in the 1560s, in Catalonia and Portugal in the 1640s, the rebels found it easier to rally support, because the oppression came from foreign rulers, foreign officials and foreign troops on native soil. In these circumstances, a revolt originally sparked by religious protest or sectional discontents was capable of gathering support and momentum by combining in a common patriotism the constitutionalism of the privileged classes and the general antipathy to the outsider felt by the population at large.

This combination almost always proved fragile and transitory, because the idea of a national community to which all sections of society owed their prime allegiance was still so weakly developed. The national community was shot through with rival allegiances, and riven by sectional and social hatreds. Moreover, the constitutionalism of the privileged was all too often no more than a convenient device for defending the interests of an exclusive caste on the basis of bogus history and bogus law. Yet, in recognizing this, one must also recognize that the defence of liberties could, in certain circumstances, broaden into the defence of liberty; and that the pursuit of sectional advantage was not necessarily incompatible with the furtherance of a genuinely constitutional cause. For all its obvious deficiencies, constitutionalism provided the political nation with an ideal standard against which to measure current realities. Once this ideal standard existed, it was always capable of extension by a leader of political genius. The *patrie*, as glimpsed by William of Orange, was something more than a society in which the rights and liberties of the privileged were safe from the exercise of arbitrary power. It was also a society that included freedom of conscience among its liberties; an essentially open society, in which men were free to come and go and educate themselves without restrictions from above.[51]

Given the existence of an idealized vision of the community, however restricted that vision, movements of protest are likely to occur within the political nation when the discrepancy between the image and the reality comes to seem intolerably wide. In Early Modern Europe it is these movements of protest from above, and not the popular uprisings, that are capable of leading to a 'mutation in the State'. The problem, though, is to relate them to other manifestations of discontent, simultaneous or complementary, which have their origin in religious, fiscal or social grievances among the general population. 'Then is the danger,' as Bacon appreciated, 'when the greater sort do but wait for the troubling of the waters among the meaner, that then they may declare themselves.'[52] But it is impossible to establish here any common pattern of revolt. In the Netherlands of the 1560s an aristocratic movement benefited from simultaneous movements of religious and patriotic protest. But the aristocratic movement was halted in its tracks by the popular uprising – the iconoclastic fury – of August 1566. In Catalonia in 1640 the popular uprising, provoked by the behaviour of foreign troops, encouraged the leaders of the political nation to seize the initiative, and to transform a long-standing movement of protest into a decisive break with the Crown. In the England of the 1640s, it was only *after* the political nation had seized the initiative, and then itself split down the middle, that the people began to move. In Naples in 1647 the popular movement failed to evoke an effective response among the dominant social classes, and doomed itself to destruction.

In states displaying such varieties of political and social organization great variations in the pattern of revolt are only to be expected. There will always be men bold enough, angry enough, or frightened enough to seize the opportunity afforded by an upsurge of popular fury or by a sudden weakening of the State. The crucial question then becomes the attitude adopted by the mass of the uncommitted among the ruling class. Will they rally behind the Crown and the agents of royal authority in an emergency, or will they allow the leaders of the insurrection to have their way? The answer is likely to depend on a delicate balance between the ruling class's persistent fear of social upheaval, and its feeling of alienation from the Crown. In the Netherlands in 1566, for example, the political nation rallied to the government of Margaret of Parma when social upheaval threatened it. But in 1572, after five years of repressive government by the Duke of Alba, it had become so alienated from a regime that had launched an assault on its liberties, that it adopted a position of neutrality when the emergency came. The same is true of the Catalan political nation in the summer of 1640: the extent to which it had been alienated from Madrid by the policies of Olivares over the previous twenty years was sufficient to prevent it making any serious move to check the course of the revolt. In Naples, on the other hand, the nobles and gentry, for all their discontents, had remained closely associated with the viceregal administration, which had bribed them with favours and privileges because it needed their help in mobilizing the resources of Naples for war. This association made them the immediate objects of popular hatred in 1647; and they had nothing to gain from breaking with a regime which had shown itself more responsive to their interests than any that was likely to replace it.[53]

If the 1560s and the 1640s prove to be decades of more than usual unrest in Europe, it does not seem a coincidence that they were both periods in which the traditional loyalty of ruling classes to their princes had been subjected to very considerable strain. In both decades, several states were still engaged in, or were only just emerging from, a long period of warfare which had imposed heavy demands on national resources. In both decades, too, there was deep discontent among the ruling classes over the prevailing style of government. In the 1560s resentment was focused in particular on the rule of secretaries and professional civil servants: Cecil in England, Persson in Sweden,[54] Granvelle in the Netherlands. In the 1640s, it was focused on the rule of favourites – Strafford, Richelieu, Olivares – all of whom had shown a degree of political ruthlessness which was all the more objectionable because, as nobles, they had been traitors to their kind.

At a time when there was already something of a coolness between the Crown and the political nation, the situation was aggravated in both periods by signs of unusually energetic activity on the part of the State. In the late 1550s or early 1560s, the State's preoccupation with religious dissidence as a threat to its own authority had made it exceptionally vigorous in its employment of counter-measures. These brought the central power into conflict with sectional interests and those of local communities, and aroused widespread disquiet about the infringement of rights and liberties. In the 1630s and 1640s the main thrust of state power was fiscal rather than religious, but the consequences were not dissimilar. The financial demands of the State brought it into direct conflict with important sections of the political nation, which expressed its discontent through its representative institutions, where these still existed, and through the tacit withdrawal of allegiance.

In these circumstances, a group of determined rebels is well placed to make the running. The Crown, and those sections of the governing class immediately dependent upon it, finds itself temporarily isolated. The privileged and propertied classes hold aloof, or lend their sympathy and support to the rebels. But in practice the rebels have very little time at their disposal. Not only do their actions give rise to new feuds and vendettas, but a society that thinks essentially in terms of restoration is likely to baulk at measures that smack of innovation. 'From the beginning of the rebellion,' wrote Hobbes, 'the method of ambition was constantly this: first to destroy, and then to consider what they should set up.'[55] Rebels who contrived to give this impression were bound to alienate the body of uncommitted but conservative opinion in a political nation that was anyhow terrified that its own internal disputes would place power in the hands of the populace.

Rebels, therefore, could not count on continuing support from within the ruling class. Their movement, too, was likely to have only a narrow social base in a vertically articulated society. In the circumstances, they were bound to be driven back on alternative sources of help – and these could only come from outside. Merriman, with world revolution at the back of his mind, was impressed by the lack of co-operation between rebel regimes in different states. But much more impressive is the extent to which rebels sought, and secured, foreign assistance at vital stages in their revolts. Foreign aid, in fact, seems to have been an indispensable requirement for any revolt, if it were to have a chance of perpetuating itself. It was English military assistance that enabled the Scottish rebels to triumph in 1560. It was the French, the Germans and the English who saved William of Orange and the Dutch. It was the support of foreign Protestant or Roman Catholic powers that gave an additional lease of life to the rebel factions in France. In the 1640s the story was the same. The Scots came to the help of the English, the French to the help of the Catalans, the French and English to the help of the Portuguese.

The dependence of Early Modern revolts on external assistance suggests something of their character and their limitations. Sometimes they were furthered, sometimes impeded, by popular uprisings; but these were ephemeral movements, which could achieve little or nothing without assistance from groups within the ruling class. The prime aim of this class was to conserve and restore; and this aim at once determined the scope of the rebels' action, and the extent of their support. A ruling class alienated from the Crown by encroachment upon its liberties was prepared to let royal authority be challenged, and this allowed the rebels such successes as they in fact achieved. But once the heritage had been saved, the political nation reverted to its traditional allegiance, and those rebels who chose to persist in rebellion were compelled to look abroad for help.

The sixteenth and seventeenth centuries did indeed see significant changes in the texture of European life, but these changes occurred inside the resilient framework of the aristocratic–monarchical state. Violent attempts were made at times to disrupt this framework from below, but without any lasting degree of success. The only effective challenge to state power, and to the manner of its exercise, could come from within the political nation – from within a governing class whose vision scarcely reached beyond the idea of a traditional community possessed of traditional liberties. But this proved to be less constricting than it might at first sight appear. Renovation in theory does not of itself preclude innovation in practice; and the deliberate attempt to return to old ways may lead men, in spite of themselves, into startlingly new departures. There remained, too, sufficient room for the ruling class to be able to challenge the State at the two points where its activities were most likely to influence the character of national life. By resisting the State in the matter of taxation, it might destroy, or prevent the establishment of, a major obstacle to economic development; and by resisting its claims to enforce religious uniformity, it might remove a major obstacle to intellectual advance. If significant change came to certain European societies in the sixteenth and seventeenth centuries, it came because this challenge was effectively carried through.

By the eighteenth century, the growing awareness of man's capacity to control and improve his environment would make it more fashionable than it had been in the seventeenth century to think in terms of innovation. At this point the character of revolt would also begin to change; and rebellion might come to assume the characteristics of revolution. Until then, revolts continued to be played out within the context of the ambitions of the State on the one hand, and the determination of the dominant social groups to preserve their heritage on the other. If this determination came to be expressed in an increasingly sophisticated language, this was because the political nation itself was becoming more sophisticated. National constitutionalism learnt the language of law, of history and antiquity. Perhaps, then, it is to the rise of a literate and educated lay establishment, not to the rise of new social classes, that we should look if we are to understand the eventually decisive achievement of Early Modern revolts – the transformation of liberties into liberty. That one man, at least, guessed as much, we can see from the dialogue of the *Behemoth*:[56]

B. For aught I see, all the states of Christendom will be subject to these fits of rebellion, as long as the world lasteth.

A. Like enough; and yet the fault (as I have said) may be easily mended, by mending the Universities.

Notes

1 Many of the contributions to the debate are to be found reprinted in Trevor Aston (ed.), *Crisis in Europe, 1560–1660* (London, 1965). For expressions of dissent, see E. H. Kossmann, 'Trevor-Roper's "general crisis" ', *Past and Present*, XVIII (November, 1960), pp. 8–11; Lublinskaya, *French Absolutism: The Crucial Phase, 1620–1629* (Cambridge, 1968); and I. Schöffer, 'Did Holland's Golden Age coincide with a period of crisis?', pp. 83–119 above. Dr Schöffer's admirable article, of which I was unaware when I originally drafted this essay, makes a number of points that coincide closely with my own.

2 R. Mousnier, *Les XVIe et XVIIe Siècles* (Paris, 1954).

3 Aston, op. cit., pp. 5–58.

4 ibid., pp. 59–95.

5 ibid., p. 59.

6 ibid., p. 221.

7 R. B. Merriman, *Six Contemporaneous Revolutions* (Oxford, 1938), p. 89.

8 Aston, op. cit., pp. 62 and 63.

9 *John Knox's History of the Reformation in Scotland*, ed. W. C. Dickinson, I (London, 1949), p. 367.

10 R. Nürnberger, *Die Politisierung des Französichen Protestantismus* (Tübingen, 1948), p. 91 n. 57.

11 The links between the Huguenot and the Dutch revolts have, of course, received considerable attention, especially from nineteenth-century historians. Cf. in particular Kervyn de Lettenhove, *Les Huguenots et Les Gueux*, 6 vols (Bruges, 1883–5). See also H. G. Koenigsberger, 'The organization of revolutionary parties in France and the Netherlands', *Journal of Modern History*, XXVII (1955), which draws interesting parallels between the organization of the revolts in France, the Netherlands and Scotland. See also p. 89 above.

12 Merriman, op. cit., pp. 209 and 213.

13 Boris Porchnev (Porshnev), *Les Soulèvements Populaires en France de 1623 à 1648* (Paris, 1963), pp. 537, 17, 47.

14 R. Mousnier, *Peasant Uprisings* (London, 1972), p. xvii.

15 J. A. Maravall, *Las Comunidades de Castilla* (Madrid, 1963), pp. 243–4.

16 A, Giraffi, *Le Rivolutioni di Napoli* (Venice, 1647); Luca Assarino, *Le Rivolutioni di Catalogna* (Bologna, 1648). See also Vernon F. Snow, 'The concept of revolution in seventeenth-century England', *The Historical Journal*, V (1962), pp. 167–74.

17 K. Griewank, *Der Neuzeitliche Revolutionsbegriff* (Weimar, 1955).

18 Knox, op. cit., I, p. 193.

19 Griewank, op. cit., p. 7.

20 See Mousnier, *Peasant Uprisings*, pp. 18–19 and also p. 320 n. 9 for reference to his debate with Porshnev. Further discussion of the question of class in Early Modern society may be found in R. Mandrou, *Introduction à la France moderne* (Paris, 1961), pp. 138–64, and F. Mauro, *Le XVIe Siècle Européen, Aspects économiques* (Paris, 1966), pp. 337–44.

21 R. Villari, *La Rivolta antispagnola a Napoli* (Bari, 1967), p. 44.

22 J. H. Elliott, *The Revolt of the Catalans* (Cambridge, 1963), pp. 462–5.

23 For a classic example, see Gene A. Brucker, *Florentine Politics and Society, 1347–1378* (Princeton, 1962), p. 55.

24 A. Gerschenkron, *Continuity in History and Other Essays* (Cambridge, Mass., 1968), p. 65.

25 H. Kaminsky, *A History of the Hussite Revolution* (Berkeley, 1967), pp. 481ff.

26 Griewank, op. cit., p. 102.

27 Nürnberger, op. cit., pp. 19–21.

28 M. Walzer, *The Revolution of the Saints* (London, 1966), p. x.

29 See J. W. Smit, 'The present position of studies regarding the revolt of the Netherlands', *Britain and the Netherlands*, ed. J. S. Bromley and E. H. Kossmann (London, 1960), pp. 23–5.

30 E. Pasquier, *Lettres Historiques (1556–1594)*, ed. D. Thickett (Geneva, 1966), p. 100.

31 ibid., p. 47.

32 J. Hopperus, 'Recueil et mémorial des troubles des Pays Bas', *Mémoires de Viglius et d'Hopperus sur le commencement des troubles des Pays Bas*, ed. A. Wauters (Brussels, 1868), p. 237.

33 It is significant that Olivares was greatly exercised by the problem of how to educate and employ the Infantes Don Carlos and Don Fernando, and complained of the lack of precedents to guide him: British Library, Egerton MS. 2081 f.268, *Papel del Conde Duque sobre los Infantes*.

34 A. De Rublé, *Le Traité de Cateau-Cambrésis* (Paris, 1889), p. 77.

35 G. Malengreau, *L'Esprit particulariste et la révolution des Pays-Bas au XVIe siècle* (Louvain, 1936), p. 82 n. 4.

36 T. Hobbes, *Behemoth*, ed. F. Tönnies (London, 1889), p. 119.

37 A. Giraffi, *An Exact Historie of the Late Revolutions in Naples* (London, 1650), p. 160.

38 Lord Acton, *Lectures on Modern History* (London, 1907), p. 205.

39 Cf. the description of Barcelona as his *pàtria* by Pujades (Elliott, op. cit., p. 42).

40 As it is by Malengreau, op. cit.

41 Maravall, op. cit., p. 55. See also G. Dupont-Ferrier, 'Le sens des mots "patria" et "patrie" en France au Moyen Age et jusqu'au début du xviie siècle', *Revue historique*, CLXXXVIII (1940), pp. 89–104.

42 Elliott, op. cit., p. 253.

43 Brucker, op. cit., p. 396.

44 Elliott, op. cit., p. 344.

45 Julian H. Franklin, *Jean Bodin and the Sixteenth-Century Revolution in the Methodology of Law and History* (New York, 1963), esp. Ch. 3.

46 Ralph E. Giesey, *If Not, Not* (Princeton, 1968), p. 245. On the general question of constitutionalism, see in particular J. G. A. Pocock, *The Ancient Constitution and the Feudal Law* (Cambridge, 1957) and Michael Roberts, 'On aristocratic constitutionalism in Swedish history', *Essays in Swedish History* (London, 1967). I have also greatly benefited from discussions on this subject with Mr Quentin Skinner of Christ's College, Cambridge, who kindly read an early draft of this essay and made valuable comments on it.

47 For the influence of classical polities on seventeenth-century English thought, see Zera S. Fink, *The Classical Republicans* (Evanston, 1945).

48 Hobbes, op. cit., pp. 3, 40, 58.

49 A. Everitt, *The Community of Kent and the Great Rebellion* (Leicester, 1966), p. 269.

50 Knox, op. cit., I, p. 225.

51 *Apologie ou défense de . . . Prince Guillaume* (Leyden, 1581), esp. p. 91.

52 'Of seditions and troubles', *The Works of Francis Bacon*, ed. J. Spedding, VI (London, 1858), p. 411.

53 The extent of the Crown's concessions to the Neapolitan nobility, and the political consequences of this policy, emerge very clearly from Villari, op. cit.

54 Michael Roberts, *The Early Vasas* (Cambridge, 1968), p. 224.

55 Hobbes, op. cit., p. 192.

56 ibid., p. 71.

Chapter six

The Preconditions of Revolution in Early Modern Europe: did they really exist?*

A. Lloyd Moote

Despite our general understanding of the wave of Early Modern European revolts that began with the Wars of Religion after 1560 and ended with a cluster of political rebellions during the 1640s, we still do not know to what extent and in what ways those upheavals constituted a revolutionary situation. Here is an excellent laboratory for comparative history by the traditionalist scholar daring enough to escape old generalizations about the uniqueness of this or that revolt. Here is also a mass of useful data for social scientists who specialize in testing revolutionary models. Yet until quite recently traditionalist historical scholarship has been content with brief critiques or bland acceptance of Trevor-Roper's thesis of a mid-seventeenth-century 'general crisis',[1] while sociologists and political scientists have generally applied their model-building technique to the period since the late eighteenth century, which boasted political changes that were more intelligible to twentieth-century man than those of 1560–1660.[2]

Now, some of this timidity and evasiveness has been swept aside. Early Modern historians have not yet found a Robert Palmer to give us another 'Age of Revolution', but Helmut G. Koenigsberger has produced three essays that pull together his long standing views on revolution and crisis in the states influenced by the Spanish Habsburgs between 1516 and 1660.[3] His traditionalist approach is complemented by a multi-authored book in which five distinguished scholars discuss particular uprisings of the period 1560–1775 from the perspective of what social scientists call the 'preconditions' of revolution. The editors of this innovative work, Robert Forster and Jack P. Greene, have made their own contribution by extracting from the discussions of

* First published in the *Canadian Journal of History*, VIII (1973), pp. 207–34 and reprinted here by permission of the Editor of the journal and the author.

specific uprisings some provocative generalizations about Early Modern revolt and revolution. In their introductory essay, the editors categorize the uprisings according to 'types', and sort out the overall preconditions of revolution that lie behind those types that seem to be revolutionary in scope.[4] Even a cursory reading of both books reveals that the fundamental questions raised by the authors and editors cannot be discussed adequately in a brief, conventional review. Some sort of extended analysis seems in order.

The most obvious question concerns the very meaning of that troublesome word 'revolution'. Professor Koenigsberger takes it for granted that truly revolutionary movements were involved in the rise of Dutch, Scottish, French Leaguer, and French Huguenot 'parties' during the late sixteenth century. He goes on to describe the Bohemian phase of the Thirty Years' War as a 'revolution', and he labels the movements that followed in France, England, the Swiss Cantons, Naples, Palermo, Catalonia, Portugal, Sweden, Poland and the Dutch Republic as 'revolutions and coups'. Not to be outdone by Trevor-Roper, the author expands the mid-seventeenth-century political crisis into what he calls 'a genuine crisis of societies and of their political constitutions', and adds his own 'great political crisis of the mid-sixteenth century'.[5] The very title of the Forster–Greene volume implies what Koenigsberger assumes by its assertion that there were 'Preconditions of Revolution in Early Modern Europe'. And the first two essays of that multi-authored work make it clear that preconditions actually led to a 'Dutch Revolution' and an 'English Revolution'. As if to convince those who may believe these historians are merely superimposing a new terminology on what we used to call the Dutch Revolt and the Great Rebellion, Forster and Greene are quite explicit in their meaning of revolution. According to the definition that they have borrowed from a social scientist, revolution is:

> sharp, sudden change or attempted change in the location of political power which involved either the use or the threat of violence, and, if successful, expressed itself in the manifest and perhaps radical transformation of the process of government, the accepted foundations of sovereignty or legitimacy, and the conception of the political and/or social orders.[6]

Of course the wary reader is still tempted to reject the renaming of so many revolts as revolutions or revolutionary movements. Indeed, it is appropriate to object that ideological, social, and political conditions prior to the late eighteenth century were unconducive to revolution, in the sense of some basic, lasting structural change in government or society. Especially in the realm of ideas, Europe before the Age of Democratic Revolution was non-revolutionary, looking forlornly back to a lost Golden Age rather than forward to a better life. Such a generalization seems to hold even if we include those waves of millennial movements that combined the Garden of Eden with the Second Coming.

In their efforts to type political upheavals, social scientists have sensed the existence of this premodern mentality and consequently of an ideological dividing line between premodern revolt and modern revolution. Note, for example, Chalmers Johnson's scheme. It starts with (a) simple rebellions designed to restore a system betrayed by an entrenched élite, exemplified by a Jacquerie such as Pugachev's revolt against the late eighteenth-century Russian state and society. It then turns to (b) advanced rebellions by declining social groups seeking an idealized form of the past system. Finally it turns to two types of revolution, both of which are illustrated exclusively by uprisings from the period since the late 1700s. The first is (c) the simple revolution that goes beyond rebellion in consciously aiming at some basic and unprecedented changes in the existing system, and which apparently dates from the American Revolution. The second revolutionary type is (d) the total revolution, allegedly involving a conscious break with all existing values, and best illustrated by the French Revolution of 1789.[7] The obvious conclusion is that the assumption of progress implicit in the Enlightenment constituted the ideological breakthrough necessary for turning aside Early Modern mental blocks against revolution, and making types (c) and (d) possible.

In social structure and attitudes, the late eighteenth century seems to have been just as much of a watershed. Its 'élites', in the broad sense of the well-to-do whose values and habits were considered the ideal by lower social orders and who had direct or indirect control over governmental policies, were vulnerable to criticism and attack from below on their *raison d'être*. This contrasts with the immediately preceding eras, when blind attacks on the upper orders failed to make much headway against the deeply ingrained ideas of hierarchy and stratification, even in England, where wealth worked more than elsewhere to undermine the importance of status.

Politically, too, there was a shift, though it may have been more gradual. In the sixteenth and seventeenth centuries no state, with the possible exception of England, had progressed far towards centralization. In one country after another, there was lacking a long-established fixed capital for both court and bureaucracy. Hence it was far more difficult for would-be rebels to overthrow and replace a political system than it would be a century later. Most uprisings could aspire to little more than breaking from or changing the personnel of their rather amorphous governments.

It may be mere coincidence that the eighteenth-century specialists, Forster and Greene, deal more directly with the nature of Early Modern revolution than the sixteenth-century-oriented Koenigsberger. In any case, they have established the first typology of Early Modern revolution, and in the process forced us to start asking what distinguishes different upheavals of the time. Descending from the most to the least revolutionary, their types of uprisings are as follows: (a) great national revolutions, specifically the Dutch break with Spanish rule in the late sixteenth century and the English overthrow of the Stuarts in the 1640s; (b) national revolts such as the French Fronde of 1648–53 and the almost contemporaneous Catalan rebellion against Spain, which according to Forster and Greene had the potential of becoming genuine revolutions; (c) large-scale regional rebellions with limited revolutionary potential, as shown by Pugachev's movement; (d) secessionist *coups d'état*, exemplified by the Portuguese overthrow of Spanish rule 1640–68; and (e) urban Jacqueries, such as those in mid-seventeenth-century Sicily and Naples.[8]

The main weakness in Forster and Greene's scheme is that it does not spell out exactly what distinguishes one type of upheaval from another, despite an interesting discussion leading up to their typology. The reader is therefore forced to draw inferences, and he is unfortunately led to the conclusion that quantitative measurements, particularly 'bigness', have determined the Forster–Greene types. That is, the more people, the larger the territory and the greater the violence involved, the more revolutionary an upheaval was. And in so far as this scheme is quantitative, it looks strikingly similar to one by George Pettee, whose social science-oriented typology included the categories of 'great national revolution', 'rebellion in one area against rule by the government of another country' and 'public palace revolution'.[9]

Fortunately it is not necessary to accept either the Pettee or Forster–Greene approach. Other model-builders have managed to offset the weakness of such elusive quantitative yardsticks as body counts, duration and mass participation with qualitative, yet rather precise, criteria. Especially noteworthy is James Rosenau's emphasis on the 'object' of rebel attacks. We historians could well ask, with him, whether particular uprisings had the object of opposing merely (a) the personnel of a regime, (b) its authority, or some institutional base, or (c) its very structure.[10]

The reader should be warned that the actual typologies that Chalmers Johnson and others derive from a combination of quantitative and qualitative criteria are not as useful as the criteria themselves. Probably the main reason for this is that not all of the yardsticks have been used consistently. Johnson does try to take into account the rebels' targets, ideals, and ideologies, as well as their social background. Yet by virtually ignoring the role of social élites and by concentrating on mass movements he renders invalid his criterion of social background.[11] At the present time, it would appear that social scientists cannot integrate more than a few variables.

This imperfection can have serious consequences. In his scheme Johnson uses so few variables that the lines between types of revolt and revolution remain blurred. For example, by admitting that both his 'simple revolution' and 'advanced rebellion' types have the same target – the regime – he begs the question of the distinction between the two. The same sort of confusion bedevils the less complex typology of Forster and Greene. For they establish five types of 'political upheaval', of which only the 'great national revolution' is clearly revolutionary; and then they blur the line between revolution and revolt by placing that revolutionary category together with national revolts and large-scale regional uprisings in a vague grouping of 'actual or potential' revolutions.[12]

For all the weaknesses of the Forster–Greene scheme, and of even the most sophisticated typologies by social scientists, it must be emphasized that models can be usefully applied by traditionalist historians to particular upheavals. We all know that the types are imperfect, theoretical concepts, so there is no danger of distorting

sense of modern nationalism but the rallying by a local or national community and its leading elements in support of its established constitutional system. The *patria* was a precondition of rebellion in the sense that it could produce spontaneous resistance to any outsiders or other persons who dared to tamper with the *status quo*.[19] Despite the backward-looking nature of this rebelliousness, Forster and Greene can view it as a potential precondition of revolution. As they point out, such appeals to tradition could be turned into forward-looking 'demands for basic alterations in the political system or constitutional structure'. Without developing this theme, the editors tantalizingly speculate that 'religious divisions and a strong moral content may have been powerful catalytic agents in pushing the thought of discontented groups beyond traditional bonds'. And they conjecture further that 'a major intellectual breakthrough was possible only in large up-heavals [e.g. the Dutch and English revolutions] that stimulated prolonged and intense debates about the fundamental postulates of political and social organization'.[20]

Two other preconditions appear in Forster and Greene's list. One is the existence of an institutional vehicle of protest – a House of Commons, the Catalan Diputats, Dutch States-General and provincial estates, or the Parlement of Paris. This is the Forster–Greene category that most precisely fits the meaning of precondition as opposed to an actual 'cause'. The final pre-condition is really a combination of the long-range emergence of an opposition and its short-term initial acts of rebellion. Specifically, there must be a feeling that success lies around the next barricade, an atmosphere that is essential for bringing wavering members of the upper social orders into open support of the rebel side.[21]

This is an impressive list of preconditions. It shows quite dramatically how far we have come from the once-celebrated analysis in Crane Brinton's *Anatomy of Revolution*. Admittedly, that trail-blazing scheme was partially predetermined by the author's decision to restrict his analysis to four 'major' revolutions, the Puritan, American, French, and Russian. In any case, Brinton's categories contained preconditions now considered too general to be of much use: economic progress, intensified hostility between social groups, the alienation of the intelligentsia, and a weak, insecure regime faced with a fiscal crisis.[22]

Some social scientists who are more experienced in the craft than Forster and Greene can go still farther in probing into revolutionary origins, weighing as well as counting preconditions, linking them to each other, and in the process developing them into highly complex, extremely plausible factors lying behind upheaval. What Brinton called the alienation of the intelligentsia, Forster and Greene the defection of the élite, and Koenigsberger the intensified opposition of old privileged classes, can be utilized in surprisingly new ways. Merely by rephrasing these descriptions as hostility towards a regime by persons normally non-criminal in behaviour, scholars are forced to ask why such people would become political criminals. Immediately, Brinton's explanation that these persons were progressing economically has to be discarded as psychologically shallow. Social scientists can then bring out a point that is implicit only in Brinton, namely that political criminality stems from the general frustration of expectations rising far beyond actual economic benefits. Moreover, this thesis can be pursued to the conclusion that the frustration occurs under differing circumstances. A prosperous person may envy a rival, idealized social group that enjoys greater economic success. A similar individual may feel bitter when caught in a short-run recession after prolonged prosperity. These factors are not even implicit in Brinton, and they are all but missing from Forster and Greene. Yet they are well known as the complex economic–psychological precondition labelled the 'J curve'.[23]

If one asks 'how' as well as 'why' seemingly prosperous establishment types can turn against a system, social scientists provide an answer by linking psychological factors with ideological and political as well as economic preconditions. There is the interesting hypothesis that a new ideology focuses an individual's attention on a single objective by destroying the delicately balanced multiple-role-playing that normally keeps him going in so many directions that his rebelliousness is stifled. The same person is thereby psychologically prepared to become bolder when the existing regime exhibits by bankruptcy or foreign defeat that it cannot and will not cope with internal frustrations and discontent. While it is fair to note that this last factor is almost identical with the Forster–Greene precondition of the feeling of imminent success, that partial explanation of revolution has been made more intelligible through its incorporation in the cohesive economic–intellectual–psychological analysis.[24]

Even the most sophisticated treatment of revolutionary preconditions by social scientists remains unconvincing for the historian who wants models discarded ultimately in favour of actual historical situations. Unfortunately, the Forster–Greene scheme does not shake itself entirely free from the hypothetical approach it has inherited from the social sciences, despite the factual buttressing of the succeeding essays on individual revolts and revolutions. We are presented with factors that could lead to revolution, but are left asking whether they actually did, since many revolutionary preconditions turn out to be the norm in early modern Europe, existing in places that did not revolt as well as in rebellious and revolutionary regions.[25] Thus the *patria* was a very widespread Early Modern concept; we need to compare its ideological importance in areas that revolted with its impact on those that remained docile. Almost as intriguing is the role of institutions that could become vehicles of protest. The one state that lacked the social estates and political provinces necessary for representative institutions to thrive was Russia; yet there has been virtually no comparison of Russian uprisings with Western ones, or – with the exception of Elliott's essay in the Forster–Greene volume – of docile and rebellious Western assemblies.

If it is retorted that Early Modern revolutions were caused by a combination of preconditions, thus rendering any comparative study of one precondition irrelevant, a second objection can be raised. The supposed preconditions that are most crucial to such a combination theory, because they occurred more often in rebellious than in peaceful states, are not really preconditions after all. Rather they most closely resemble 'precipitants' and 'triggers', precisely the types of short-run causes that the editors Forster and Greene have warned the other contributors in their volume to avoid discussing.[26] For example, the defection of the élite, a frequent possibility throughout Europe during the Early Modern period, occurred prior to other defections in only one major upheaval, the Puritan Revolution. In Catalonia, it came after rebellion by the lower social orders, and in Portugal well after that stage. One could argue the priority of either popular revolt or élite defection in the coming of the Fronde, and the Dutch revolt.

The 'weakness of regime' concept is perhaps the chronologically weakest candidate for 'revolutionary precondition' status. Vulnerability was a universal trait of Early Modern times, becoming more and less pronounced almost in geographic and chronological cycles. Was not Christina of Sweden's regime dangerously weak right after the Thirty Years' War, being hard pressed to handle an unhappy nobility, disgruntled clergy, merchants and peasants, and a remarkably viable parliamentary tradition? Denmark was more vulnerable still, having lost its foreign wars against Austria and Sweden. Russia had perhaps the weakest of all the mid-seventeenth-century regimes, if we take into consideration the after-shocks of the Time of Troubles, the freezing of social status and domicile by the 1649 Law Code and the impact of the Nikonian religious reforms. The point is that governmental weaknesses, élite dissatisfaction, and institutional vehicles of protest all had to be tested by political crisis.

In effect, the two basic questions regarding the nature and preconditions of revolution raised by the Forster–Greene and Koenigsberger volumes have converged with the same positive suggestion. It has become clear that we can most effectively test theories of preconditions and explore the nature of revolution in Early Modern times by studying the background of individual uprisings. For this study, the analyses of specific upheavals in the Forster–Greene volume by Professors Raeff, Mousnier, Elliott, Stone and Smit are particularly helpful.

Marc Raeff's essay on Pugachev's late eighteenth-century regional revolt against tsarist Russia, though clearly out of place in a discussion of sixteenth- and seventeenth-century western European uprisings, does tell us some things. First, it indicates how indispensable the western European institutional bases of opposition were for even a mere rebellion, and especially for a revolution. Lacking the West's built-in protest vehicles of representative assemblies and royal princes, Russian rebels worked clumsily time and again on behalf of a poor substitute – the almost mythical 'true Tsar'.[27] Second, though Raeff handles skilfully the complex relations of the many rebel groups, from Cossacks to Bashkir and monastery peasants, he fails to convince the reader that their movement had either a workable programme or hope of overthrowing the distant central regime. This underscores the generalization that those missing ideological ingredients must exist before historians can apply the term 'revolution', in either the potential or the actual sense. Raeff tries to link the Pugachev affair to Western traditions of rebellion by suggesting that both 'exemplified the discontent and rebelliousness of a traditional group in the fact of the transformations wrought (or threatened) by a centralized absolute monarchy'.[28] He only succeeds in conveying the impression that the Cossacks were closer to primitive rebels than to rebellious system-builders. Indeed, it seems reasonable to accept the social scientists' labelling of Pugachev's revolt as another Jacquerie, or 'simple rebellion'. After all, it was essentially a church and king protest on behalf of existing traditional authority, aiming solely at purging State and society of bad personnel.

The ideological and institutional bases of major, violent change are much more apparent in Roland Mousnier's analysis of the pre-Fronde. His description of France's government fits the 'weakness of regime' theme in so far as its ministers were hated for fiscally harsh internal programmes and aggressive foreign policies which remained unclear to many subjects. More important still for Mousnier was the façade of constitutionalism on the side of the opposition. Combining ideological and institutional factors, he notes that many within the upper echelons of society thought the king should rule in accordance with 'royal edicts registered by the parlements and . . . certain habits and customs, . . . the so-called fundamental laws of the kingdom'. Acting on such a belief were princes who claimed a right to participate in upholding this constitution, either by advising the king or rebelling against his 'evil' ministers, the corporate bodies of officials (notably the parlements which, in their capacity as judicial guardians of equity for subjects, blocked legislation) and finally the organizational elements of single provinces which reacted against royal 'violation' of their customary tax exemptions and other privileges.[29]

Mousnier's argument falters only when he begins to contend that this opposition's attack on the actual constitution in the name of their idealized constitution created a revolutionary situation. In practical terms, their institutional vehicles were incapable of either overthrowing or taking the place of absolute monarchy. For the key opposition institution, the Parlement of Paris, antagonized rival law courts in the capital, and never spoke for the provinces outside central France. Moreover, that tribunal continually drew upon the monarchy's own principle of divine right absolutism, although it did so in a highly complex manner. Revolution was also prevented socially by divisions between the judicial and princely–noble branches of the opposition, as well as by the primarily neutralist role of the peasantry. While many urban artisans and petty bourgeois did rebel against royal authority, peasants frequently tried to fend off royalist and opposition attacks on their possessions.[30] Thus, despite strong ideological and institutional bases of revolt, plus the existence of alienated elements within the upper social orders, some popular discontent, a somewhat discredited regime, and many socioeconomic factors such as climatic adversity, frequent plagues and economic recession, these preconditions of revolt do not add up to preconditions of revolution.

Perhaps one could type the Fronde as a very 'advanced rebellion', in the Chalmers Johnson scheme. It acted on behalf of an idealized past and against existing personnel, with a few attacks on some elements of authority such as intendancies and extralegal courts. What it did not and probably could not do was break with absolute monarchy, question the social structure, or develop an ideological alternative to existing beliefs. In short, it fell far short of being potentially or actually a 'simple revolution'.

The mid-seventeenth-century cluster of uprisings against Spain is even more illuminating than the Fronde, thanks to Professor Elliott's decision to compare all the revolts and his refusal to read more into them than the evidence warrants. He underscores Koenigsberger's finding that 'popular' revolt, lacking leadership from higher social echelons, could not be sustained for long in the sixteenth and seventeenth centuries. Indeed, he sees Early Modern Europe's hunger riots as a danger constantly threatening both the upper orders and monarchy – a perspective that contrasts sharply with Mousnier's view of the poor as largely directed by their social superiors against governments.[31]

The social role of the élite in the Iberian peninsula and Spanish Italy is, instead, linked by Elliott with its institutional and ideological context. Where the upper orders had reasons to be hostile to the central regime because of a threat to their prosperity, and where they enjoyed an institutional base like a Cortes as well as a sense of belonging to a *patria*, a successful revolt could take place. That is precisely what occurred in the case of Portugal's war of independence against Spain from 1640 to 1668, though we should note with Elliott that this was not a revolution. (After all it did not abolish monarchy, it did not alter basic institutions, and it changed nothing socially.) By contrast to this successful revolt, the nobles in Sicily and Naples lacked the preconditions of Portugal's rebellion, and, in particular, were relatively satisfied with their role in government and hence more than willing to suppress rebellion by the restive native poor.

Between these two types of Hispanic experience was Catalonia, which had both the élite revolt experienced in Portugal and the popular uprisings associated with Sicily and Naples. The result was an upheaval with far greater potential for change than the Portuguese political revolt, thanks to popular, radical involvement. Yet, ironically, the Catalan leaders' fear of popular revolt turning against them gave the general Catalan uprising against Spain far less chance of succeeding than the Portuguese. Because of this balancing of tendencies, Elliott stops short of Forster and Greene's editorial suggestion that revolution might have come out of the breadth and depth of Catalan hostility to Spain.[32]

The Russian, French, and Hispanic cases show that institutional and ideological factors were preconditions to Early Modern rebellion, and, just as clearly, that uncertain social conditions thwarted successful revolt or attempted revolution. With these findings in mind, it is pertinent to concentrate on the troublesome social aspect of pre-revolution within those uprisings which their particular historians claim were revolutions.

In the case of the Dutch uprising against Spanish rule, social factors would seem to be the only explanation for an otherwise baffling phenomenon. Indeed, the other rebellious ingredients stressed by Elliott and Mousnier were largely lacking in the Low Countries. There was such deeprooted localism throughout the provinces of that region that one would never have predicted the emergence of an independent United Netherlands – *patria* might work to rebellion, but *patriae* cancelled out each other or at best went their separate ways. The most that can be said for institutional factors is that Habsburg centralizing efforts stiffened local oppositions, while the development of the relatively new but traditionalist States-General into a successful organ of revolt in the northern provinces was the result and not the cause of rebellion. Religion provided only a negative ideological force, as people of various religious views agreed only in hating the established church.

Initially, social conditions were equally unconducive to united revolt. Nevertheless, Professor J. W. Smit is able to expose the underlying rebellious and revolutionary aspects of Dutch society in a brilliant analysis that also buries the pet theories of Marxists, conservative scholars and social scientists. He contends that the economic situation gradually eroded the docility and particularism of one group after another. Briefly, a period of prosperity for 'middle class' elements and lagging wages for poorer subjects gave way to a recession in the 1560s that coincided with imperious

Spanish tax demands. Consequently, 'the frustrated prosperous bourgeois of the booming towns joined the desperate declassed craftsmen and thriving or declining nobles'. In Smit's words, 'local riots coalesced into general revolution'.[33]

By itself, this initial coalescing of economically diverse interests against the scapegoat of the State does not explain the outcome of the rebellion that began in the 1560s. The story might have ended the way the Catalan revolt of the 1640s would. And, in fact, the same social flaws detected in sixteenth-century rebellions by Koenigsberger appear in Smit's account. In 1566 and again in 1576–9 waves of popular iconoclasm throughout the southern towns of the Low Countries destroyed what possibility there had been of a united Great Netherlands state by turning the nobles and patricians against the poor.

Still, Smit insists on looking beyond those debâcles to the ultimate winning of independence by the northern provinces, and speculates on the reasons for that partial revival of the rebel cause. There is the important, if obvious, point that the northern provinces' revolt succeeded because their middling bourgeoisie were threatened neither by the nobility, which was weaker than in the south, nor by the poor, whose lack of numbers and confusion after immigration from the south may have caused their rather mysterious docility. But this absence of social conflict, even if true, explains only a Portuguese-style successful fight for independence, not a revolution. Hence Smit has to reinterpret the nature of the independent Dutch state. In general, it can be agreed that the Dutch were revolutionary by their act of abolishing (reluctantly) the monarchy. Yet how innovative was the structure that replaced it, since the new regime had, at best, a moderately unified, flexible government combining provincial and town particularism with some centralization through the States-General? In historiographical terms, Smit's version of Dutch political change lies somewhere between the weakly federated and backward-looking state depicted by hostile, pro-absolutist historians on the one hand, and the image of a forward-looking, economically *laissez-faire* state conjured up by the nineteenth century's liberal–bourgeois historians. Politically, this peculiarly past- and present-oriented Dutch republic does not take us very far in our quest for an understanding of the Dutch 'revolution'. But just as in his initial discussion, Smit looks to the emerging state's economic and social bases to provide the answers.

In trying to fathom how so many groups could initially rise up against Spain, Smit suggests the possibility of an underlying change in the economic and social structure which might have broken up traditional patterns of life. He speculates in particular on the sort of psycho-economic–intellectual history that Pierre Chaunu's students have employed in analysing criminal behaviour. Smit returns to this broad precondition of underlying socio-economic change when he discusses the successful northern movement. He claims, if in qualified tones, that 'the new republic became the first real capitalist and bourgeois nation with a strongly marked, very mercantile national identity'. Just what the bourgeois 'mentality' and 'consciousness' were is precisely what he says we need to explore.[34] But at least Smit's emphasis on the changing role and nature of the rebellious Dutch élite marks an advance on the revolutionary precondition of the mere alienation of a traditional and entrenched élite. As we shall see, Lawrence Stone's account of the Puritan Revolution demonstrates that Smit's hypothesis is worthy of serious consideration.

Professor Stone has the best assignment of the Forster–Greene volume in explaining the one upheaval most historians agree was a true revolution, and he does full justice to his subject. He refuses to become entrapped in historiographical arguments, methodological quibbles, or the morass of revolutionary events themselves. And, ideally for the issues raised in this review essay, his examination of the long-range preconditions brings out the social as well as the ideological and institutional background of revolution.[35]

The most obvious precondition of the Puritan Revolution was the existing regime's ineptness. Yet the way Stone develops that theme helps to show how the government not only triggered rebellion but unwittingly prepared the way for a revolutionary on-slaught that temporarily swept away Crown, Church and Lords, that is the institutional aspects of political, religious and social structure. As in the case of the Portuguese, Catalan and Frondeur uprisings, there was a heavy-handed centralizing move-ment by the monarchy that acted as a precondition of upheaval. But in England the complementary precondition of the regime's loss of inner vitality had also been at work, a self-destructiveness that can be traced back from the regime of Buckingham in the 1620s to Henrician–Elizabethan policies. That weakness was so fundamental that, when revolt came against Charles I's personnel and authority, it quickly became revolution against the structure of the regime as well.

Stone is particularly convincing in probing the weakness of the Tudors' religious settlement, a masterful political step that staved off continental-style religious strife only at the terrible price of manufacturing a compromise church from which few subjects could receive spiritual nourishment. The same clever, but ultimately disastrous, political negativism is evident in the fiscal, military and courtly areas. In all three spheres, Elizabeth and the Stuarts were too wary of antagonizing powerful subjects to gamble on centralizing measures that would have provided greater fiscal strength as well as a broader base of social support.[36]

Stone's analysis of the opposition's institutional, ideological and social bases goes still farther than the 'weakness of regime' in explaining how rebelliousness could become revolution. Institutionally, there was of course a single Parliament for the entire realm. In the author's words, it was 'a powerful national representative body',[37] though one could qualify the point by arguing that its power derived less from medieval roots than from its revitalization as the agent of Reformation legislation. There was certainly a contrast with the other great national assembly of the period, the French Estates-General, which eventually got on the losing side of the religious wars after being the pathetic plaything of court factions. No other assembly in a state that rebelled was truly national. Both the short-lived States-General of the entire Low Countries and its successor in the northern, Dutch, provinces represented regional assemblies and corporate interests rather than the upper socioeconomic orders throughout the realm as in England.

Stone's arguments about the ideological foundations of the opposition are more debatable than his convincing picture of an ideologically weak regime. Even so, his general emphasis on early modern sceptical ideas, country virtue versus courtly vice, and puritanism in the broadest sense is well placed.[38] The difficulty lies mainly in his insistence on seeing the English situation in a vacuum. If English sceptical ideas undermined support of the Stuart regime, how do we account for the fact that leading French intellectuals such as Montaigne, Pascal, Descartes and Bayle used scepticism and intellectual doubt as an argument on behalf of absolute monarchy?[39] And in contrast to the revolutionary outcome in England of the ideological struggle by the virtuous 'country' against courtly vices, a strongly imbedded 'country' reformist ideology in Philip III's and Philip IV's Spain failed to merge with rebel political and social opposition.[40] Pre-revolutionary legalism in England needs also to be tested in a comparative context, though Stone's assumption of its uniqueness will probably stand up to close scrutiny. Even the pre-Fronde legalism of the parlementary judges was too closely associated with absolutism, perhaps because of the lack of a French common law tradition, to provide the sort of alternative ideology for outright revolution that English law did.

Stone's best case for ideological preconditions of the English revolution of the 1640s rests with the 'puritan' mood, and he opts for the broadest definition of puritanism – 'a desire . . . to moralize Church, society, and state'.[41] This drive to purify and purge, together with the self-confidence, organization and leadership of the Puritans in the stricter, religious, sense, contrasts sufficiently with Caroline courtly attitudes to justify the old term, Puritan Revolution. Yet, as Stone says, the consequences of Puritanism are plainer than its very obscure causes. We still cannot explain why there were so many mystical conversions in the decades before the revolution, including some among parliamentary leaders.[42] Nor is there a completely satisfactory explanation for the quite different behaviour of those French Catholic 'Puritans' known as Jansenists. Potential leaders of political rebellion like Saint Cyran underwent religious conversion, only to take up a fatalistic, almost otherworldly, stand.[43] The failure of the conservative but religiously reformist Devout movement and the ultimate collapse of the zealously moralistic Company of the Holy Sacrament in France are equally puzzling. Together, these negative French counterparts of dynamic English religious currents point to a conclusion that is obvious, significant, and virtually ignored in Early Modern historical studies: the country most approaching England in ideological roots of revolution nevertheless lacked the intellectual climate necessary for the growth of a radical political opposition.

We are thus left with the rather bald generalization that ideology was a key, and may be the key to the institutional changes of the Puritan upheaval. It may well have been the motor, the driving force of the opposition. Yet it was not an all-powerful precondition of revolution. It could not fuse the anti-absolutism of the upper echelons of society with any radical rebelliousness by their social inferiors, any more than religion could in the Dutch revolt. Nor could it turn political revolution into any kind of social revolution. In both respects, seventeenth-century English ideology of the opposition fell far short of the work of the pre-1789 Enlightenment.

The socioeconomic aspects of the English opposition are equally interesting, particularly since Stone avoids the upper- versus lower-class dichotomy so evident in most accounts of Early Modern rebelliousness. Instead, he contends that men of the middling sort swelled the ranks of the discontented. Behind this move, the author detects a massive shift of relative wealth from the very rich and the poor toward the 'upper middle and middle classes'. Thus friction increased between the traditional wielders of power – the Crown, courtiers, higher clergy, the aristocracy – and the growing forces of gentry, lawyers, merchants, yeomen and small tradesmen. Hostility intensified when the monarchy failed to assimilate into the ranks of the old sociopolitical élite the aggressive elements of the middling sort whose political power did not match their increase in wealth or their social aspirations.[44]

Can it be that Stone has hit upon one of the missing revolutionary links in most Early Modern revolts by stressing the restructuring of élites? On the surface, it is a more plausible precondition of revolution than either the mere alienation of an existing sociopolitical élite (that could lead to rebellion at the very most) or the currently popular historical view of a split right down the ranks of an élite (which could tear apart an Early Modern state in an inconclusive civil war). Moreover, from our study of the so-called bourgeois role in the Coming of 1789 we have evidence that a basic changing of the balance among élites and their values can be crucial to the shift from rebellion to revolution, from political to social revolution, and from hope of success to sweeping triumph. Despite Professor Smit's failure to prove the existence of such a socioeconomic metamorphosis in the breakaway northern Netherlands, he is also on the right track in suggesting a partial reordering of society as a precondition of Dutch revolution. And the very fact that the Dutch were not as revolutionary as the English can be attributed to the lack of an emotional target which could increase their emerging élite's self-consciousness. To be more specific, the Dutch, in contrast to the English, could not vent their rage on a sizeable court aristocracy.

In England, as in the northern Netherlands, one other social factor made it possible for aspiring segments of the well-to-do to revolt. This was the relative absence of widespread agitation by the lower orders. The Dutch rebels did not need to compromise with Spain in order to keep their own social inferiors in check. The English rebels made their peace with monarchy only after the death of their leader, Oliver Cromwell. However, it is a mystery how the English and Dutch joined the Portuguese in escaping the contemporary European onslaught of popular discontent, which was as marked in Russia as in Catalonia, in Sweden as in Sicily.

Thanks to the specialists' analyses of particular Early Modern revolts, the broad interpretive essays by Koenigsberger, and the suggestions for organizing revolutionary studies made by Forster and Greene as well as by social scientists, we have arrived at a broader view of Early Modern upheaval than any one scholar could have provided. To be sure, this new perspective is merely a halting preliminary to what can be done in the field of comparative Early Modern rebelliousness. For that reason some of the ground already covered deserves to be recrossed in a brief recapitulation.

First, we have isolated several preconditions of revolt in Early Modern Europe: a discredited regime; alienated elements of the upper orders comprising a socioeconomic élite; economic and political stresses that threatened their position; some vehicle of protest; and perhaps the concept of a *patria*. Once those preconditions existed, the injection of short-term triggers could stampede rebel elements into rallying together and either altering some personnel and policies, as the Portuguese rebels did, or forcing the central regime to restore local or group privileges, as occurred in Catalonia.

In the second place, additional preconditions were needed to lead to a revolution in the sense of an attack not just on governmental personnel, policies or authority but against fundamentals like the regime or type of governmental structure, the existing socioeconomic élite, and the very way in which social and economic structure shaped and upheld its upper orders. Political revolutions against governmental structure were possible in England and the Netherlands because the existing regimes were not only aggressive and disliked, but to a greater or lesser degree lacking in inner vitality. In the English case, this self-destructive tendency existed in virtually every sphere of governmental activity. In the Dutch case, it was revealed in at least two ways – the thorough unpopularity of the state church, and the Habsburgs' failure to develop unifying and dynamic organs of central government for the entire Low Countries.

Quite clearly, too, something had to happen in the socio-economic sphere before either a 'simple' political revolution or a 'great national' social and political revolution could erupt. Even a political revolution had to have more than the support and leadership of elements from the existing élite, whether this came from nobles, high office-holders or well-to-do commoners. Some change in the nature of the socioeconomic élite was essential, as Smit suggests tantalizingly, for the 'bourgeois–capitalist' Dutch revolution, and Stone argues more elaborately and convincingly for the revolution of the middling sort in England.

Great difficulties remain in showing how such a transformation of élites could get under way. Here we can draw negatively on the findings of Koenigsberger, Elliott and Smit, our knowledge of positive social factors at the beginning of the French Revolution of 1789, and several ideological factors.

To take negative clues first, it is evident that during the sixteenth and seventeenth centuries anything more than a minimal, docile role by the lower orders could immediately dampen or extinguish the flames of an élite rebellion. Yet some sort of terrorizing by the poorer sort was, paradoxically, a major factor in radicalizing élite movements. Even the popular 'furies' during the early stages of the Dutch revolt loosened bonds with the State as well as retightening them. It has also been argued that the Puritan Revolution was accompanied by just enough agitation from below to force the upper orders more to the left than they were prepared to go.[45]

Even more radicalizing was to be the effect of peasant Jacqueries on France's so-called bourgeois revolution of 1789. Yet we cannot help asking how these French-style popular furies which had terrified upper-order rebels in the religious wars and frightened them during the Fronde, could work such revolutionary magic a few generations later. The answer lies partly in the shifting position of the French bourgeoisie between 1648 and 1789, a shift that was largely determined by bourgeois hostility to growing co-operation between the older, noble élite and the monarchical regime. An anticipation of that situation can be found in England prior to its Puritan Revolution. The existence of an English aristocracy more prominent than the Dutch one and having elements closely identified with the Stuart court helps to explain a political revolution greater than the Dutch one, and a social revolution (against the House of Lords) that approached the intensity of the initial stages of the French Revolution. Of course in 1789, the aristocratic–royal alliance, being much stronger than the English one of the 1620s and 1630s, drove the French 'bourgeoisie' not only to attack monarchy but towards a new social concept of élitism based on talent and wealth instead of birth and status.[46]

Some of the mystery surrounding changing élitism can perhaps be dispelled by social psychologists. They already have a convenient scheme in the 'J curve' economic theory. Hence it should be easy to add to the psychological and other factors now encompassed in that explanation – the coming of prosperity, subsequent new élite power, followed by short-run recession or fear of the loss of benefits, frustration caused by rivalry with a previously established élite, and sudden, almost unresolvable, political problems.

Yet even if such a complex of factors makes a revolutionary act by well-to-do persons intelligible, some sort of long-term ideological preparation seems to be necessary to explain fully the outbreak of a revolutionary psychology. There had to be some generalized moral and intellectual concepts undergirding grievances, dissolving habits of obedience and articulating new aspirations. The Enlightenment provided these, giving the late eighteenth century what the previous two centuries had lacked, something that could not be provided by any brand of Christian belief, any revolutionary 'party', any concept of a *patria*, any charismatic leader, or even a millennial futuristic or idealized traditional goal. In a sense, this means that full-blown revolution was not really possible before the late eighteenth century, that is not until people looked to the future rather than to the past for hope, to earth and not to heaven, to written constitutions, not to eternal, God-given natural law. In another sense, revolution is a modern phenomenon; as stated at the outset, there has to be a regime sufficiently centralized to be overthrown and replaced, not just deprived of a province or a prime minister.

Ironically, too, revolution was possible by the eighteenth century precisely because the political stability that accompanied centralization made men think revolution would not erupt. If Forster and Greene are correct in saying that revolts occur because would-be rebels think they can realize their aims, the fact remains that Early Modern peoples, in general, dreaded the effects of a major upheaval. It is no coincidence that the most profound upheaval of the sixteenth and seventeenth centuries occurred in England. As Lawrence Stone so astutely notes, fears of a succession dispute turning into civil war, of uprisings by poor against rich, and of foreign invasion had died down between the mid-sixteenth and the mid-seventeenth century; it proved ironically fateful for Charles I that he was the first king since Henry VIII with a fully undisputed title.[47] The contrast between the English revolutionaries and the French Frondeurs, who tried to avoid any comparison with the Leaguers of the French Wars of Religion and were horrified by the judicial murder of Charles I, cannot be stressed too much.[48]

Late in the seventeenth century John Locke added important ideological underpinnings to this English 'revolution-without-fear' mentality. Picking up the loose ends of a double contract theory of government that several continentalists were developing, Locke implied that rebellion in the sense of removal of personnel (legislative or executive) would not cause serious turmoil. Rebellion would dissolve the political contract between society and governors, only to leave intact the prior social contract which had established a stable society and made possible the second, political agreement.[49] It would be interesting to pursue the development of that mental and ideological sense of security in eighteenth-century continental circles and within the thirteen of the British American colonies that ultimately engineered the American Revolution.

The other side of this ideological coin shows the absence of that secure feeling during most of the Early Modern period. It is an anti-revolutionary precondition we historians should not ignore. This does not mean that we should write off the word 'revolution' as irrelevant to historical studies of Europe before the late eighteenth century, for sometimes backward-looking movements, aided by an unusual coalescing of factors, can become revolutionary. The English and Dutch revolutions were, indeed, partly the product of backward-looking, confused peoples thrust in the midst of a muddled political situation, though those upheavals also anticipated aspects of the forward-looking preconditions lying behind late eighteenth-century revolutions. What we should try to avoid is the glib use of question-begging labels like 'revolution', or that even more honoured term of our time, 'crisis'.[50] With these qualifications, we can still take advantage of the admittedly rigid models of types of upheaval and categories of revolutionary and rebellious preconditions. Both devices can open up questions and

develop answers about upheavals between 1560 and 1660 that
have been obscured too long by lack of historical imagination and
daring.

Notes

1 H. R. Trevor-Roper, 'The general crisis of the seventeenth
century', *Past and Present*, XVI (1959), pp. 31–64. The ways in
which this 'crisis' thesis has been superimposed on traditional
textbook accounts vary. Compare J. Blum, R. Cameron and
T. G. Barnes, *The Emergence of the European World* (Boston and
Toronto, 1966), Ch. 9, 'The age of crisis, 1600–1660: absolutist
solution', especially the Introduction, pp. 206–7; J. R. Strayer,
H. W. Gatzke, E. H. Harbison and E. L. Dunbaugh, *Western
Civilization since 1500* (New York, 1969), Ch. 4, 'Political and
economic crises of the seventeenth century', especially p. 111; and
the more sophisticated J. R. Major, *Civilization in the Western
World: Renaissance to 1815* (Philadelphia and New York, 1966),
part 4, 'The seventeenth-century crisis, c. 1560–1715', especially
pp. 232–5, 282–4. For criticisms of Trevor-Roper's 'crisis' see
especially *Past and Present*, XVIII (1960), pp. 8–42, notably the
comments by R. Mousnier, who contrasts France and England,
and who had earlier developed the crisis theme in his *Les XVIe
et XVIIe Siècles* (1st edn, 1954) constituting vol. IV of M. Crouzet,
ed., *Histoire générale des civilisations*; by J. H. Elliott, who
questions the applicability of the English type of revolutionary
crisis to Europe; and by E. H. Kossmann, who does not believe
there was a mid-seventeenth-century crisis. The most constructive
use of the Trevor-Roper thesis has been by M. Roberts, 'Queen
Christina and the general crisis of the seventeenth century', *Past
and Present*, XXII (1962), pp. 36–59. The published version of a
conference on 'Seventeenth Century Revolutions', *Past and
Present*, XIII (1958), pp. 63–72, shows what specialists can do when
confronted with the opportunity to compare several revolts.

2 The most helpful treatment for me has been by Chalmers
Johnson, *Revolutionary Change* (Boston, 1966). All historians will
enjoy and profit from the critique of the work of social scientists
by Lawrence Stone, 'Theories of revolution', *World Politics*,
XVIII (1966), pp. 159–76. See also the wide-ranging essay by P.
Zagorin, 'Prolegomena to the Comparative History of Revolution
in Early Modern Europe', *Comparative Studies in Society and
History*, XVIII (1976), pp. 151–74.

3 H. G. Koenigsberger, *The Habsburgs and Europe 1516–1660*
(Ithaca and London, 1971), pp. xv, 304. The three chapters were
originally published separately in volumes II and III of the
New Cambridge Modern History (1958, 1968), and in H. R. Trevor-
Roper (ed.), *The Age of Expansion* (London, 1968). The main

theme of the essays concerns interstate relations: the Spanish
Habsburgs' imperial mission shifted from Charles V's ideal of
universal Christian empire to Philip II's less grandiose groping
towards a Spanish–Catholic imperialism on behalf of Counter-
Reformation, and culminated during the Thirty Years' War in the
collapse of the still more restricted vision of a Castile-dominated
Spain playing a 'Catholic–Christian and politically pre-eminent
role in Europe and the world'. Despite the provocativeness of that
interpretation of Early Modern imperialism, and the equally striking
conclusion that Westphalia replaced Charles V's 'old, imperialist
ideal' with the 'idea of a universal guarantee of peace', the
author's treatment of foreign affairs is not as conducive to debate
and innovative work among historians as sketchier, but bolder
allusions to internal affairs and revolution in particular, at various
points in all three chapters.

4 Robert Forster and Jack P. Greene (eds), *Preconditions of
Revolution in Early Modern Europe* (Baltimore and London, 1970),
p. 214. The book was the product of a colloquium on modern
revolutions by the editors, a series of talks by experts of
particular Early Modern uprisings, and commentaries, involving
J. W. Smit and Herbert H. Rowen, Lawrence Stone and Perez
Zagorin, J. H. Elliott and Ruth Pike, Roland Mousnier and Orest
Ranum, and Marc Raeff and Michael Cherniavsky, all undertaken
under the auspices of the Department of History at the Johns
Hopkins University in 1968–9.

5 Koenigsberger, *The Habsburgs and Europe*, pp. 64, 217, 276, 283.

6 Forster and Greene, *Preconditions of Revolution*, p. 1, quoting
Eugene Kamenka, 'The concept of a political revolution', in
Carl J. Friedrich (ed.), *Revolution* (New York, 1966), p. 124.

7 Johnson, *Revolutionary Change*, Ch. 7.

8 Forster and Greene, *Preconditions of Revolution*, p. 12.

9 G. Pettee, 'Revolution – typology and process', in Friedrich,
Revolution, pp. 10–33.

10 J. Rosenau (ed.), *International Aspects of Civil Strife* (Princeton,
1964). I prefer Roseneau's terms to the more ambiguous
'government', 'regime', and 'society' or 'community' in Chalmers
Johnson's similar scheme. The body-counting quantitative
approach is exemplified by R. Tanter and M. Midlarsky, 'A
theory of revolution', *Journal of Conflict Resolution*, XI (1967),
264–79. This approach creeps into Stone's essay in the Forster–
Greene volume, where he notes the wordiness of the English
Revolution (22,000 pamphlets and newspapers in twenty years).

11 This criticism is based on Johnson's *Revolutionary Change*, Ch. 7,
which has lost as well as gained some things in reducing the six
types of violent upheaval in his earlier work, *Revolution and the
Social System* (Stanford, 1964). Stone's favourable evaluation is
based on the earlier six-part scheme. See his 'Theories of
revolution', p. 162.

12 Forster and Greene, *Preconditions of Revolution*, p. 12. The
   dustjacket, incidentally, omits the Dutch uprising from the only
   truly revolutionary category, calling the English Revolution 'the
   one great national revolution of the period'.

13 Koenigsberger, *The Habsburgs and Europe*, Ch. 2, especially
   pp. 64, 196.

14 Koenigsberger, *The Habsburgs and Europe*, p. 197. The author's
   idea of 'revolutionary parties' goes back to his justly celebrated
   essay, 'The organization of revolutionary parties in France and the
   Netherlands during the sixteenth century', originally published in
   the *Journal of Modern History*, XXVII (1955), and now reprinted
   along with a host of other interesting Koenigsberger essays in his
   Estates and Revolutions: Essays in Early Modern History (Ithaca,
   1971).

15 Koenigsberger, *The Habsburgs and Europe*, pp. 281, 283.

16 Koenigsberger, *The Habsburgs and Europe*, pp. 35–9, 43, 48–9,
   51–3, 64–7, 279. I find it difficult to take seriously the author's
   emphasis on the weakness of female rule during the 1560s in a
   'society whose ethos was masculine and military'. Elizabeth of
   England survived, while Mary Queen of Scots, Margaret of
   Parma in the Netherlands, and Catherine de Medici in France
   failed because of many personal and circumstantial factors. See
   p. 66 of his work.

17 Koenigsberger, *The Habsburgs and Europe*, pp. 64, 197, 223–35.

18 Forster and Greene, *Preconditions of Revolution*, pp. 13–14,
   contains the discussion of the socioeconomic precondition as well
   as the long quotation.

19 Elliott, 'Revolution and continuity', pp. 110–33 above; Forster and
   Greene, *Preconditions of Revolution*, pp. 15–16.

20 Forster and Greene, *Preconditions of Revolution*, p. 16.

21 Forster and Greene, *Preconditions of Revolution*, pp. 16–17.

22 Crane Brinton, *The Anatomy of Revolution* (1st edn 1938, rev. edn
   1952), Ch. 2.

23 See James C. Davies, 'Toward a theory of revolution', *American
   Sociological Review*, XXVII (1962), pp. 5–13.

24 These themes are particularly well developed throughout Johnson,
   Revolutionary Change.

25 Taking into account the title of the Forster–Greene book and
   various statements in the introduction, it is also not clear whether
   the editors are distinguishing between 'preconditions of
   revolution', 'preconditions for political upheaval . . . and the
   character of the five early modern revolutions or potentially
   revolutionary uprisings . . .' and 'preconditions of political and
   social disturbance'. The dustjacket does clarify somewhat by
   stating that 'this volume examines the preconditions – or
   underlying causes – of eight of these [Early Modern] upheavals
   in an attempt to throw additional light upon the origins of the now
   familiar phenomenon of *revolution*'. Unfortunately the dustjacket
   ends by broadening this statement with the assurance that the

individual essays on the 'long-range causes of each of these disturbances' allow the editors to 'register some general observations about the nature and range of the preconditions and character of revolutions and revolts in early modern Europe'.

26 See Forster and Greene, *Preconditions of Revolution*, p. 2.

27 The Russian difficulties bear some resemblance to the traditional Chinese problem of questioning political legitimacy. Cf. the review essay on Roland Mousnier, *Fureurs Paysannes: les Paysans dans les Révoltes du XVIIe Siècle (France, Russie, Chine)* (Paris, 1967), by M. O. Gately, A. L. Moote and J. E. Wills, Jr, 'Seventeenth-century peasant "Furies": some problems of comparative history', *Past and Present*, LI (1971), p. 67. The striking contrast between such ideological contexts as the Russian Communist glorification of past revolts, successful or not, as a norm and the traditional Chinese situation that did not even have a term for revolution except in reference to legitimacy, i.e. the 'removal' of the Mandate of Heaven, does raise the basic question of whether order or upheaval is the norm in a given society's value system. Here is a fundamental question that historians, sociologists, political scientists and psychologists have barely begun to raise. J. W. Smit's opening remarks about the theory that sees revolution as 'internal war', constituting a breakdown of the peaceful, normal political process rather than an intensification of it, is sufficiently devastating to scare any modish scholar from trying to get away with a superficial exploration of the issue. See Forster and Greene, *Preconditions of Revolution*, pp. 22–3.

28 Forster and Greene, *Preconditions of Revolution*, p. 161.

29 Forster and Greene, *Preconditions of Revolution*, pp. 138–9, 142–3, 149–50.

30 In general the reader can contrast Mousnier's views, in Forster and Greene, *Preconditions of Revolution*, pp. 149, 156–7; and A. L. Moote's *The Revolt of the Judges: the Parlement of Paris and the Fronde, 1643–1652* (Princeton, 1971). There are, nevertheless, striking modifications by Mousnier of some of his long-standing interpretations, stressing now the carelessness of the monarchy's articulation of its policies, the weakness as opposed to the strengths of royal manipulation of sale of offices to control parlementarians and other *officiers*, and the degree of popular revolt that was not manipulated by the upper social orders.

31 Compare Forster and Greene, *Preconditions of Revolution*, pp. 110–11 (Elliott), and p. 157 (Mousnier).

32 Compare Forster and Greene, *Preconditions of Revolution*, p. 9 (Forster and Greene), and p. 110 where Elliott states categorically that 'To search for the "preconditions" of revolution in the Spanish Monarchy, then, is to search for something rather grander than the revolts themselves appear to warrant.'

33 Forster and Greene, *Preconditions of Revolution*, p. 41.

34 See Forster and Greene, *Preconditions of Revolution*, pp. 41, 43, 51–3.

35 Of course, some of Stone's present themes are elaborations on his major social study, *The Crisis of the Aristocracy, 1558–1641* (Oxford, 1965; abridged edn, 1967), just as J. W. Smit has built his own contribution partly on his earlier, sparkling historiographical essay, 'The present position of studies regarding the revolt of the Netherlands', in J. S. Bromley and E. H. Kossmann (eds), *Britain and the Netherlands*, I (London, 1960). J. H. Elliott's basic work behind the present contribution is well known: *The Revolt of the Catalans* (Cambridge, 1963).

36 Forster and Greene, *Preconditions of Revolution*, pp. 78–86, 95–6.

37 Forster and Greene, *Preconditions of Revolution*, p. 73.

38 See Forster and Greene, *Preconditions of Revolution*, pp. 86–93.

39 See the doctoral dissertation by Dale Daily, 'Early Modern Scepticism on Political Society: Montaign, Pascal, Bayle and Hume' (University of Southern California, 1974).

40 This fact emerges in the unpublished doctoral dissertation by Theodore G. Corbett, 'The elements of reform in early seventeenth-century Spain' (University of Southern California, 1970).

41 Forster and Greene, *Preconditions of Revolution*, p. 89.

42 This fact was first brought to my attention by Professor Paul Christianson of Queen's University, Canada.

43 The sociopolitical study by L. Goldmann, *Le Dieu caché: Etude sur la vision tragique dans les Pensées de Pascal et dans le théâtre de Racine* (Paris, 1955), is fascinating, though the author's explanations of that 'tragic vision' are not entirely convincing. Dorothy Backer is now probing the psychology of Jansenist–précieuse connections. See her *Precious Women* (New York, 1974).

44 Forster and Greene, *Preconditions of Revolution*, pp. 62–5, 94–5.

45 Brian Manning, 'The nobles, the people, and the constitution', *Past and Present*, IX (1956), pp. 42–64.

46 Several scholars are now working on this crucial question concerning 1789, including Marcel Reinhard in France, George V. Taylor in the United States and Colin Lucas in England.

47 Forster and Greene, *Preconditions of Revolution*, pp. 76–8.

48 See P. Knachel, *England and the Fronde: the Impact of the English Civil War on France* (Ithaca, 1967), an interesting genre of comparative rebellion studies that should stimulate further work of its kind.

49 Cf. A. L. Moote's *The Seventeenth Century: Europe in Ferment* (Lexington, Mass., 1970), Ch. 15, especially p. 391. I would accept Chalmers Johnson's suggestion that Locke was describing a conservative rebellion designed to preserve the existing social structure by removing offending personnel. However, one must add that the effect of Locke's *Second Treatise of Government* was to make rebellion respectable, and hence to make revolution possible. See Johnson, *Revolutionary Change*, p. 136.

50 Two important essays on that term have recently appeared: R. Starn, 'Historians and "crisis" ', *Past and Present*, LII (1971),

pp. 3–22, which warns us of that word's double threat by creating vagueness in place of the precision of 'revolt' as well as by diagnosing short term, surface sickness out of the context of long term healthy continuity of a State or society; and N. Steensgaard, 'The seventeenth-century crisis', pp. 26–56 above, which, in the process of taking on the Marxist left, Mousnier right and Trevor-Roper in the middle, suggests that we play down the idea of crisis impinging on the hapless State, and instead concentrate on the State itself as neither the captive of classes nor the victim of wartime pressures but a living being playing out the role of the persons who staffed it, in the social and economic realms of the individual country.

Since the initial publication of the present article, an invaluable study of seventeenth-century France has appeared: P. J. Coveney, ed., *France in Crisis, 1620–1675* (Totawa, N.J., 1977), a unique collection of essays by Mousnier, Porshnev, and others, with a sophisticated introductory essay on the historiography of the 'crisis' (by Coveney, pp. 1–63).

Chapter seven

Between the Sixteenth and Seventeenth Centuries: the Economic Crisis of 1619-22[*]

Ruggiero Romano

A few words are necessary to explain the title of this article. Why does it include the words 'between the sixteenth and seventeenth centuries' when the discussion is to be about the economic crisis of the years 1619–22? It is obvious that historical periods do not necessarily tally with the partitions of centuries: the life of a sovereign, the term of office of a minister, or a war, cannot be accommodated in the neat divisions of the calendar. The same applies to price tendencies and commercial affairs. Economic history has its own chronology. A comparatively new science, it requires a periodization of its own. For the European economy, the sixteenth century ends in 1640 (although some would maintain that it ends in 1630). It is not just a matter of taking ten or twenty years from the seventeenth century and attributing them to the sixteenth, since this would be a rather pointless exercise and of little intellectual reward. My aim is, instead, to show how the crisis of 1619–22 did not merely represent a break between the centuries, but determined the character of the new century, marked the failure of the ambitions of a long period in history and, finally, was the point at which the great hopes of capitalism (obviously a mercantilist capitalism) in the sixteenth century were shattered.

In this way, the displacement of a group of ten (or twenty) years acquires a precise significance, determining the birth of the seventeenth century and engendering the spirit and characteristics that were to accompany it throughout its duration.[1]

* Translated by Margaret Wallis. First published in Italian in *Rivista storica italiana*, LXXIV (1962), pp. 480–531. The article summarizes a series of lectures given during the academic year 1960–1 at the Ecole Pratique des Hautes Etudes, VIe Section (Sorbonne). In addition to this, it draws on a previous article, 'A Florence, au XVIIe siècle: industries textiles et conjoncture', *Annales ESC*, VII (1952), pp. 508–12. I should like to thank my friend B. Geremek for assisting me with the editing and also for his criticisms.

The paper has a further aim. Studying the internal workings of an economy in the process of development, it is possible to see the causes of recession. But it is worthwhile taking into consideration a problem known to economic historians: that while structural movements, circumstances (of long and short duration) and recessions seem to be well defined, it is in fact through a random combination of factors and their mutual interaction that economic history attains its substance and its concrete significance.

In historiographical terms, what is the sixteenth century and what is the seventeenth century? The scholar has a plethora of definitions at his disposal. To characterize the first, there is: the century of 'price revolutions', of 'American silver', of 'modernism', of 'early capitalism', of 'economic expansion' – the list could be continued indefinitely. For the second, however, the definitions can all be contracted to a single phrase: the century of 'economic stagnation'. I am convinced that this reasoning depends to a large degree on the history of prices. A truism has been created that a price rise equals economic expansion, while a stagnation in prices equals economic contraction. I mentioned a truism: if it were only a question of a truism, it would not matter. But the fact remains that this identity is often, too often, cited as an explanation. If the results of modern history of prices are accepted, it is necessary to recognize the dichotomy existing between the sixteenth century (c. 1540 to 1640) of expansion and the seventeenth century (c. 1640 to 1740) of stagnation. But it may well be asked if it is really necessary to accept 'the results of the modern history of prices'. These results are, for the most part, the fruit of arbitrary transformations into precious metals of prices that were originally expressed in local currencies. In fact, they are no longer 'prices' but 'silver prices' and 'gold prices'. And because of this, we are no longer speaking about the history of money, but about the history of 'metals'. Now, so far, all the definitions put forward for the two centuries with which we are concerned are determined by the movement of silver prices. This shows very clearly that there was a price rise in Europe until 1640; this rise was followed not so much by a direct fall but by a stagnation, hence the definitions of the two centuries noted above. But is this movement a good criterion for analysis? I do not believe that it is, and I shall try to show why not in the following pages.

At this point, I should like to remind the reader of a similar misunderstanding which has been established for a different period, that of the fifteenth century. It is significant that, for a long period, historians divided into two distinct groups and argued about the existence, or not, of a crisis (in the sense of a general exhaustion) in the fifteenth century. The reasons for the opposing interpretations centred on the different constructions of the price curves. With silver prices, there is the crisis of the fifteenth century, whereas with prices in local currencies the crisis is dissolved.

Returning to the period that interests us, we see at once that, if the criterion of silver prices is abandoned, the chronological partitions obtained previously are different. For example, in Basse Provence, a long period of price rises ended in 1594; this was followed by a phase of stagnation, which continued until 1689, after which there was another rise, which ended in 1785.[2] How is this to be reconciled with the old chronological definitions of the sixteenth (c. 1540 to 1640) and seventeenth (c. 1640 to 1740) centuries? Which is right? This is neither the place to solve the debate, nor the time to decide in favour of one or other argument.[3] It merely shows that it is useless to ask the history of prices for what it is unable to give, whether in silver prices or in what we should like to call, to avoid any misunderstanding, 'real prices'. The important point is that it is extremely difficult to try to determine the characteristics of a total economy (that is, in its aspects of production and distribution) on the evidence of prices alone. In addition to this, I should like to deny the truism mentioned above (the discussion of which was postponed). If I deny, at least to a great extent, this function of prices as a 'thermometer' to measure the economy, it is because I think that one should always argue in terms of a total economy. Prices only act as a 'thermometer' to gauge trends in trade, production and revenue: on consideration, these may have internal discordant elements, and prices could reflect these. I say 'could', for it is by no means certain that they do. The 'thermometer' is, then, subject to change, and cannot measure pure economic reality. It does not pretend to show, with absolute precision, the characteristics, functions and rhythms of the whole. It is because the intervening factors are so complicated that prices cannot accurately reflect the situation in all its intricacy. If we deny the value of silver prices and of their chronology, and accept the 'real prices' and the chronology that comes with them, even then our new periods have no validity in determining the chronological sequence of a whole economic age. Nevertheless, I do not believe that the sixteenth century ends in 1594–5, as the figures for Basse Provence suggest. In this sense, the title of this paper retains its full significance: researching into the characteristics of a crisis that by its very nature separated two economies, the two 'global' economies of the two centuries.

In order to study the transition from the sixteenth to the seventeenth century, this paper will concentrate on those elements that are basic to life, curtailing discussion of those that I consider to be only peripheral. The pages that follow can be divided into two distinct sections. The first is characterized by facts and figures that I believe should be put before the reader in order to give weight to my argument. In addition to this, they will clearly show that there is a distinct turning-point between the second and third decades of the seventeenth century. In order to illustrate this turning-point, I have been obliged to take the time-honoured period of 1561–1660 for examination.

As there is only one idea to be demonstrated, and as there is a wealth of evidence, there will be some monotony, which I excuse as inevitable. The second part, which I feel is more animated and 'alive', endeavours to illustrate the internal mechanism of the crisis. It surveys the period 1614–25 and applies to it the observations of the first part. Thus the two sections are linked together rather like documents and commentary. The dynamic nature of the latter will, I hope, compensate the reader for the pedestrian nature of the former.

I   Facts and Figures

TRADE

Turning first to the currents of international trade, there are two major sources of information at our disposal. The first concerns Seville and the Atlantic, and has been imaginatively and diligently researched by Huguette and Pierre Chaunu.[4] The second is that of the Sound, which has been investigated by Nina Ellinger Bang in a series of volumes[5] which, although they are often criticized,[6] remain of incontestable value, inasmuch as they refer to the (then) contemporary trends.

Let us enlarge our sphere of observation in order to sharpen our judgement. From 1560 to 1650, the total movement of tonnage leaving from, and arriving at, Seville over five-yearly periods, as shown by the Chaunus, is as shown in Table 7.1.[7]

TABLE 7.1

Years	Tons	Years	Tons
1561–5	87,048	1606–10	273,560
1566–70	111,039	1611–15	228,705
1571–5	129,480	1616–20	248,214
1576–80	135,926	1621–5	229,828
1581–5	166,057	1626–30	221,522
1586–90	191,589	1631–5	158,414
1591–5	162,323	1636–40	158,475
1596–1600	218,988	1641–5	126,498
1601–5	216,701	1646–50	121,308

On the evidence of the tonnage, the turning-point appears clearly in 1610 (exactly in 1610, since in the annual record of tonnage, that is the year that shows the highest level); but up until this point, can tonnage be regarded as a true expression of the vitality of trade? With this documentation, we are in sight, not just of a linear movement in trade which happens to be well defined, but of a system of distribution of American products in Europe, and of the distribution of products from Seville – from Europe, to the new continent. The latter, being in the process of development, needed everything, at least everything that it was able to buy. Because of this, the figures for the value of the merchandise will be more significant than those of tonnage (see Table 7.2).[8]

TABLE 7.2

Years	Value (*maravedis*)	Years	Value (*maravedis*)
1566–70	10,828,567,382	1601–5	17,210,271,982
1571–5	10,319,197,700	1606–10	22,945,977,430
1576–80	14,666,341,625	1611–15	20,492,651,323
1581–5	22,059,667,844	1616–20	24,652,885,326
1586–90	20,926,428,610	1621–5	19,744,823,361
1591–5	26,127,615,905	1626–30	—
1596–1600	26,604,787,326	1631–5	13,842,413,722

Now, in the light of the value of trade, which is more significant than its tonnage, a different picture emerges. From 1566 there is a rise continuing until 1596–1600, when it reaches its maximum; then there is a sharp recession during the quinquennium 1601–05, a recovery from 1606–15 and finally a boom in the succeeding five years. But, since Pierre Chaunu has not merely edited a mass of data on the subject, but has also written a shrewd commentary, it would be best to quote him:[9]

> At the heart of the crisis, 1622–23, the Carrera de las Indias was confronted with a thoroughly abnormal situation. The winding-up of an ancient and accustomed prosperity was nearly completed. . . . After 1622, we can say that there are no more turning-points.[10] The break occurred a little after 1622, and we could look in vain for something similar at the height of the preceding crisis, that of 1609–13. After the 1609 crisis, the Carrera, although reduced, retained its recuperative abilities, which it lost in the following crisis. Crisis in volume, yes; but also an irreversible change in values. This is the main convincing reason which leads us to place the change in the 1620s, despite the many and excellent reasons for locating it in the structural *pré-crise* of the years 1609–13.[11]

These passages – and others that I could have cited – expound the trends already indicated by the figures above. They show that the years 1609–13 – which we shall consider again and again – saw a real reversal of the general trend, so that we are, as Chaunu affirms, in sight of a structural crisis. I shall have occasion to return to this again.

Let us now observe another dominant sector of international trade in the world of the seventeenth century, that of the Sound. Through the work of Nina Ellinger Bang we can begin to perceive the commercial relationships between two worlds, namely that of the Baltic and western Europe.

TABLE 7.3

Period	Number of vessels (annual average)	Period	Number of vessels (annual average)
1497–1547	1,336	1600–09	4,525
1557–8	2,251	1610–19	4,779
1560–9	3,158	1620–9	3,726
1574–9	4,300	1630–9	3,383
1580–9	4,921	1640–9	3,499
1590–9	5,623	1650–7	3,015

We may gain our first impression from the annual average of ships passing through the Sound during the periods shown in Table 7.3.[12] If, in the case of Seville, the figures for tonnage show a turning-point in 1610, here, on the sole evidence of the number of ships, the turning-point is situated in 1600. This is followed by a recovery, which is sustained (strongly in the second decade) until 1619, after which there is a significant fall.

But what do the above figures indicate? Is the number of ships a good measurement of the flow of trade? Unfortunately, for the Sound, we have neither the total tonnage, nor general data on the value of trade at our disposal. However, through the work of Aksel E. Christensen, we can attempt to make some concrete observations on the commercial relationships between western Europe and Baltic Europe. Christensen has calculated the lastage duty levied by the customs officials at Elsinore. 'Lastage', he rightly notes, 'was an artificial attempt at joining together the two completely incommensurable and independent functions: [the] value and volume of commodities.'[13] Now, these figures are expressed as in Table 7.4.[14]

TABLE 7.4

Period	Total	Annual average
1581–90	579.1	57.91
1591–1600	780.7	78.07
1601–10	868.1	86.81
1611–20	1008.1	100.81
1621–30	964.9	96.49

Unfortunately, as there are some gaps in the documentation of succeeding years, it is not possible to calculate the total average. Despite this, it is evident that from 1581 to 1620 there is a steady increase, which reaches its maximum in 1619, after which there is a maintenance of a high level until 1623. Then there is a clear fall which continues in succeeding years.

I realize that my evaluation of the figures given by Aksel E. Christensen can easily be attacked. It is significant that after 1618 there was a radical alteration in the customs system of the Sound. This makes any comparison between the figures relating to the years before 1618 and those relating to the years after 1618 impossible. Despite this, each of the two periods (especially that of the years 1618–39) has its own intrinsic value and so we may conclude that after the maximum, reached in 1618, until the end, there was a steady decline.

But other elements make it possible for us to assess the trade of the Sound with more accuracy and more success. Firstly, it is possible to take into consideration, among the total number of vessels passing through the Sound, those that were exclusively Dutch (Table 7.5). They represent almost half the total number of voyages, and they express international commercial relationships with the greatest clarity.[15]

TABLE 7.5

Years	Total number of Dutch ships	Annual average
1576–80	13,501	2,700
1581–5	11,810	2,362
1586–90	16,072	3,214
1591–5	19,616	3,923
1596–1600	18,009	3,601
1601–05	13,167	2,633
1606–10	16,732	3,346
1611–15	16,877	3,375
1616–20	19,455	3,891
1621–5	13,852	2,770
1626–30	9,110	1,822

It seems to me that the figures show that there are two phases: a first, which spans the maximum of the years 1591–5, and another, which occurs after the depths had been plumbed in 1601–5, in the years 1616–20, when the high levels have been restored. So we have 1616–20, with 19,455 voyages, to set against the old maximum of 1591–5, with 19,616 voyages. These figures become more significant if, as well as the number of ships, their tonnage is considered. It is valued as in Table 7.6 by Christensen.[16] Here, we have a further element confirming my argument. It is possible

TABLE 7.6

Years	Tonnage in lasts
1591–1600	126,000
1601–10	121,000
1611–20	182,000
1621–30	117,000
1631–40	130,000

to cite various others in order to show the clear 'turning-point' that occurred in the second decade of the seventeenth century, and which was manifested in the trade between the Baltic and western Europe. The two products that were central to the importance of trade in the Baltic were grain (sent from the Baltic to western Europe) and salt (sent from western Europe to the Baltic). Between 1565 and 1635 grain represented 55 to 65 per cent of the total of commodities bound for the West. Salt represented between 51 and 72 per cent of trade bound for the East during the period 1565–1615, but this fell to between 40 and 48 per cent during the period 1625–35.[17] Basically, we have two products, which we may legitimately assume are valid expressions of the importance of the Sound, in terms of global trade. If these two leading products are observed, it appears that between 1562 and 1640 the grain trade follows a tendency to increase until 1618 and to decline thereafter. For salt, which was mainly carried in Dutch ships, the trend is the same.[18]

These splendid series of statistics bring clear proof of the turning-point in international trade after 1620. I said 'splendid' series: not in the sense of extensive, or in the sense of being well defined (in the case of Seville especially), but splendid in that they refer to incontrovertible facts. The decline of one port at a certain time may not be very significant. It is always possible, for example, that it will lead to the rise of another. Thus 'malheur des uns, bonheur des autres', or even 'mors tua, vita mea', may apply. This is not the case with our figures. It is possible to argue that the trade of Seville represented the total trade of the vast Spanish Atlantic and that the trade of the Sound represented all commercial communication between the Baltic and Europe. This being so, the decline in the trade of the Sound did not give way to the rise of another trade current. Similarly, the recession of Seville did not precipitate the new life of another port (Cadiz began to become important somewhat later).[19]

The weight of the conclusions produced from the data of the Sound and the Spanish Atlantic is such that it is now possible to take into consideration various specific trade movements in different major centres. These will confirm the conclusions already reached and at the same time will reinforce them.

First we shall enter the Mediterranean world. A preliminary sounding of the rhythms of economic life here can be made by means of a strange document which indicates the number of Dutch ships that were captured and taken to Algiers. During the seven years between 1617 and 1623, 186 ships were captured (to this, 24 ships that were captured and released should be added). We may see the annual distribution of these captures in the following list: 1617:30, 1618:22, 1619:16, 1620:82, 1621:35, 1622:1, 1623:0, 1624:4, 1625:1.[20] Is it possible to believe that this is merely a matter of the fluctuating fortunes of war, that it is a reflection of purely military circumstance? Or rather, should it not be taken into consideration that the greater or lesser number of ships captured must have been proportional to the number of Dutch ships present in the Mediterranean? Since it concerns *Dutch* ships, does this not suggest that their presence was a faithful reflection of the favourability, or not, of circumstances? Is it not striking that, in 1620, 82 ships were captured, yet only one was captured in 1622? And this in spite of the fact that in 1622 there was a famine which affected the whole Mediterranean area. It should have constituted a strong attraction for the Dutch ships, which had specialized since 1591 in the transportation of grain from the North to the countries of the South. But a famine is an accidental occurrence. However favourable the economic context may be that it creates, any advantages vanish when a general economic crisis rages.

I believe that it is worth spending some time on the problem of the Dutch presence in the Mediterranean. It is significant that, because of favourable circumstances initiated by the famine of 1591–3,[21] Dutch ships began to frequent the Mediterranean ports. But they were involved essentially in transportation, since the Italians already had the role of merchants, often supported and protected by the State.[22] It was, however, during these years that the Dutch presence in the Mediterranean became more vigorous and significantly better organized. In 1610 a group of Dutch merchants boasted that they were among the first to organize a commercial enterprise with the countries of the Ottoman Empire; they indicated clearly that before their time there had never been such a commercial relationship with the Mediterranean Levant. They do not give the exact date of their installation in the Levant,[23] and it seems significant that they had always worked under the aegis of the French and the English.[24] It is only in 1611 that the States-General nominated the first consul for Syria, Palestine, Cyprus and Egypt.[25] In this year, a letter to the States-General pointed out that this trade comprised 'A great number of ships whose capital during the previous year amounted to twelve tons of gold'.[26] Meanwhile another report, also of 1611, did not hesitate to define the importance of this trade as superior to that of the East India Company, valuing it at 40 tons of gold[27] per annum.

The turning-point of the Dutch presence in the Mediterranean occurs between 1611 and 1612. In May 1612, the ambassador of the States-General arrived in Constantinople and won the favour of the Sultan by the gifts that he offered him,[28] and in September the first treaty ('capitulation') was signed.[29] At least twelve Dutch ships arrived at Aleppo in 1614, nine in 1615 and nine in 1616.[30] In this last year, the tax of 3 per cent on silk was abolished, to the advantage of the Dutch.[31] In 1620 the consul in Aleppo noted that 'trade is increasing'.[32] But, on 23 November 1623, a letter sent to the States-General by a Dutch *orateur* in Constantinople indicated that a combination of factors (rising prices, piracy, higher security costs) had ruined every trade, 'so that for *two years* I have not received any directives from the ports of Smyrna, Cairo, Alexandria and Constantinople'.[33] It could be that this is an example of the usual protests of a diplomatic consular agent, who complained in order to justify a demand for a supplementary subsidy to his government. But this was not how the States-General chose to see the situation in 1625. In order to gild the pill of the 'adverse period of twenty-two months', they declared that 'The previous years have been extraordinarily prosperous', and maintained that, in general, the consul did not have occasion to complain.[34]

But it is not the complaints of consuls or the semi-philosophical consolations of the government that interest us; the important point is that in 1621 the great phase of expansion seems to have suffered a sharp recession, which continued even until 1626, when the consul at Aleppo commented, 'Very few ships are sent now', meaning ships under Dutch jurisdiction. He went on to say, 'Trade has been declining for the past few years.'[35] This is confirmed by two documents concerning negotiations in the Mediterranean Levant. The first was signed in August 1619 by sixty-three merchants, while a similar document of June 1625 carried only thirty-seven signatures.[36]

But the Levantine situation was not a reflection of general Dutch dealings in the Mediterranean. This is shown by the fact that in the second decade of the seventeenth century Dutch consuls were appointed to the more important places of Italy

(Livorno 1612, Venice 1614, Genoa 1615, Sicily 1617).[37] In 1615 twenty-three 'Flemish' merchants were established in Venice[38] and between September 1615 and April 1616, eighty-five Dutch *bertoni* (ships) arrived at that port.[39] In 1619, the consul in Venice wrote to the States-General, 'It is a long time since I have seen so great a number of ships in the Gulf.'[40]

It seems that this descent of the 'Flemings' on to the Mediterranean began during the last decade of the sixteenth century with transportation; that it was consolidated commercially in the first decade of the seventeenth century; and that it flourished in the next decade. However, by the end of this decade (the 1610s) there was a marked recession. These phases are really only expressions of the Dutch expansion, which in its turn followed the more general phases of Mediterranean trade. If there was a recession in Dutch trade in the Mediterranean, this was not necessarily because Amsterdam itself suffered a setback, but rather because the whole of the Mediterranean found itself in difficulty.[41]

If we now take a cursory glance at Venice, the problems will appear somewhat different, but there should be a recognizable general trend. Let us take the customs duties for a significant period in order to gauge the economic life of this ancient port (see Table 7.7).[42] There are two distinct periods, which I should

TABLE 7.7

Year	Wine	Exports	Imports	German traders	Maritime customs	Olive oil	Excise
				Yield of duties on:			
1582	168,580	183,000	87,059	4,280	39,500	79,840	9,801
1587	291,157	208,532	81,255	45,998	27,481	61,978	8,615
1594	280,133	227,265	80,235	49,940	91,637	79,500	9,666
1602	293,655	264,724	91,353	63,168	118,658	106,148	11,500
1621	320,624	236,563		42,695	71,000	110,213	10,568
1633	241,191	156,917		26,772	59,112	93,629	8,728
1640	221,673	156,374		24,661	48,705	88,014	6,664

like to call the preparation, between 1580 and 1595–1600, and the boom, in the following years. It is true that the extreme gap between 1602 and 1621 prevents us drawing many conclusions, but it is still possible to recognize the climax of 1621 and the phase of deflation that followed. But there is another factor that may be particularly significant in the case of Venice. I am referring to the tax on anchorage, as reconstructed by F. C. Lane in Table 7.8.[43]

TABLE 7.8 '

Years	Ducats	Years	Ducats
1587–9	2,006	1620–2	2,701
1589–91	1,760	1622	2,401
1591–3	1,500	1623	1,600
1593–5	1,850	1624–6	1,300
1595–7	2,014	1626–8	750
1597–9	2,513	1628–30	1,000
1599–1601	2,953	1630–2	1,005
1601–03	3,930	1633	1,159
1603–05	6,647	1637	1,160
1605–07	4,760	1638	1,159
1607–09	5,210	1641	1,029
1618–20	1,701	—	—

This series of figures can illustrate the argument that is sustained here in two ways. The first is the clear rise that took place between the last years of the sixteenth century and the year 1609, while the second is the catastrophic fall after 1618 (it will be noted that the great fall of the years 1626–8 was *before* the plague of 1630). What took place between the two phases?

The gap in the excellent table of F. C. Lane is probably destined to stay unfilled, since during these years the State took over 'anchorage' and it was not released until 1618. It may well be asked why the State assumed the management of this tariff in this period. Was it that the 'easy' times were over? Why was the tariff relinquished in 1618? Is it not significant that in Naples as well, in 1619, they ceded the revenue from the customs duties belonging to the king to the State creditors?[44]

After the confident explanation that we have given on the evidence of the figures for the Sound and for Seville, the reader has probably found much of what we have said about the Mediterranean unconvincing. In economic history it is only well-constructed tables of data that are considered valid.

In spite of the paucity of the figures presented for Venice (I could have cited similar ones for the ports of Livorno, Marseilles and Ragusa,[45] but they would have taken up too much space), I should like to look at those elements that affected the Dutch. It is significant that the 'foreigners' in the Mediterranean soon reached an enviable prosperity. This was not merely because they were a strong power in a confined sea. It was above all because this was a time of general economic expansion. New centres, notably Livorno and Algiers, established themselves, and not just at the expense of the old centres, which, on the contrary, enjoyed a revival during this period. Similarly, when we see the Dutch in the throes of a sharp recession the cause is, *as a rule*, to be found in the general difficulties of the Mediterranean. In the Dutch presence, as in their difficulties, nothing depends upon its own contingencies; everything, on the contrary, aligns with the various Mediterranean trends. But let us sail to other seas.

Inside the Baltic, Danzig was the great trading centre, the port on which focuses the hinterland of the Vistula. It is a world that has been thoroughly investigated.[46] S. Hoszowski[47] states, interestingly, that 'between the end of the fifteenth century and the 1620s, grain exports increased twelve-fold (from 10,000 to more than 120,000 lasts), which is eloquent testimony to the dynamic growth of Polish agricultural production and also Danzig trade'.[48] Since we know how important the grain trade was in the general trade of Danzig, the fact that Hoszowski takes the 1620s as the end of his comparison, which spans a long historical period, seems to me significant. This is all the more important when, following an inconsistent historical scheme, he speaks of a 'period of stagnation of Danzig trade, 1650–1772'. What of the period 1620–50? Graph 1 in Hoszowski's article clearly shows that the fall in exports of grain continued throughout the seventeenth century – and beyond.[49] Linked almost directly to this fall in the exports of cereals was the decline of shipping from Danzig passing through the Sound. This is shown in the same graph, and is illustrated by the figures of Table 7.9, which refer not only to Danzig, but also to lesser ports of the region.[50] The fall appears decisively after 1620 for all ports except Riga,

TABLE 7.9

| Period | Danzig | Provenance of ships leaving Sound | | | |
		W. Prussia	E. Prussia	Kurland	Riga
1580–9	12,509	1,152	3,163	366	1,341
1590–9	11,188	1,312	4,566	534	2,183
1600–09	9,589	793	4,270	381	960
1610–19	10,329	748	4,928	322	1,113
1620–9	4,910	410	4,873	280	540
1630–9	5,200	130	2,830	240	2,200
1640–9	6,880	240	2,270	270	2,790

whose expansion cannot compensate for the general trend of decline.

In the specific case of Danzig, the fall in the number of ships is accompanied by a sinking in the value of goods traded. This is shown by the imports between 1615 and 1628 (see Table 7.10).[51]

TABLE 7.10

Year	Value of imports	Year	Value of imports
1615	9,300,600	1622	13,239,400
1616	10,164,200	1623	17,455,300
1617	11,614,900	1624	14,486,000
1618	14,411,500	1625	14,894,400
1619	12,904,500	1626	11,073,500
1620	13,860,200	1627	3,665,500
1621	12,672,000	1628	4,386,200

The repetition of this trend is strongly significant, and at the same time it is reminiscent of that already cited for the Sound.[52] This suggests that in this sector of the Baltic there is a clear difference in the periods before and after 1620. There is a turning-point in this year that is so clear as to be indisputable.

The examination of Europe at this time is not complete unless the cases of England and Holland are considered. Unfortunately, the documentation is poor. For England, the only figures at our disposal are those of English ships (along with all other nationalities) sailing from England for the Sound. This, for the most part, reiterates what has been said previously à propos of the Sound. In addition to this, we have figures for the export of cloth from London,[53] but these reflect the situation in industrial production rather than that in trade.[54] I shall, however, return to these figures.

The case of Holland is more complicated. The excellent tables of data published by J. C. Westermann[55] concerning Amsterdam begin only in 1624. And, in any case, it would be difficult to approach the 'Metropolitan' commercial life of Holland before this date, as a recent article by I. J. Brugmans makes clear.[56] So, setting aside much of what has already been said about the Dutch presence in the Mediterranean and Dutch shipping in the Sound, I shall consider some other aspects of Dutch economic life later on in this article, bringing together those things that will illustrate, albeit indirectly, the movement of trade.[57]

In the world of the seventeenth century, it is difficult to think of geographical zones closed off one from another. We may presume that geographical distances were very important in the transmission of economic events. If there was a crisis today, for example over shipping in London, this would have immediate repercussions in the ports of America and Asia. We suppose that, in the seventeenth century, this transmission of economic trends was less rapid and less intensive. But in fact we find surprising concordance in places far from Europe with the phases I have so far described. For instance, in Buenos Aires, the imports and exports correspond as shown in Table 7.11.[58]

TABLE 7.11

Period	Imports	Exports
1586–95	1,810,314	84,758
1596–1605	1,411,282	753,436
1606–15	7,534,123	1,151,678
1616–25	7,957,579	360,904
1626–35	1,792,427	255,974
1636–45	1,708,204	288,196
1646–55	1,875,537	98,500

Unfortunately, the figures, published by Juan García, are expressed in decades of years that end in five, thus differing from all the other tables that I have used so far. While I would not dismiss them on these grounds, I cannot really elaborate on them. Is it merely the love of my theory that makes me imagine that the maximum of imports shown in the period 1606–25 would appear even more clearly were it expressed over the two decades 1601–10 and 1611–20? It would give immense weight to my argument if it could be shown by data expressed over decades ending in noughts that the great fall appeared immediately after 1620–1. As it is, the hypothesis can be evaluated by trends in a particular 'product' of Buenos Aires that was essential to trade (and also to general economic development): slavery. The figures in Table 7.12 for the importation of black slaves in Brazil (they were brought from the coast of Africa to Brazil by Portuguese merchants)[59] are highly significant and are presented here not merely for decades, but for each year. (This is necessary to avoid doubtful interpretations.)

TABLE 7.12

Year	Number of slaves	Year	Number of slaves
1606	517	1631	339
1607	226	1632	470
1608	39	1633	297
1609	60	1634	78
1610	37	1635	187
1611	348	1636	175
1612	666	1637	225
1613	780	1638	145
1614	831	1639	211
1615	1,089	1640	295
1616	14	1641	175
1617	9	1642	0
1618	8	1643	0
1619	218	1644	0
1620	760	1645	0
1621	1,834	1646	0
1622	630	1647	0
1623	718	1648	0
1624	74	1649	303
1625	106	1650	0
1626	73	1651	10
1627	20	1652	0
1628	189	1653	0
1629	186	1654	2
1630	334	1655	0

It seems clear to me that the boom, after 1606, reaches its maximum in 1621. I stress that an enterprise such as the slave trade was, during the early years of the seventeenth century, of crucial importance to economic development. The great demand for slaves shows that the city was, until 1621-3, experiencing an extraordinary phase of expansion in all aspects of its economic life. Now, is it merely accidental that the highest number of slaves imported appears in 1621, while a little after this date the decline continues inexorably, despite such a dynamic start?

Is this an exception? I do not believe that it is. The documents for the study of Spanish America are many. There are *almojarifazgos*, *alcabalas* and other customs regulations, which exist in great quantity and with which Pierre Chaunu has dealt very successfully.[60] But with the aims of this paper in mind, I do not know how far this type of documentation truly reflects the reality of the economic trend *ad annum*. It is a good guide for the long term, but I very much doubt whether it can be used to study short-term trends, or, more simply, to observe the profound change in commercial activity.

Basically, the figures for the money exacted for payments of *almojarifazgos*, *alcabalas*, etc., are valid only in so far as they show general rather than commercial aspects of the fiscal finances. It would be necessary to examine the duties themselves in order to know which precisely were taxes of imposition. It is possible to affirm that in the long term the figures are strongly representative of the general tendency, but they may not deceive us into finding in them the statistical documentation of a 'turning-point'. However, Pierre Chaunu, with his knowledge of this type of source, maintains with regard to the 'Pacifique des Ibériques' that there is

> nothing, absolutely nothing, that would not fit into the most classic models of the European conjuncture and, *a fortiori*, Seville and her Atlantic trade. Pushing the analogy beyond what is undoubtedley reasonable, we observe that the most important date here is at the end of the 1610s – broadly speaking, 1618–20; more specifically, 1619. That is to say, ὁhe date at which the volume of Seville's Atlantic trade began to fail.[61]

Since we have been wending our way in a kind of round-the-world tour, let us continue the journey. Excellent guides for us will be C. R. Boxer,[62] and, once more, Pierre Chaunu.[63] They will take us to Macao, the port that opened up the world of continental Asia. Macao, being Portuguese, was in opposition to the Spanish Philippines. They were two 'worlds', which, though they detested each other, were often obliged to sink their differences. Their two roles became defined through this *concordia discors*. Now if, as we have already seen for Manila, 'the downturn in the secular trend occurred in the second decade of the seventeenth century'[64] (that is for commercial activity, excluding the Japanese), this suggests that this 'either would remain at a high level, or even continue to increase, albeit slowly, between 1612 and 1619'.[65] It is possible to cite the same cause for Macao's difficulties, which began during the period 1615–20 and were accentuated after 1621 with 'official renewal of the war with the Dutch'.[66]

Frankly, I do not think that the influence of the war was very great. In the case of Macao, Pierre Chaunu considers the revival of hostilities as an element bringing about the end of the boom. At the same time, the Dutch attributed much of their misfortune to the same war.[67] They referred, above all, to the rivalry of the English, and it seems certain that the English also found themselves in difficulty, because of the Dutch or for some other reason. It should be noted that, because of all the complications, the inconveniences and the recessions that occurred during the 1620s, merchants, politicians and bankers had a real need to rationalize the causes of the difficulties encountered. We ought not to pay too much attention to their complaints. It seems to me that we should look not just at those economic aspects that brought about the structural change, but at the collective mentality as well. The men of the time did not face up to the real situation in which they found themselves, and they believed the crisis to be of the kind that often appeared.[68] They did not expect it to last long. In fact, they were faced at this time by a genuine, structural crisis of the sort that changes the character of an epoch.

INDUSTRY

Turning to industrial production, it is difficult to undertake a cursory observation of industry during the transitional period of the sixteenth and seventeenth centuries. There are a number of reasons for this, but I shall cite just some of them. In the first place, there are not usually many extensive tables of data on industrial production. But even when we have long columns of figures at our disposal, it is easy to raise objections to them. In few sectors other than the industrial can the success or failure of a city's economic activity be interpreted as the success or failure of that city alone. To give a simple example, if the cloth industry declines in Florence, it is always possible to argue that Prato, Siena and the other minor centres will increase their cloth industries so that the 'Tuscan' balance sheet ought to stay the same. The same argument can be applied for various sectors of production. If the production of woollen cloth declines in a certain locality, that of silk may undergo considerable development in compensation. In addition to this, it is almost impossible to find tables of figures (production keys) for industry, of the sort used for Seville and the Sound in the sphere of trade, that may be a measurement of so wide a sector.[69]

We should mention the intrinsic limits of industry during these centuries. What in fact is 'industry'? It is essentially textile productions, mineral extractions and shipbuilding. The rest of industrial activity is of the individual, artisan variety. I stress that, however important all these forms of activity may be, they do not represent more than a tiny percentage of world production at this time. The considerations that follow must be accepted (if, indeed, they are accepted) with one important reservation in mind: the role of industry in the development of economic trends was always one of acceleration, not of traction. In early modern Europe, industry could speed up growth but it could not start it.

First, let us see what materials we have at our disposal. The first source is that of textile production at Leiden as shown by N. W. Posthumus in his work[70] which is one of the greatest pillars of economic history, and one that should be a model. Then there is the production of cloth in Venice,[71] the textile industry of Florence,[72] the cloth exports from London[73] (the last figures are more an expression of production than of distribution, so we are not simply studying commercial movements); the total consumption of mercury in Spanish America and the production of this metal in the mines of Huancavelica[74] (expressions of the mining industry of that continent); the production of silver from the mines of Potosí;[75] and finally other figures, more or less complete and representative of other trends in assorted sectors.

We shall begin with the case of Venice and the production of woollen cloth. This is a particularly significant case because the output increased from 1,310 pieces of cloth in 1516 to 28,729 pieces in 1602, following a steady rhythm of increase. After that, it fell to 1,721 pieces in 1712 with an equally steady rhythm of decrease. For the first time in this paper, we have a series of figures that does not show a clear boom in the first twenty years of the seventeenth century. Neither do they indicate a clear

TABLE 7.13

Years	Cloths	Years	Cloths
1561–70	171,946	1611–20	192,833
1571–80	178,403	1621–30	162,999
1581–90	194,459	1631–40	123,677
1591–1600	223,804	1641–50	112,902
1601–10	216,701	1651–60	97,064

progression or even a sustained movement. But I hope that my argument will not lose force because of this.

The important point (I mention this for the first time here, but shall return to it) is that we are not seeking to find in these figures curves rising to dizzy heights, thereafter to fall. Our aim is to observe the differences in the speed of growth at different times. The production of woollen cloth is shown (in decades) in Table 7.13.[76] A good way of penetrating beyond the superficial would be to calculate the average percentage increase or decrease over the decades during the period 1561–1660 (Table 7.14).

TABLE 7.14

Years	Increase or decrease over preceding decade %	Years	Increase or decrease over preceding decade %
1561–70	+2.66	1611–20	+15.13
1571–80	+6.52	1621–30	−7.61
1581–90	+16.11	1631–40	−26.16
1591–1600	+33.63	1641–50	−32.59
1601–10	+29.39	1651–60	−42.05

These figures show clearly the profound trends over the two centuries. It is evident that there were positive phases until 1620, even though the maximum increase came during the period 1591–1600. After this date, the potential capacity of the industry remained the same until 1620.

TABLE 7.15

Year	Looms	Year	Looms
1602	1,722	1614	1,522
1603	—	1615	1,463
1604	1,342	1616	1,334
1605	1,179	1617	1,464
1606	1,174	1618	1,505
1607	1,255	1619	1,910
1608	1,388	1620	1,591
1609	1,355	1621	1,226
1610	1,400	1622	904
1611	1,335	1623	—
1612	1,498	1624	1,563
1613	1,662	—	—

But I stress that Venice is a special, limited case. We are, in fact, in front of a descending curve;[77] this is shown clearly after 1590. However, after that there was no real structural fall. This did not occur until after the decade 1611–20.

Confirmation of much of what has been said may be found in the number of silk looms in operation in Venice between 1592 and 1624.[78] If the totals are compared, it is impossible to discern anything other than a tendency to increase between 1592 and 1602 and a period of stability in the years following. But this total is a false indication, in that it includes a number of looms associated with the production of *ormesini*. Now there is no doubt that Venice, during the sixteenth century, had tended to abandon this sort of cloth (mainly to concentrate on the production of brocade, which was more profitable). If we look at the looms engaged in the production of brocades and silks, we have the figures shown in Table 7.15.[79] There is a clear increase, which finds its maximum in 1619, to be followed by a significant drop. Again, the figures correlate with a chronology that is indisputable.[80]

The case of England is of particular interest. We have not, I repeat, the figures for the textile production of this country at our disposal, but we may take a first measurement of this production through the commercial trends expressed by wool exports from London (Table 7.16).[81]

TABLE 7.16

Years	Woolsacks exported	Year	Woolsacks exported
1571–3	73,204 (ave.)	1606	126,022
1574–6	100,024 (ave.)	1614	127,215
1577–9	97,728 (ave.)	1616	88,172
1580–2	98,002 (ave.)	1618	102,332
1583–5	101,214 (ave.)	1620	85,741
1586–8	95,087 (ave.)	1622	76,624
1589–91	98,806 (ave.)	1626	c. 91,000
1592–4	101,678 (ave.)	1627	c. 88,000
1598	100,551	1628	108,021
1598–1600	97,737 (ave.)	1631	84,334
1601	100,380	1632	99,020
1602	113,512	1633	80,244
1603	89,619	1640	86,924
1604	112,785	—	—

The frequent gaps prevent us from reaching precise conclusions; neither can we make an exact distinction between the 'commercial' and 'industrial' aspects of the trend.[82] Besides this, we lack the data for some years (1619 and 1621 in particular), which are very important in the specific case of England.

However, there are other means available to us. We may look at English cloth carried by ships of all nationalities through the Sound (Table 7.17).[83]

TABLE 7.17

Years	Total	Cloths Annual average
1591–1600	287,000	(28,700)
1601–10	320,000	(32,000)
1611–20	312,000	(31,200)
1621–30	281,000	(28,100)
1631–40	271,000	(34,000) (only 8 years)
1641–50	207,000	(20,700)
1651–60	87,000	(12,420) (only 7 years)
1661–70	150,000	(15,000)
1671–80	163,000	(16,300)
1681–90	209,000	(20,900)

What stands out in this group of figures is that from 1590 to 1610 there is the clear, characteristic increase, followed by a period of stability during the second decade of the seventeenth century. Then there is a fall, followed by a revival during the 1630s and after that a very significant fall. But it will be necessary to look at other figures, which will show that, in all the tables compiled by Supple over the period 1591–1693, the absolute maximum was reached in 1623 with 60,000 pieces, and the minimum (9,000 pieces) was recorded in 1629.

Another argument of fundamental importance should be taken into consideration. I am referring to the strengthening of the customs system of the Sound, which occurred in 1618. Because of this, Supple's table of figures should be divided into two sections, on either side of this date. The figures of the second section reflect quite accurately the number of pieces of cloth carried. In the first section, however, the influence of smuggling was so great that the figures given are almost certainly inaccurate. However, if a (hypothetical) increase of 30 per cent smuggling is allowed, the correct totals appear as shown, in Table 7.18.

TABLE 7.18

Years	English cloths passing Sound	
1591–1600	37,310	
1601–10	41,600	annual averages
1611–20	40,560	

In the periods that follow, the original figures are correct. At this point, and only at this point, the 60,000 pieces of cloth of 1623, indicated by the annual trend, acquires its full significance. Similarly, what had seemed to be a maximum during the decade 1631–40 appears instead as a steady period of stagnation.

I am quite aware that the authority of these figures can be challenged, especially if my corrections are not accepted. It would, however, be possible to question the smuggling figure that I propose without rejecting the conclusions established in many critical works of the last few years that are concerned with the problems of the Baltic. However, other indicators show that

TABLE 7.19

Years	Apprentices	Members
1572–6	20	24
1577–81	7	14
1582–6	7	11
1587–91	1	12
1592–6	4	5
1597–1601	19	5
1602–06	14	—
1602–07	—	6 (6 years)
1607–09	6 (3 years)	—
1609–10	8 (2 years)	—
1608–10	—	24 (3 years)
1611–15	29	11
1616–20	43	22
1621–5	16	21
1626–30	27	17
1631–5	34	21
1636–40	25	14
1641–5	16	14
1645–50	38	15
1651–5	46	32
1656–60	36 (4 years)	12 (4 years)

the rhythm of productivity in the English textile industry underwent a change between the second and third decades of the
seventeenth century. The number of apprentices and freemen
in the Shrewsbury Drapers' Company developed as shown in
Table 7.19.[84]

Again, I insist that the real problem is not that of finding the
high points and low points. The idea is not to lead these figures
into some pre-ordained pattern. What it is important to realize
is that the maximum number of matriculated apprentices is
reached during the years 1616–20 and that the maximum will not
be reached again until the years 1651–5. The same trend is found
in the matriculation of members.

It seems to me that the clearest confirmation of the 'global'
development of European textile production is to be found in the
case of Holland, and particularly in the magnificent study of the
Leiden cloth industry by N. W. Posthumus. Rich in data and full
of intelligent commentary and explanations, it makes clear the
development of production in this key textile centre. The total
production of wool, which it is possible to estimate only after
1591, shows a clear upward movement, which reaches its first
maximum in the decade 1621–30. There is a marginal decline in
the following twenty years and a recovery (which moves back
towards the old maximum) in the last decade studied.[85] But
perhaps it is possible to study this trend in a different way,
following, instead of doubtful figures, the percentage increase or
decrease (Table 7.20).

TABLE 7.20

Years	Increase or decrease %	Years	Increase or decrease %
1591–1600	—	1631–40	− 1.14
1601–10	+33.66	1641–50	− 9.81
1611–20	+30.54	1651–60	+18.83
1621–30	+14.34	—	—

Here we see that the two highest rates of development occur
during the first twenty years of the century, to be followed by a
notable decline. This, in turn, is followed by a recovery, lacking,
however, the force of a 'boom'. There is evidence of a significant
recovery in an excellent graph published by Posthumus.[86] This

shows clearly that the maximum of 1619 is followed by years of fluctuation until 1653, when the final increase occurs, which continues until 1664.

It is possible to maintain that the number of pieces of cloth produced is not a very significant guide; that what really matters is the total value, and the quality (poor or luxury) of the wool produced. It seems clear, following the qualitative details of the figures for total production,[87] that the changes that are shown are all to the advantage of the poorer goods.[88] This element reinforces the impressions that we have already gained from the percentages of increase or decrease shown by Table 7.20.[89]

Much of what has been said à propos the textile industry, is confirmed in other sectors of production in Holland. The production of soap in Amsterdam is shown in Table 7.21.[90] Thus,

TABLE 7.21

Years*	Tons of soap	Years*	Tons of soap
1595–1600	140,787	1615–20	200,746
1600–05	139,900	1620–5	177,469
1605–10	157,639	1625–30	159,798
1610–15	180,030	—	—

* The years run from 1 August to 31 July.

it may be said that production reached its height between 1617 and 1620. This maximum was attained through a steady growth, which began in 1595 and was over by 1620.

The other sector that is outstandingly important in the case of Holland is that of shipbuilding. In Rotterdam, the number of ships built rose from 20 in 1613 to 30 in 1620, 23 in 1630, 23 again in 1650, falling to 11 in 1673 and 5 at the beginning of the eighteenth century.[91] It is true that the long series of figures over the period 1613–1700 is marginally less significant because of the concentration of this activity in Rotterdam itself on behalf of other ports, but in spite of this, the increase in the number of ships built between 1613 and 1620 and the decrease in those built between 1621 and 1630 cannot be ignored. It was not only the dockyards that increased their productivity: the industries that were associated with shipbuilding, such as rope-making and saw-milling, developed in the same way.[92]

It was during the first twenty years of the seventeenth century that conditions were ripe for the extraordinary industrial development of Amsterdam. It was then that the premises were created (which soon became more than premises) for the sugar-refining industry,[93] for the glass industry[94] and for the distillation of alcohol.[95] There was immense enthusiasm and animation, which was reflected in the influx of new citizens to Leiden, Amsterdam, Middleburg, Delft and Gouda (Table 7.22).[96]

TABLE 7.22

| | Number of new citizens admitted | | | | |
Dates	Leiden	Amsterdam	Middelburg	Delft	Gouda
1575–9	193	334	437	146	69
1580–4	328	440	426	165	108
1585–9	400	724	939	191	126
1590–4	580	853	1,064	205	72
1595–9	353	973	676	158	51
1600–04	314	1,481	382	138	95
1605–09	424	1,822	396	142	110
1610–14	485	2,605	340	176	115
1615–19	577	2,768	334	124	173
1620–4	488	2,703	354		
1625–9	414	1,986	290		
1630–4	337	1,987	317		
1635–9	579	—	348		
1640–4	609	—	391		
1645–9	596	—	386		
1650–4	605	—	390		
1655–9	799	c. 1,900	599		

As in the case of industrial production, we find an increase in population that continued steadily until 1620. After this, the level fluctuated somewhat and in some instances rose further than before. But despite this, the driving force was gone, especially in Amsterdam. These figures should be seen as expressions of urbanization,[97] which means that they are more important than any of the other tables concerned with industrial production. Basically, if the migration rate to the towns is reduced, or at least stabilizes, this means that the town is offering fewer prospects of work. It is surely significant that in a centre such as Amsterdam, where there had been no real textile industry (apart from the preparation of imported unbleached cloth) since the middle of the sixteenth century, there was a revival of woollen cloth production between 1617 and 1619. The municipality even offered assistance to the serge-producers at the end of 1619. Can this be seen as a mere coincidence, or do these dates of recovery coincide with the others, so linking them to the wider economic trend ?[98]

Finally, before proceeding to another argument, I should like to point out that a certain similarity exists between the figures shown above and those for the members and apprentices of the Shrewsbury Drapers' Company.

Are these trends peculiar to Holland, or can they be found throughout the wider economic spectrum ? There are many factors that suggest the latter. There were sugar refineries flourishing in other centres at this time, for example in Copenhagen.[99] And once again, we have what is probably the best testimony in the well-documented textile industry. In Hondschoote there is a sustained rhythm of exportation (of almost all production) during the period 1590–1630. As in the case of Leiden, it is important to realize that the first maximum (57,310 pieces) was reached in 1618, as a result of the boom, whereas the second maximum (60,730 pieces) was reached during a decade when the production level was already high. Thus the percentage increase of the second maximum is less than that of the first.[100]

The various minor centres of Flanders and Germany,[101] though not statistically documented, seem to follow a parallel movement of a boom during the last few years of the sixteenth century and the first twenty years of the seventeenth. Any increase thereafter was not due to this early trend. In addition to this, we may assume that the constriction of the economy during 1619–22 was clearly manifest in this region, which in time was to become one of the greatest industrial centres of Europe.

Once again, we shall sail the seas. The continent of America should prove an excellent target for our observations. Let us study the total consumption of mercury; this will give us a most accurate insight into the mining industry of Spanish America, since from around 1570 all silver extraction was done by the process of amalgamating the mineral silver with mercury. This last was brought from Europe in large quantities, but was also produced locally, in the mines of Huancavelica in Peru.

The figures for mercury mining have been tabulated by Pierre Chaunu with his customary accuracy. Here, I am limited to producing those shown in Table 7.23.[102]

What may be deduced from these figures? If the column showing the total consumption is studied, this gives the impression that the maximum is reached during the decade 1620–30. In

TABLE 7.23

Years	Production of Huancavelica (quintals)	Total consumption: production plus imports (quintals)
1561–70	—	8,750
1571–80	33,974	56,462
1581–90	67,786	94,470
1591–1600	65,755	94,886
1601–10	35,355	70,709
1611–20	61,896	106,675
1621–30	39,857	108,388
1631–40	48,717	95,818
1641–50	53,350	68,174
1651–60	67,260	93,280

fact, this is false, since it must not be forgotten that these figures include the quantities sent from Europe. Now, as 'the mercury exported from Seville could only be used two or three years later',[103] this creates chronological alterations in our quinquennial averages. If, on the other hand, we look at the production of mercury in Huancavelica alone, it is evident that the maximum is established in 1611–20, with 61,896 quintals (there is also an unexpected recovery from 1651–5).

We may now consider the production of silver in the mines of Potosí. The reader may think it odd to mention Potosí in this context of industrial production, since if Potosí is discussed it is always *à propos* of Europe's money supply. But in the former sector, as in the latter, there are the customary concordances and discordances. As far as production was concerned, it eventually became difficult to exploit the metal and it involved high costs. Hence the decline of the argentiferous possibilities of America, which goes far towards explaining why the seventeenth century was a 'century of economic stagnation'. In response to such arguments, it is sufficient to remember that the production of the American silver continued, though on a reduced scale, during the stagnation in question. In addition to this, the reduced scale of silver production was not the cause of stagnation, but only a reflection of it. Economic historians often seem to forget that the production of precious metals is not so much proportional to the wealth of the deposits as to the needs, in terms of precious metals, of the world economy at different times. Gold and silver are extracted because they are necessary, not because mines happen to be discovered at a certain time. Mines are 'found' when they are needed; there is not some casual discovery of them (the same applies to geographical and technical 'discoveries').

It is in the light of these considerations that we should study the figures in Table 7.24, indicative of the 'reales quintos y $1\frac{1}{2}$ per cent de cobos' (levies on the production of the mines) of Potosí between 1561 and 1660.[104] Once more, the turning-point seems

TABLE 7.24

Years	Tax revenue	Increase or decrease %
1561–70	4,205,379	− 58.06
1571–80	5,811,456	− 43.47
1581–90	13,729,510	+ 33.66
1591–1600	14,458,165	+ 40.75
1601–10	13,656,749	+ 32.05
1611–20	12,022,943	+ 17.05
1621–30	10,597,768	+ 3.17
1631–40	10,870,266	+ 5.82
1641–50	9,391,833	− 8.57
1651–60	7,971,170	− 22.40

to occur during the period 1591–1600, but again, we should remember that we do not seek mere records of figures but real, structural changes. If the figures of wastage, averaged throughout the century are studied, it is evident that the decline sets in only after 1620.

AGRICULTURE

We shall now turn to agricultural production. There is no doubt that, in the present state of historical knowledge, a discussion of agriculture, agricultural production and the peasants' life is a difficult, one may even say risky, undertaking. It will be necessary to circumvent this difficulty in order to show the panorama of economic events between the sixteenth and seventeenth centuries, as they concerned the majority of the people, and not just the small minority of merchants, bankers, industrialists and the few who moved in their circle.

I should stress (even if the reader is aware of the relevant bibliography) that I am not able to produce very much statistical documentation in support of my argument. Unfortunately, there are few tables of data showing increases or decreases in production, movements of land reclamation (or flooding), or the contrasting trends between cereal cultivation and cattle-rearing. It will be necessary to expound theories in a general way, to make general references, which may be supported by some not altogether reliable figures. We are studying a sector where progression is slow, less slow than is commonly believed, but still not rapid. Hence, we shall not expect to find a 'turning-point' in the span of so few years. It will be a matter, rather, of showing the chronological relationship between the weakening of the agricultural structure and the effect of this upon the structure of industry and trade.

There is no doubt that, throughout the sixteenth century, agriculture was sensitive to price rises and to demographic expansion. Thus, we have two good reasons for the boost in the cultivation of agricultural produce, especially grain. The price rise secured the increased value of crops and land, while the population growth guaranteed a good market and provided the labour necessary for this increase in production. At the same time, the production increase accentuated the price rise. In the absence of technical innovations,[105] this increase in production was obtained by placing more land under cultivation. Assarts, land reclamations, and deforestations were all factors in European agrarian life during the sixteenth century in Venetia, Tuscany, Holland, France and England. In fact, there was scarcely a part of Europe that was not engaged, at this time, in placing new land under cultivation.[106]

With the exception of southern Italy, Europe shows a marked tendency to limit the space set apart for the rearing of animals. In this way, cereal cultivation was increased. The innovation was widespread in Europe and was most commonly established in the flatter parts of France, Holland, Spain and Germany. Europe had thus been able to cope with the exigencies of producing food over the years, and at the same time agricultural production had improved. Not only was cereal cultivation increased, but new varieties of cereal were introduced (such as rice and maize) and (in the case of rice) were produced on a larger scale. However, if production had increased, there seems little doubt that this increase was accompanied by a clear deterioration in the peasant class, which lost privileges and ancient constitutions. But, looking at the balance sheets at this time, it would be quite in order to speak of an agricultural expansion in the sixteenth century. It was at the end of this century and at the beginning of the next that the situation deteriorated. I believe that throughout the sixteenth century (though the phenomenon had already begun towards the end of the fifteenth century) many engaged in agriculture were drawn to speculative enterprises. The reclamation of land entailed the investment of money in precarious operations, which in spite of all precautions (political, technical and economic) might come to grief. In comparison with secularized church lands, bought by similar means, land reclamation was an insecure investment. It required much work and money to make land that had been badly neglected productive once more. This phenomenon of 'returning to the land' (much cited in the case of Italy) is not regarded by some historians as a sign of apathy in a spirit once adventurous, but simply as a different manifestation of the same spirit in the practice of speculation.[107] We are discussing an agricultural economy of the sixteenth century, which is 'capitalist' and 'bourgeois' (though we should not forget to put these words in inverted commas). During the course of the sixteenth century, what was 'bourgeois' at the beginning of the century was transformed into 'noble' at the end of it (this was valid only for proprietors of sufficiently vast lands); each great 'bourgeoisie' was destined to be turned into 'nobility'. Whereas an ancient nobility could be adventurous and sensitive to the problems of their time, the new nobility, with the conceit born of their ersatz title, could not be other than reactionary, or at best conservative.

These great phenomena, one of which Fernand Braudel has called the *'trahison de la bourgeoisie'*, and the other *'réaction seigneuriale'*,[108] did not comprise two distinct classes for very long. There was basically one class, comprising more or less the same people, who were at least the descendants of the same families. Thus, they brought their bourgeois origins and, above all, their bourgeois functions and offices into the *réaction seigneuriale*, a reaction that, in the case of Italy, I have termed 'refeudalization'.[109]

I believe that this word may be applied not only to Italy and the Mediterranean, but also to a much wider area of Europe, with the exception of Holland. I believe that the new nobility, together with the descendants of the old, considered it possible that the profits made by their ancestors in commercial operations could be equalled by their own diligence and wise investment in the 'refeudalization' of landed property.

But what is meant, exactly, by this word? It does not refer merely to the restoration of a juridicial or a political system but primarily to an economic system. If the old privileges were not revived *de jure*, they came to be re-established *de facto*. Since the privileges are liable to abuse, coercion became the inevitable 'currency', which replaced the old, 'bourgeois' metal coinage. Land reclamations made in the seventeenth century were paid for not with money, but with corvées, feudal services and seigneurial demands.

It is possible to conclude that 'agricultural production, in contrast with all other production, decreased very little in the seventeenth century'.[110] It has been stated in relation to northern Italy, but I believe that it may be applied to almost all of Europe, that it was not so much agricultural production that remained constant, as the total return of the land (that is, the purely economic profits, and the value – difficult to measure in figures – of services due to the lord) that remained constant.

For the lord in the seventeenth century, economic affairs favoured him in that many of the services owed to him were free. If the availability of manual labour had increased (reflecting a general demographic contraction), it was possible to reduce crop cultivation and increase animal-rearing. And if new land was required, there was always the common land. These alternating movements in crop cultivation and animal-rearing are a means of gauging the rhythms of agrarian life. There seems little doubt that the increase in animal-rearing was to the great detriment of agriculture. It should not be forgotten that animal-rearing requires fewer people; the tilling of fields requires many more. It is enough to consider the alterations in cereal cultivation and animal-rearing (and the social consequences that these entailed) in the Argentine Pampas during the nineteenth and twentieth centuries, to gain some insight into this situation. In the Europe of the sixteenth and seventeenth centuries, it seems clear that the sixteenth century saw the development of cereal production, and the subsequent decline in animal-rearing, while the reverse is true for the seventeenth.

Animal-rearing is a sign of widespread poverty. It signifies that there are problems in cultivation, and it necessarily subjects the people to a hazardous life-style. The lord may have been able to derive great benefits; the peasant masses could not. For the purposes of the total economy, it is not the level of the lord's profit that determines the wellbeing of an economic organization. It is rather the average standard of the peasant's life, and his monetary situation, that serves as an indication.

Let us leave these generalizations and look instead at three detailed cases that seem to me to be very important. The first is that of the Company of the Millers of Cesena, which has been illustrated in an excellent book by Antonio Domeniconi.[111] Their case seems particularly significant, in so far as milling is an activity that is central to three economic sectors: agriculture, trade and industry. We find that the number of 'shares' in the company increased from 28 in 1418 to 120 in 1591 and to 149 in 1640. This level was maintained until the end of the century. But what seems to me to be more significant is that, while the number of 'shares' in the period under consideration increased regularly at least until 1640 and stagnated after this date, the number of holders showed a tendency to increase (indicating an expression of the dispersion of capital) until 1600, after which there is a contraction (signifying the concentration of capital) which continues to the end of the century, despite the brief recovery of 1650–60. This gives the impression that, in the first decade taken into consideration, more people (nobles and artisans) showed an interest in this kind of investment, an interest that later diminished. The figures show that:

1 until 1600 there was widespread interest in investing money in this enterprise;

2 between 1600 and 1620, this interest was somewhat uncertain;

3 after 1620, there was general determination not to risk anything more.

We may find another example in the rural benefices of the five bishoprics of Cracow, Plock, Poznari, Wrocław and Gniezno, in Poland. Between them, they included 1,400 villages, 46 cities and about 300 'seigneurial domains', which have been studied recently in the enthusiastic and intelligent work of Leonid Zytkowicz.[112] It is possible to discern in the contradictory texts certain basic characteristics. During the course of the sixteenth century, the peasants were able to save money, but after the end of the century there was a progressive and widespread pauperization. This is shown by the fact that in the sixteenth century, the peasants were able to redeem a good part of the duties owed to their lord by making payments in money. In the period after this, they were unable to do so. In the case of Wolborz, in 1604, more than 50 per cent of the peasant landholders were free, while the inventory of 1623 showed a clear diminution in their numbers. This may have been because the lord renovated (in order to make more efficient) the system of corvées: or it may have been that he conceded the tax at a particular time. The old types of corvées were very rigid (for example, the corvées of transport) and were a great burden on new developments at the time (the increasing trade with foreign ports and the number of workshops created for the production of beer).

These interchanges between landlord and peasant could not but have had their effect on the harvests, so that between 1532 and 1583 we find an increase of about 50 per cent on seeds planted in the domains of Kujawy, in the bishopric of Wrocław.[113] We do not know what followed in this area, although all the factors point to a contraction in production. But, we may be enlightened by the excellent work of Jerzy Topolski, which considers the rural economy of the domains of the bishop of Gniezno, showing that in the first half of the sixteenth century the increase in crops was considerable, was less so in the second half, while the first half of the seventeenth century saw the beginning of a decline that, by the second half of the century, had turned into a drastic regression.[114]

It is possible to object that much of what has been said so far refers to ecclesiastical property. Leaving aside the fact that this last is a good representation of the general conditions of agricultural property in Poland, it remains true that if the agrarian economy of the rural domain of the city of Poznan is studied, we find the same trends, during the period 1582–1644, as elsewhere.[115] The most striking confirmation comes, it seems to me, from the work of Andrzej Wyczański, somewhat dubious regarding method, but full of vitality, intelligence and considered conclusions.[116] This indicates that between 1564 and 1660, production of four cereal crops (wheat, oats, barley and rye) in 160 agricultural enterprises, throughout the six regions of Poland, show almost complete stagnation, which is followed, after 1660, by a drastic fall, attributed mainly to the war.

So, the case of Poland shows that there was:

1 an expansion of production until the end of the sixteenth century, which was followed by a stagnation during the next few decades, which in turn was followed by a sharp recession;

2 a certain wellbeing (obviously relative) in the peasant class throughout the sixteenth century. The lord in this century was not a philanthropist, but there were possibilities for the majority of peasants to improve their lot, for example, in the commutation of their duties;

3 a reaction that, I stress, did not follow a halcyon period, but that was so oppressive and indiscriminate that it was, in effect, a regression to serfdom. It appeared to run parallel in the seventeenth century, with the contracting of cereal cultivation.[117]

Finally, we have the third example, that of land reclamation in Holland. The struggle against the sea is crucial in the economic history of Holland – and in the history of the whole Netherlands. The intensity of the war waged by the Dutch to keep the land out of the sea, or the marshes, reflects the vitality of agricultural life in their country. Between 1540 and 1864, the figures for the

TABLE 7.25

Years	Index*	Years	Index*
1540–64	346.0	1715–39	100.0
1565–89	75.3	1740–64	94.8
1590–1614	339.9	1765–89	168.3
1615–39	418.5	1790–1814	148.8
1640–64	273.0	1815–39	160.6
1665–89	115.7	1840–64	368.0
1690–1714	117.6	—	—

* 1715–39 = 100

reclamation of the land appear as shown in Table 7.25.[118] A similar trend is shown in the cultivations of East Frisia between 1633 and 1794 as shown in Table 7.26.[119] These two sets of figures show that the recession comes only after the period 1660–70, in contrast to the previous cases, where the signs of recession are already present at the end of the sixteenth century. In addition to this, looking at the figures for the Polders, we see

TABLE 7.26

Years	Area
1633–60	6,043 diemath (1 diemath = 0.9822 hectare)
1661–1735	0
1736–94	8,139

that this reclamation began on a large scale only at the end of the sixteenth century. Thus, we are faced with a contradiction that we already know about regarding the chronology of the sixteenth-century economy: the century of Dutch agricultural expansion (c. 1590–1670) contrasts with the agricultural sixteenth century of the rest of Europe (about the end of the fifteenth century to the end of the sixteenth century). It seems to me that this discrepancy is important, and I shall return to it later.

Thus we have three examples, Italy, Poland and Holland, two of which accord while the third is an exception. The cases of Italy and Poland are confirmed by those of France,[120] Spain[121] and Germany,[122] while that of Holland corresponds, to some extent, with England.[123]

I realize that it is easy to find exceptions to the rule in the agricultural sector. A corner of a province, the accounts of a particular estate, the development of a certain enterprise can have their own, exceptional characteristics. Neither is the seigneurial reaction manifest in the same way in all countries. For example, in Italy money was invested in official acquisitions (which conferred a certain 'official' status on to some domains); in Poland the nobility sought to compensate for the decrease in cereal production by distilling, so they used grain to create an industrial monopoly on beer and brandy. But the net result was the same in most places at this time: agricultural production declined, or at best stagnated. The growing 'feudalization', evident in the collection of revenues, was sterile in itself and sterilizing in its consequences. It produced a structural economic stagnation.

Turning away from the particular characteristics and postponing our study of Holland and England, we shall try to make some observations that may be applied to Europe as a whole.

First of all, it may be asked how it is that trade or industry develops in an economic sphere, where the majority of inhabitants do not participate in the life of the commercial market? The two shillings that a peasant may spend at the market during a prosperous period go to maintain, directly or indirectly, much of international trade. When he does not spend the two shillings, who will buy the spices and cloth imported? The lord? The latter is, in spite of his wishes, not able to proceed beyond a limited consumption of spices and cloth. *Luxus und Kapitalismus*, the fine formula of Werner Sombart, is valid mainly for the Middle Ages, but should be revised seriously if the economic historians of the modern world would have a similar vision: it is useless to look for commercial or industrial development when agriculture is faring badly. In these centuries before the nineteenth, trade and industry prospered during the times when agriculture retained its vitality. This was not solely because the peasants were the direct consumers, but because they promoted (indirectly) a class of consumers in the cities which outnumbered the lord and his entourage.

We should reflect on these elements before embarking on explanations that cannot be proved, other than by arbitrary illustrations. It is an illusion to think that there were completely autonomous fluctuations in trade and industry before the nineteenth century. The great phases (positive and negative) of commercial life (and of industry) responded, in these societies of markedly agricultural character, to the significant rhythms of agrarian life. When agriculture goes, everything goes, for want of a better phrase.

To return to our theme, after the end of the sixteenth century European agriculture showed definite signs of exhaustion. Refeudalization began to make its effects felt, and the agrarian structure of almost all Europe was weighed down by the strain. This is shown not only in the qualitative data of production, but also in other sectors beyond the purely economic. The phenomenon was general. Trade and industry managed to circumvent this weakening of the agrarian structure, overcoming the pre-crisis of 1609–13 and forging ahead again. They had, however, recourse to a particular 'stimulant': credit. I shall return to this aspect in the second section of this article. In spite of every 'stimulant', trade and industry did not manage to pass through the major crisis of 1619–22. Originally a normal, cyclical crisis, it was transformed into a structural crisis because the support of agriculture was no longer there. If, at the back of Seville, or Danzig or Florence or Lübeck, there had been a healthy agrarian economy, this crisis of 1619–22 would have remained a (more or less) minor event. Is this an oversimplification? How else are we to explain such significant exceptions, discordances and agreements?

By examining the great trades and industrial production as a whole, we have seen that the depression in these economic sectors was not so drastic in Holland and England as in other regions of Europe. Perhaps, instead of a depression, it should be described as a stagnation, or merely as a decrease in vitality. We shall now return to the conclusions previously advanced for the case of Holland. Basically, I put forward the idea of a 'Dutch agricultural century' (c. 1590–1670) and placed this against the wider agricultural sixteenth century of Europe (the end of the fifteenth century to the end of the sixteenth century). I do not know how far this idea will be accepted, but either way, what seems to me important to emphasize is that many of the Dutch trade regulations coincide perfectly with the agrarian chronology that I have suggested. For example, the number of ships engaged in the trade of the East India Company is shown in Table 7.27.[124]

TABLE 7.27

Years	Number of ships	Years	Number of ships
1611/12–1620/1	117	1701/2–1710/1	271
1621/2–1630/1	148	1711/2–1720/1	327
1631/2–1640/1	151	1721/2–1730/1	379
1641/2–1650/1	162	1731/2–1740/1	365
1651/2–1660/1	226	1741/2–1750/1	315
1661/2–1670/1	257	1751/2–1760/1	276
1671/2–1680/1	219	1761/2–1770/1	303
1681/2–1690/1	209	1771/2–1780/1	294
1691/2–1700/1	241	—	—

It is not difficult to observe in this different chronological arrangement the affinity of movement between the series of figures and those previously cited for land reclamation. Does not the reduction in the number of ships between 1671 and 1701, at least to a great extent, coincide with the period of contraction in land reclamation? Is this a coincidence? If it is not a mere coincidence, we may surmise either that it was the decline in trade with the East Indies that decreased agricultural production, or, more accurately, that it was the stagnation of agricultural life that brought about the decline in trade.

Holland and England are, however, exceptional regarding the absence of a massive and unequivocal 'turning-point' that seemed to affect all other places. They are exceptions that, so to speak, prove the rule. It seems that Holland and England were the only two countries that escaped the phenomenon of refeudalization. Holland and England, the former more than the latter, continued throughout the seventeenth century to maintain an agricultural life of a higher level than the rest of Europe. We may recall, for instance, the curious phenomenon in Holland of the 'tulip mania'.[125] This passion (which incidentally caught the attention of the rest of Europe, because tulips, bought by the bag, grew into beautiful flowers) could never have occurred in countries such as Italy, or Spain, or Poland or Germany. Was this an isolated example of agrarian enterprise? But then, how are we to explain that, while all Europe was struggling with agricultural decline Holland maintained an equilibrium? Certainly, not everything concerning agriculture in Holland and England was idyllic, but the fact remains that these two countries continued throughout the seventeenth century to invest large amounts of money in land. It was this that not only gave vitality to the existing economic life, but established the preconditions for the agricultural and industrial revolutions that followed.

SUMMARY

We are now able to draw up a sort of balance sheet of the characteristics of the two centuries, which we have reviewed somewhat hastily.

1 The sixteenth century, a century that begins at the end of the fifteenth century and ends between 1600 and 1620, was marked in Europe (and beyond Europe) by a general economic development, brought about by an expansion in agriculture, which also allowed the boom in trade and industry.

2 After 1600, the commercial and industrial sectors, lacking the support of agriculture, were maintained for another twenty years, to lose their driving force only after 1620.

3 The seventeenth century seems to have been characterized by a stagnation in economic life. Holland escaped from this and so, to some extent, did England.

The reader may well be surprised that I should attribute so much to the effects of the crisis of 1619–22. He may say: how is it possible that even so important a crisis could shake the foundations of industrial production and commercial distribution previously so secure and extensive? What happened to the investments of businessmen and merchants? The answer is simple. It is necessary to remember that in the industrial and commercial sectors of the world, until the eighteenth century, the proportion of fixed capital was minimal in relation to that of floating capital; consequently, it was very easy to pull out after a round of business affairs bearing real capital.

In addition to this, I should like to point out that in the six-teenth century the old Mediterranean economies, such as that of Florence, were expanding, as were those of England, France and Holland. In the seventeenth century, however, the Dutch and English economies stood alone (and they did not abandon their old rivalry). Thus, the seventeenth century was for all Europe, indisputably, a time of regression.

We may conclude that the sixteenth century tried to break out of the web of a 'medieval economy', to enter a 'modern economy'. The resistance was too strong, and the old forms of production, and the old relationships in production, prevailed. The 'capitalist' experiment of the sixteenth century ended in the return of the feudal type of economy. It was the eighteenth century that allowed the definitive departure of a good number of European regions from these old economic systems, thus resuming the movement that failed in the sixteenth century.

II The Internal Mechanism of the Crisis

We must now move from the long term to the short term and try to identify the hinge that joins together the two long phases of the sixteenth and seventeenth centuries. It should not have escaped the reader's notice that, in the first part of this paper, there was no mention of money, prices (there was a very rapid allusion to these), exchange or banking. These matters, which I now wish to discuss, were essentially facts of production and distribution, not facts *connected* with production and distribution. If prices fall, and if monetary issues show a contraction, this is because production has contracted, and this contraction obviously cannot be attributed to the fall in prices. This principle is indisputably correct as regards long term trends, but with the short term in view, it may fairly be said that prices, money, banking and exchange are all factors that have their own value, as far as trends are concerned. These must, therefore, be considered.

We shall now turn to money and the metals used for money. There is an abundant supply of material at our disposal. But before entering into the details of specific situations, I think that it is important to note the relationships between the types of precious metals. Basically, after 1620, it was the reserves of gold that could dictate events.[126] As a general rule, each surplus of wealth tended to transform its capital, or the profits created by it, into gold, thus hoarding wealth and making it sterile. There was some attempt to counteract this by the introduction of small change and of copper in particular, but this was doomed to failure.[127]

We shall now embark on a more detailed examination of the monetary situation in the period 1613–22. I believe we may look at this from two viewpoints, one being the totals of money issued, and the other being the relationship that existed between credit and real money. This last aspect concerns a phenomenon common without exception to all Europe: the progressive increase in the value of metal coinage in terms of money of account. This is not a new factor, peculiar to the period we are now studying. What seems to me important is that, while this evaluation continued regularly, and sharply, after 1619, all European money, without exception, underwent a drastic devaluation.[128] I stress: what was important was the *intensity* of the phenomenon, together with its epidemic character, and the severe aggravation of the problem clearly shown in the years 1619–22.

The coinage figures are, obviously, less clearly characterized. In their case there are a number of external factors – the reissue of old money, issues using old stocks of metals, issues to cover the overspending of the State – that obscure or alter the real situation of the money market. However, I think it is possible to maintain that:

1 In the case of France, during the period 1608–35 (with the sole exception of the year 1615), the issues of money show a considerable reduction. From this vantage point, it is possible to say that the crisis of 1609–13 was never resolved. The minimum issue was reached in 1622, with £163,236 tournois; this was

TABLE 7.28

Years	Coinage issued (£)	Years	Coinage issued (£)
1561–70	12,633,438	1601–10	14,527,552
1571–80	18,832,520	1611–20	7,351,539
1581–90	29,737,772	1621–30	2,888,829
1591–1600	11,896,571	1631–40	30,103,704

preceded by another low point of £165,785 in 1620. If the totals for the decades between 1561 and 1640 are studied, these minima assume a greater significance (see Table 7.28).[129] Leaving

aside the inflationary figures of the last decade (they are inflationary owing to the reissue of old money), it is evident that there is a
steady contraction in issues of money which begins in the last
decade of the sixteenth century. The two minimum issues are
significant in so far as they occur in the context of a progressively
falling monetary stock.

2 In the case of Milan, rather than citing figures I shall quote
C. M. Cipolla:

> Without much searching, we see, in the level of coinage
> issues, the occurrence of the 1607–9 crisis, that very acute
> crisis of 1619–22, and again that of 1686. The extent of the
> fluctuations corresponds surprisingly well to the movements
> of the conjuncture. During the 1619–22 crisis, the total
> issue falls from 4,770,000 *lire imperiale* to 250,000. If,
> moreover, we take into consideration the fact that these
> figures should be set within the context of a deflationary
> movement of the exchange rate, and therefore that the real
> value of these issues was far in excess of 4,770,000 lire at
> the optimum point of the boom, it follows that the crisis of
> 1619–22 saw a contraction of issues at least equal to 97 per
> cent. Further, during the crisis of 1619–22, just as during
> that of 1686 (and later), it is obvious that the contraction
> only touched the issue of *monete grossi* [gold and silver
> coins], while that of *monete piccoli* [copper coins] followed an
> inverse path.[130]

Everything appears more clearly if, as Cipolla has done, all the
period 1580–1630 is taken into consideration.[131] Over these
years, despite the generally high level of issues between 1590 and
1605, there is a boom which is followed by a stagnation.

3 The situation in Lisbon shows a downward trend between
1609 and 1615; from this date until 1619 there is a recovery that
is overwhelmed by a violent fall. This reaches its nadir in 1622,
after which there is a recovery until 1626, which in turn is followed
by another violent fall, lasting until 1634.[132] Unfortunately, data
at our disposal do not go beyond 1604, but F. Mauro, a specialist
in Portuguese economic history during the sixteenth and seventeenth centuries, writes of 1604–40 as a 'période de grand stabilité
monétaire'.[133] However, this period of great stability was also
characterized by violent oscillations. The stability is achieved

only when the maxima and minima have been averaged out, and their own polarities discarded!

4 The case of London is very similar to that of Portugal.[134] There is a limitation of issues between 1609 and 1612; a recovery until 1617, a fall until 1620, a recovery until 1627, a stagnation until 1636. The oscillations here are, however, much less pronounced than they were in the case of Lisbon; there is notable stability, which I should like to call a stagnation, in the issues of money (apart, that is, from the important contraction of 1619–20).

What conclusions may we draw from these four cases ? I believe it is possible to maintain that the first forty years of the century showed the signs of a steady, or sometimes direct, contraction in the issue of money. This is reinforced by E. J. Hamilton's work on the arrival of gold and silver in Seville: the maximum was reached between 1591 and 1600, to be followed by a steady diminution.[135] The intense and sudden fall of the years 1619–22 takes place against the background of this chronic contraction.

I believe that what I have said so far will arouse little opposition. The crisis of 1619–22 has often been noted in the sphere of monetary policy, ever since the vintage study of W. A. Shaw.[136] Perhaps because of this, English (and also Polish) historians have found it easy to believe that the origin of the crisis was monetary, which is like looking at a shadow rather than at reality. We ought to remember that, as regards money, the years 1613–25 were years of insufficient monetary issues and that between 1619 and 1622 a severe drop in monetary issues was experienced everywhere. However, we cannot further elaborate on this for the data are not available.

There is an anomaly that may be discerned at once. If monetary issues contracted, if during the years 1619–22 the nadir was reached, how are we to explain the fact that,

> in Genoa, at the beginning of the seventeenth century [that is, in its first twenty years], there was regular lending of capital at one and two per cent. It was the first time in the history of Western Europe, since the fall of the Roman Empire, that capital was offered so cheaply, and this constituted a major revolution.[137]

How do we reconcile the fact that in 1619 money was offered at one and two per cent, the absolute minimum interest rate throughout the period 1522–1625 ?[138] On the one hand we have a very low rate of interest, while on the other we have a reduction in the issues of money. The contradiction seems flagrant and insoluble. In fact, I believe that a solution can be found in at least two ways.

The first concerns the banking situation. I believe that there are few periods so extraordinary in the history of banking as that of 1613–22. We may follow the case of banks in Naples, Siena, Strasbourg and Colmar in order to obtain a fair geographical and economic representation. Although they are in different zones, they show the same characteristics.

In the case of Naples, we may observe two banks: the Banco dello Spirito Sancto (from 1591 to 1664) and the Banco dei Poveri (from 1605 to 1624).[139] What is at first striking is that in both cases there is a clear manifestation of inflation of credit during the period 1610–22, above all in 1615. In the case of the Banco dei Poveri, the percentage increase on the fiduciary circulation from one year to the next is shown in Table 7.29.[140] For the

TABLE 7.29

Year	Increase %	Year	Increase %
1607	1,109,75	1617	9,08
1608	98,14	1618	21,94
1610	270,83	1619	5,36
1611	13,67	1620	6,51
1612	24,93	1621	80,11
1613	19,34	1622	47,01
1614	20,98	1623	66,87
1615	14,77	1624	56,56
1616	27,54	—	—

Banco dello Spirito Sancto, there are other factors that show similar trends and point to the same conclusions as the previous figures (Table 7.30).[141] The collapse appears here, as before, very clearly in 1622. There were, however, warnings spread abroad as early as 1617, as is shown by the order, 'all the debtors of the bank will pay what they owe'.[142] But this, and other demands, had no effect, and matters continued until their inexorable climax in 1622.

In Siena between 1570 and 1593 the Banco Pio, or 'Lombard', closed seven balance sheets with a deficit during the period of nearly twenty-four years, while between 1594 and 1624, over a

TABLE 7.30

Year	Total assets (lire)	Cash (lire)	%	Investments (lire)	%	Loans (lire)	%
1613	594,166	131,116	22.0	172,106	28.9	290,945	50.1
1614	732,516	112,628	15.3	251,850	34.2	368,038	51.5
1615	802,266	29,978	3.7	257,328	32.2	514,960	64.1
1616	1,147,979	67,425	5.9	422,543	36.8	658,011	57.3
1617	924,931	118,057	12.7	447,220	48.4	359,654	38.9
1618	872,599	120,242	13.7	362,613	41.5	389,744	44.8
1619	829,400	71,010	8.5	309,327	37.3	449,063	54.2
1620	946,785	57,846	6.1	332,015	35.1	556,924	58.8
1621	1,132,262	225,187	19.8	366,385	32.5	540,690	47.7
1622[1]	1,420,996	517,790	43 4	356,412	25.0	546,794	31.6
1622[2]	1,392,463	151,969	10 9	353,412	23.3	887,082	63.8
1622[3]	1,245,946	51,249	4 1	353,412	28.3	841,825	67.6
1622[4]	1,100,139	35,473	3 2	285,460	25.9	779,206	70.9
1623[5]	1,020,463	20,453	2.0	286,826	28.1	713,184	69.9
1623[6]	985,233	17,947	1.7	286,820	29.0	681,466	69.3

1 To 28 February
2 To 10 June
3 To 30 September
4 To 24 December
5 To 10 April
6 To 30 July
All other dates are to 24 December

period of thirty-one years, only one balance sheet was closed with a deficit (in 1622).[143] In addition to this, from 1596 the reserves had been rising steadily. This increase was not, however, an expression of healthy economic life. We know that the Pio Monte was engaged in the practice of making long term loans to people who, in their turn, invested this money in exchange, so that in 1619 an order was given that, 'creditors may not continue to hold any kind of letter of credit for more than a period of three years'. This had the effect of calling money back into the reserves, but at the same time it created 'shortage of money in the city of Siena'.[144] We may conclude that the development of the Banco Pio, which was a *monte di pietà* (a charitable institution which advanced money but demanded pawns or pledges in return), was governed by speculative pressures and the fluctuations of the credit market.

The Municipal Bank of Strasbourg[145] shows a series of big profits between 1591 and 1622, while the years 1623 and 1624 (especially the latter) brought few profits. After this last year, until 1670 there was a general contraction of profits. The Bank of Colmar seems to follow the same trend. It too saw the extraordinary development of credit, especially between 1614 and 1617, when there was a notable expansion of *créances actives*.[146]

To complete our investigation into European banking, we shall look at Amsterdam and Middelburg. Here, more than anywhere else, the speculative character of banking is evident. The dates of the foundations are, in themselves, significant: Amsterdam in 1610, Middelburg in 1616. In both cases, what is striking is the enormous increase in the number of holders of credit accounts (Table 7.31).[147,148] This can be interpreted in a

TABLE 7.31

Year	Amsterdam	Middelburg
1611	703	—
1617	—	484
1620	1,207	—
1627	1,312	—
1631	1,348	564

number of ways. What seems to me significant is the relationship between credit and metal reserves. In Amsterdam a strict balance was observed until 1619, after which there was a substantial divergence.[149] The same is true of Middelburg. Following a year of equilibrium, there was a dangerous distortion in the relationships of figures for 'credit' and those for metal reserves. The fact was, a euphoric atmosphere had arisen regarding credit, as is testified by the following interesting document (there are others like it):

> The Burgermaster and the Council are concerned that for some time, letters of exchange (obligations and assignations) have been used in Middelburg, to vouch for debts, instead of paying them directly in cash, and that the letters do not pass through the hands of just two people, but sometimes seven or eight, and furthermore, they all pay one and the other, with the same document.[150]

There are many other symptoms of the inordinate increase in credit. The rising numbers of agents of exchange, the fact that the municipality of Amsterdam began to lend money at the end of 1615 to the East India Company, despite all the prohibitions and all the appeals of the authorities – all these suggest that even the cities of Holland did not escape the malaise of the time.

Another way of comprehending the apparent contradiction in the low price of money and its falling quantity lies in the observation of the movement of exchange rates in many European cities based on the fairs of 'Bisenzone' held at Piacenza. I myself have studied this, in collaboration with my colleague, José Gentil da Silva, and together we arrived at the following conclusion. Between 1600 and 1619 the machinery of credit and exchange was characterized by an extraordinary amount of speculation.[151] After this last date, the trend in the fairs is such that we have referred to it as an *embourgeoisement*. How could this conclusion be avoided, after looking at graph 3 in that article, which shows that after 1619 profits were becoming smaller but, above all, more regular! Less profit was made, but less was at risk. Until 1620 the risk was considerable (relatively speaking, since the financiers were careful), but the potential profits great. After the collapse in 1620 there was a sharp recession.

How much of what we have said so far regarding money, interest and credit tallies? First of all, we may summarize the conclusions as follows:

1 a stagnation in the minting of money resulted in a reduction in the monetary stock;

2 the price of money was progressively falling;

3 there was a very considerable expansion in credit.

These three conclusions, between them, show a clear contrast (2 against 1), and an agreement (3 and 1) that explains the contradiction. It seems possible to conclude that the increase of credit, brought about by the diminution of metal reserves, not only compensated for this diminution but went beyond this, precipitating a notable reduction in the price of money.

It would be tedious to search for the exact date of the first exchange operation. It seems certain that the practice began to expand and become more common only during the last decade of the sixteenth century. A Venetian document of 14 December 1593 indicates this clearly:

> This practice has been in existence for *a certain time* [my italics] by which, instead of making payment at the bank, or in ready money, they have reduced the credit of an individual on to paper, and they pass this around from hand to hand.[152]

An odd document this, which more or less unconsciously echoes the Dutch text included on p. 211 above. 'Giros' and 'assignations' were the means which businessmen used – indeed, had adopted – to cope with the difficulties caused by the lack of precious metals. They were innovations that required a high degree of manipulative skill on the part of the businessmen, whose inadequacy bears some resemblance to that of the sorcerer's apprentice. They believed that they could control credit through monetary manoeuvers, and in fact this did solve, at least partially, the crisis of 1609–13, but it was to have no effect during 1619–22. The new stimulant was miraculous, for a little more than twenty years before its efficacy dwindled. The inflation of credit passed to monetary inflation and to the contraction of all forms of credit.

Were I an economic historian concerned, above all, with 'metals', I should stop here. I should, perhaps, emphasize the failure of credit without sufficient support of metal reserves (as if credit would be employed when the stock of metal was increasing); and the inadequacy of the mental structure of the businessman faced with an innovation such as credit (and there is certainly some truth in this); and then I should close. But I have already stated that I am firmly convinced that the crisis of 1619–22 (a normal, cyclical crisis) occurred during a structural crisis, which for some time had had its effect on the world of agriculture. It will be necessary to try to approach an understanding of this trend in the short term period.

However, we shall begin with the long term, taking the prices of agricultural products. The decade 1611–20 is characterized in all Europe by a fall in agricultural prices, which contrasts with the sustained price level of prices of industrial products. This reduction in agricultural prices (they had been decreasing steadily since the decade 1591–1600)[153] was disastrous for the peasant world, more so because the harvest yields had stagnated for some years, at least from the end of the sixteenth century.[154] Thus, the possibilities of saving and spending were reduced. From 1618 agricultural prices rose and reached their maximum in 1622.

The equilibrium (artificial in fact) that had been maintained during the previous years was broken between 1619 and 1620. But the rise in prices did not represent an increase in the value of agricultural products: it was merely an expression of poor harvests. Landlords and peasants were selling smaller quantities at higher prices, and consequently they did not manage to ameliorate the situation. On the contrary, the high prices of agricultural products made it necessary either to raise wages in the urban areas or to make large-scale dismissals.[155]

The mechanism of the crisis was as follows. The prices of industrial products fell because producers and merchants who utilized the 'giro' system were obliged to comply with the demands of the banks; the latter, in difficulty with contracting metal deposits, could not, as they had before, allow unlimited time for repayments. In addition to this, the price rise in food products forced consumers to concentrate their purchasing power in that direction, thus sacrificing industrial products, and bringing about their decline. To complete the picture, the men in government, and public opinion in general, blamed all these calamities on the monetary situation, thus forcing the government to initiate a drastic deflationary policy, which did not succeed in revitalizing the business world. The other, more important, crisis, in agriculture, was overlooked.

We shall now take a particular example. We have seen from the tables cited that the Italian commercial and industrial life expands, or at least is very stable, during the course of the second decade of the seventeenth century. In a recent study[156] of the accounts of an agency of an estate in Lombardy, it is evident that, between 1600 and 1647, there was a progressive decrease in profits, which culminated in a deficit during the last seven years. But I would sooner give the complete figures (Table 7.32).[157]

TABLE 7.32

Years	Increase %	Years	Increase or decrease %
1600–07	+35.92	1624–31	+6.37
1608–15	+31.84	1632–9	+2.37
1616–23	+28.57	1640–7	−5.07

I have produced the table in full, not merely to give greater force to my argument, but to avoid drawing false conclusions about the seventeenth century. The negative period 1640–7 occurred within the context of a decline that was already under way by the beginning of the century (unfortunately, these figures date only from 1600). It is against this background of contraction that the first crisis of 1609–13 and the later crisis of 1619–22 occurred. One event reacted upon another. The structural crisis of agriculture made the cyclical crises more serious. These, in their turn, aggravated the weakening agrarian structure, which affected the succeeding circumstantial crisis.

I repeat: what was important was the effect of the agricultural decline upon the crisis of 1609–13, a crisis of circumstance. The latter weakened the agrarian structure, which in turn affected the crisis of 1619–22.

The reader will excuse the polemical tone – somewhat excited – in the latter part of this article. Apart from the fact that I personally consider zeal to be one of the essential qualities of the historian, I wanted not merely to relate the extrinsic events of a crisis, but to expound its characteristics and its nature; and further than this, to rediscover the spirit of the two centuries, one that preceded the crisis, the other that followed it. The crucial points of contrast are the agrarian depression of the seventeenth century (which began in the last decade of the sixteenth century) and the notable conquests of the sixteenth century. These last, the fruits of ambition, and a perhaps excessive enthusiasm, failed, and the stultifying agrarian depression lumbered heavily to the fore, to characterize a long period of economic history.

Notes

1 'The seventeenth century, the last phase of the general transition from a feudal to a capitalist economy', was the judgement of E. J. Hobsbawm, 'The general crisis of the European economy in the seventeenth century', *Past and Present*, V and VI (1954), p. 33. This article seems to me fundamental in its precise assessment of the seventeenth century. It is, however, necessary to point out that, if the seventeenth century represented the last phase in the transition from a feudal to a capitalist economy, the sixteenth century contained within itself many 'liberating' elements. It seems to me that the significance of the seventeenth century lies in the fact that it was, on the one hand, a preparation for the transition to a capitalist economy, as Hobsbawm shows, and that on the other it witnessed a feudal reaction (at least during the earlier years) to those elements of capitalism (a capitalism basically mercantilist) that had already developed in the sixteenth century. In the same journal, *Past and Present*, XVI (1959), there is an article by H. Trevor-Roper, 'The general crisis of the seventeenth century'. See also the various criticisms of that article in *Past and Present*, XVIII (1960).

2 F. Baehrel, *Une Croissance: la Basse-Provence rurale (fin du XVIe siècle – 1789* (Paris, 1961), p. 57.

3 For this, see the introduction to the collection of works that I have compiled under the title *Storia dei Prezzi: Metali, Risultati, Problemi,* to be published by Einandi.

4 H. and P. Chaunu, *Séville et l'Atlantique (1504–1650),* 7 vols (Paris, 1955–7) and 1 vol. of 'construction graphique' (Paris, 1957).

5 N. Ellinger Bang, *Tabeller over Skibsfart og Varentransport gennem Oresund,* vols I and III, for the period in which we are interested (Copenhagen and Leipzig, 1906 and 1923, respectively).

6 In the first place, A. E. Christensen, *Dutch Trade to the Baltic about 1600* (Copenhagen, 1941); P. Jeannin, 'Le tonnage des navires utilisés dans la Baltique de 1550 à 1660 d'après les sources prussiennes' in *Le Navire et l'economie maritime. Travaux du troisième colloque d'histoire maritime* (Paris, 1960); A. Friis, 'Le valeur documentaire des comptes de péage du Sund. La période 1571 à 1618', in *Les Sources de l'histoire maritime du Moyen Age au XVIIIe siècle, articles présentés par M. Mollat* (Paris, 1962); P. Jeannin, 'La conjoncture commerciale à la fin du XVIe siècle et au début du XVIIe siècle: ce que donnent les comptes du Sund' in *XIe Congrès international des sciences historiques. Résumés de communications* (Stockholm, 1960); P. Jeannin, 'L'activité du port de Koenigsberg dans la seconde moitié du XVI siècle', *Bulletin de la Société d'Histoire Moderne,* LVII (1958).

7 H. and P. Chaunu, *Séville et l'Atlantique,* VI, pt. 1, p. 341.

8 ibid., p. 474.

9 P. Chaunu, *Séville et l'Atlantique. Structures et conjoncture de l'Atlantique espagnol,* 3 vols (Paris, 1959).

10 ibid., vol. 3, pt 2, 2, p. 1529.

11 ibid., p. 1132.

12 Ellinger Bang, op. cit., I, p. x.

13 Christensen, op. cit., p. 313.

14 ibid., pp. 444–5.

15 ibid., pp. 446–7. For the analogy with English trade passing through the Sound, see the reconstruction of R. W. K. Hinton, *The Eastland Trade and the Common Weal in the Seventeenth Century* (Cambridge, 1959), pp. 227–9.

16 Christensen, op. cit., p. 103, n. 1.

17 ibid., p. 465.

18 It is easy to arrive at these conclusions on the evidence of graph XVI (grain) of the work of Christensen. For salt, I have had recourse to a graph constructed by my friend Pierre Jeannin, who allowed me to use it and whom I should like to thank. Other graphs, which are part of the work that P. Jeannin has been compiling for a long time on Baltic trade during the sixteenth and seventeenth centuries, show a similar fall for rye, pitch, cinders and tar. The movement of the three latter products is

especially significant since they hardly lend themselves to
involvement in smuggling – the tariffs they carried were so small.

19 I await the volumes on the movements at the port of Cadiz,
which H. and P. Chaunu have promised, and which should
certainly equal the excellence of those that describe Seville.
Meanwhile, see A. Girard, *La Rivalité commerciale et maritime
entre Séville et Cadiz jusqu'à la fin du XVIIIe siècle* (Paris, 1932).
[But see also Steensgaard's comments on pp. 34–5 above: eds.]

20 K. Heeringa, *Bronnen tot de Geschiedenis van den Levantschen
Handel*, II (The Hague, 1910), pp. 1042ss., n. 451. And also,
H. Wätjen, *Die Niederländer im Mittelmeergebiet* (Berlin, 1909).

21 See F. Braudel and R. Romano, *Navires et marchandises à
l'entrée du Port de Livourne, 1547–1611* (Paris, 1951), pp. 49–55.

22 In the Danzig archive, 300/LIII/147, see the letters of 1590,
1591, 1592, which Florence and Venice gave their merchants,
authorizing them to buy grain for their cities.

23 It is, however, significant that a document of October 1612 in
Heeringa, op. cit., vol. 1, p. 436, n. 219, makes allusion to the
fact that the Dutch merchants in the Levant had worked there for
'twelve or thirteen years'.

24 ibid., p. 424, n. 213.

25 H. Brugmans, *Geschiedenis van Amsterdam*, III (Amsterdam,
1930), p. 30.

26 Heeringa, op. cit., I, p. 432, n. 216.

27 ibid., p. 429, n. 215.

28 ibid., p. 195, n. 127.

29 ibid., p. 256, n. 132.

30 ibid., p. 486, n. 236, n. 6.

31 ibid., p. 485, n. 234.

32 ibid., p. 494, n. 240.

33 ibid., p. 497, n. 241.

34 ibid., p. 514, n. 246.

35 ibid., p. 525, n. 249.

36 ibid., II, pp. 802–3, n. 361 and pp. 988–9, n. 426. France
also suffered a recession of trade in the Levant, as is shown by
P. Masson, *Histoire du commerce français dans le Levant au XVIIe
siècle* (Paris, 1896), pp. 118–30.

37 Heeringa, op. cit., vol. 1, pp. 53–5, n. 31.

38 ibid., pp. 58–9, n. 35.

39 ibid., pp. 61ff., n. 40; and also Brugmans, op. cit., III, p. 166.

40 ibid., p. 72, n. 55.

41 For the problem of the English presence in the Mediterranean,
see R. Davis, 'England and the Mediterranean 1570–1670' in
F. J. Fisher (ed.), *Essays in the Economic and Social History of
Tudor and Stuart England* (Cambridge, 1961).

42 The figures are taken from *Bilanci Generali della Republica di
Venezia*, I, i (Venice, 1912), pp. 284 (for 1582), 365–6 (for
the years 1587, 1594, 1602), 471–2 (for 1621), 487–9 (for 1633),
563–4 (for 1640). For the significance and details of the exaction

of customs duties, see the introduction to the above-mentioned volume.

43 See F. C. Lane, 'La marine marchande et le trafic maritime de Venise à travers les siècles' in *Les Sources de l'Histoire maritime en Europe, du Moyen Age au XVIIIe siècle, articles présentés par M. Mollat* (Paris, 1962), pp. 28–9. For other aspects of marine economy (above all, the construction of ships), see the next volume for the report on 'La marine marchande vénitienne au XVIe siècle', particulary pp. 51–5.

44 F. Borlandi, *Il Problema delle comunicazioni nei suoi rapporti col Risorgimento Italiano* (Pavia, 1932), p. 44.

45 See L. Bergasse and G. Rambert, *Histoire du commerce de Marseille*, IV (Paris, 1954), pp. 95 and 189 *à propos* the figures published here, in apparent contradiction to my argument. It should be noted that it was a matter of payments declared by '*fermiers*' and, as Bergasse observes, 'there is no guarantee that the duties levied on the items, which serve as a base from which to calculate prices, remained the same throughout the whole period'. For Livorno [Leghorn], see the excellent article of G. Mori, 'Linee e momenti dello sviluppo della città, del porto e dei traffici di Livorno', *La Regione; rivista dell' Unione Regionale delle Provincie Toscane*, III (1956), n. 12. In addition to this, is it not significant that Livorno, which had originally developed through the grain trade, should have built the greatest number of warehouses for cereals precisely in the second decade of the seventeenth century? (see M. Babuchello, *Livorno e il suo porto* [Livorno, 1932], p. 338). For Ragusa and Spalato see J. Tadic, 'Le commerce en Dalmatie et à Raguse et la décadence économique de Venise au XVIIe siècle' in *Decadenza economica veneziana nel secolo XVII, Atti del Convegno 27 giugno – 2 luglio 1957* (Venice–Rome, 1961), *passim*, and particularly p. 263. This volume, with its cross-references to English, French, German and Turkish evidence, supports the argument of this paper. Everything that has been outlined for the maritime economies is also valid for the 'landlocked' economies, as is shown by B. Caizzi, *Il Comasco sotto il dominio spagnolo* (Como, 1955), pp. 35 and 93–4.

46 C. Biernat and S. Gierszewski, *Statystyka Handlu i Zeglugi Gdańska w XVII i XVIII Wieku* (Warsaw, 1960).

47 S. Hoszowski, 'The Polish–Baltic trade in the 15th–18th centuries' in *Poland at the XIth International Congress of Historical Sciences* (Warsaw, 1960).

48 ibid., p. 144.

49 ibid., p. 153.

50 R. Rybarski, *Handel i Polityka Handlowa Polski w XVI Stuleciu*, II (Warsaw, 1958), p. 3. [On Baltic trade, there is a great deal of recent material available in English in the excellent study of A. Attman, *The Russian and Polish Markets in International Trade, 1500–1650* (Göteborg, 1973): Eds.]

51 A. Szelagowski, *Pieniadz i Przewrót cen w XVI i XVII Wieku w Polsce* (1902), pp. 126–7; I have corrected the figures for 1625 and 1627 from a manuscript in the Czartoryski Library in Cracow (no. 390 and no. 218). On Danzig trade see M. Foltz, *Geschichte des Danziger Stadthaushalts* (Danzig, 1912).

52 Hinton, op. cit., pp. 227–9.

53 F. J. Fisher, 'London's export trade in the early 17th century', *Economic History Review*, III (1952), p. 153, corrected by B. E. Supple, *Commercial Crisis and Change in England 1600–42* (Cambridge, 1959), p. 258.

54 The difficulty of compiling statistics on trade during the crisis of 1619–22 is shown by the article by J. D. Gould, which, despite its title – 'The trade depression of the early 1620's' (*Economic History Review*, VII, 1954) – is confined to industrial and monetary matters.

55 J. C. Westermann, 'Statistische gegevens over den handel van Amsterdam in de 17e eeuw', *Tijdschrift voor Geschiedenis*, LXI (1948).

56 I. J. Brugmans, 'Les sources de l'évolution quantitative du trafic maritime des Pays-Bas (XII–XVIIIe siècles)', in *Les Sources de l'histoire maritime en Europe, du Moyen Age au XVIIIe siècle, articles présentés par M. Mollat* (Paris, 1962).

57 I have put this aside here – I propose to return to it in the second part of the article. For the figures for the East India Company, see G. C. Clerk de Reus, *Geschichtlicher Ueberlick der administrativen, rechtlichen und finanzieller Entwicklung der Niederländisch-Ostindischen Compagnie* (Amsterdam, 1894), p. 118 and I. J. Brugmans, 'De Oost-Indische Compagnie en de Welvaart in de Republiek', *Tijdschrift voor Geschiedenis*, LXI (1948).

58 J. A. García, *La Ciudad indiana. Buenos Aires desde 1600 hasta mediados del siglo XVIII* (Buenos Aires, 1955), p. 183 and also A. P. Canabrava, *O Comércio portugues no Rio da Prata (1580–1640)* (Sao Paulo, 1944), p. 88.

59 E. F. S. de Studer, *La Trata de negros en el Rio de la Plata durante el siglo XVIII* (Buenos Aires, 1958), p. 102.

60 P. Chaunu, *Les Philippines et le Pacifique des Ibériques (XVIe, XVIIe, XVIIIe Siècles)* (Paris, 1960).

61 ibid., p. 250.

62 C. R. Boxer, *The Great Ship from Amacon. Annals of Macao and the Old Japan Trade (1555–1640)* (Lisbon, 1959).

63 P. Chaunu, 'Manille et Macao, face à la conjoncture des XVIe et XVIIe siècles', *Annales E.S.C.*, XVII (1962), p. 3.

64 ibid., p. 577.

65 ibid., p. 577.

66 ibid., p. 578.

67 H. Brugmans, *Geschiedenis van Amsterdam*, III, p. 147, and see also H. Dunlop, *Bronnen tot de Geschiedenis der Oostindische Compagnie in Perzië*, I (Gravenhage, 1930), particularly pp. xxxiii and 19, n. 20.

68 It seems interesting to me that F. Argelati, in his *De Monetis Italiae*, III (Milan, 1750), publishes the *Discorso Secondo* of G. D. Turbolo, in which it is mentioned, for the period 1616–29, that there is a return to seven years of prosperity and seven years of depression: an obvious biblical allusion, but still. . . .

69 Proof of the difficulty of constructing any tables to show, indirectly, the global production of industry in Europe is found in the following discussion. It is well known that alum has an important role in the woollen industry; now we know about the alum production of Civitavecchia and that of Spain, through the work of J. Delumeau and F. Ruiz Martín. But, despite this advance, we should proceed with caution, as we do not know about the alum production of Focea, and this ignorance may jeopardize our conclusions.

70 N. W. Posthumus, *De Geschiedenis van de leidsche Lakenindustrie*, 3 vols (The Hague, 1908–39).

71 Sella, *Commerci e industrie a Venezia nel secolo XVII* (Venice–Rome, 1961).

72 Romano, 'A Florence au XVIIe siècle'.

73 Fisher, op. cit.; Supple, op. cit., p. 258; Hinton, op. cit., pp. 227–9.

74 Chaunu, op. cit., VIII.ii, 2, pp. 1974–5; G. Lohmann Villena, *Las Minas de Huancavelica* (Seville, 1949), pp. 452–5.

75 M. Moreyra y Paz Soldán, *En torno a dos valiosos documentos sobre Potosí. Los quintos reales y las pragmáticas secretas sobre la moneda* (Lima, 1953).

76 Sella, op. cit., pp. 117–18.

77 I shall return to this parabolic curve to discuss the relationships with other sectors of the Venetian economy.

78 Sella, op. cit., p. 125.

79 ibid.

80 This trend in Venice finds confirmation in Milan: see C. Santoro, *Matricola dei mercanti di lana sottile di Milano* (Milan, 1940), p. 109; in Naples: see G. Coniglio, 'La rivoluzione dei prezzi nella città di Napoli nei secoli XVI e XVII' in *Atti della IX Riunione Scientifica della Società Italiana di Statistica* (Spoleto, 1952), pp. 236–7; and for Florence: see R. Romano, 'A Florence au XVIIe Siècle', p. 512. And for the situation in Italy in general – especially in the North – see G. Aleati and C. M. Cipolla, 'Il trend economico nello stato di Milano durante i secoli XVI e XVII: il caso di Pavia', *Bollettino della società pavese di storia patria*, I–II (1950); C. M. Cipolla, 'The decline of Italy: the case of a full matured economy' in *Economic History Review*, V 1952).

81 See note 73 above. Nevertheless, the qualitative composition of these exports changed considerably during the first half of the seventeenth century. Basically, the percentage of 'undressed' cloth became less in the total exports of London. See Supple, op. cit., p. 137.

82 For these aspects, I refer to the excellent book of A. Friis, *Alderman Cockayne's Project and the Cloth Trade. The Commercial Policy of England in its Major Aspects, 1603–1625* (London–Copenhagen, 1927), which will remain the definitive book on the study of commercial–industrial life of England during these years. Illuminating details may be gleaned from E. Moir, 'Benedict Weber, clothier', *Economic History Review*, X (1957).

83 See Hinton, op. cit., pp. 227–9.

84 T. C. Mendenhall, *The Shrewsbury Drapers and the Welsh Wool Trade in the XVI and XVII Centuries* (Oxford, 1953), pp. 234–5.

85 N. W. Posthumus, op. cit., II, p. 129; III, pp. 930–1. The total figures of production are as follows:

1591–1600	500,840
1601–10	669,431
1611–20	875,688
1621–30	1,001,293
1631–40	989,934
1641–50	892,835
1651–60	1,061,014

86 N. W. Posthumus, op. cit., III, p. 1163.

87 ibid., p. 933.

88 ibid., pp. 941–6.

89 Is it not significant that it was above all the dyers who developed after 1623? See J. C. van Dillen, *Bronnen tot de Geschiedenis van het Bedrijfsleven en het Gildewezen van Amsterdam*, II (The Hague, 1933), p. xix.

90 Van Dillen, op. cit., I (Gravenhage, 1929), p. xxi and II, p. 150, n. 270; p. 375, n. 642.

91 S. C. van Kampen, *De Rotterdamse particuliere Scheepsbouw in de tijd van de Republiek* (Assen, 1953), especially p. 109; see also pp. 33, 34, 106, 192. Also van Dillen, op. cit., II, p. xv.

92 Van Dillen, op. cit., p. xxx; van Kampen, op. cit., p. 148.

93 Van Dillen, op. cit., I, p. 585, n. 986; II, p. xxviii and p. 438, n. 757.

94 ibid., I, pp. 592–6.

95 Van Dillen, op. cit., vol. 2, p. xxx.

96 Posthumus, op. cit., II, p. 70 and III, p. 890; van Dillen, op. cit., I, p. xxxii, II, p. xxxi.

97 For the development of urbanization in Amsterdam in the sixteenth and seventeenth centuries, see van Dillen, op. cit., I, p. xxv. To appreciate fully the influx into Amsterdam between 1615 and 1619, it is necessary to remember that in 1617 there was an epidemic in the city: see ibid. and p. 255. Also see Brugmans, op. cit., II, pp. 4ff.

98 Van Dillen, op. cit., II, pp. 16–17.

99 ibid., p. 438, n. 757.

100 E. Coonaert, *La Draperie-Sayetterie d'Hondschoote* (Paris, 1930), p. 494.

101 For a detailed bibliography, see G. Aubin and A. Kunze, *Leinenerzeugung und Leinenabsatz im östlichen Mitteldeutschland zur Zeit der Zunftkämpfe* (Stuttgart, 1940), *passim* and especially pp. 290–361; E. Zimmermann, 'Der schlesische Garn- und Leinenhandel mit Holland im 16 und 17 Jahrhundert', *Economisch–Historisch Jaarboek*, XXVI (1956); E. Sabbe, *De Belgische Vlasnijverheid*, I (Brussels, 1953), pp. 331–45.

102 Chaunu, op. cit., VIII. ii, 2, pp. 1974–5.

103 ibid., p. 1970.

104 Moreyra y Paz Soldán, op. cit., pp. 37–9.

105 B. H. Slicher van Bath, *De agrarische Geschiedenis van West-Europa (500–1850)* (Utrecht–Amsterdam, 1960), p. 226, and also 'Agriculture in the Low Countries (*c.* 1600–1800)' in *X Congresso Internazionale di Scienze Storiche*, IV (Florence, 1955), pp. 169–203; J. M. Kulischer, *Storia Economica del Medio Evo e dell'epoca Moderna*, II (Florence, 1955), pp. 61–92.

106 See Kulischer, op. cit., pp. 92–146.

107 E. Sereni, *Storia del Paesaggio Agrario Italiano* (Bari, 1961), p. 192; R. Romano, 'Rolnictwo i chlopi we Wloszech w XV i XVI wieku', *Prezgląd Historyczny*, LIII (1962), 2, p. 255.

108 F. Braudel, *La Méditerranée et la monde méditerranéen à l'époque de Philippe II* (Paris, 1949), pp. 616–42.

109 Romano, 'Rolnictwo', pp. 246ss.

110 L. Bulferetti, 'L'oro, la terra e la societa. Un'interpretazione del nostro Seicento', *Archivio Storico Lombardo*, 8th series IV (1953), p. 44, n. 77.

111 A. Domeniconi, *La Compagnia dei molini di Cesena* (Faenza, 1956), pp. 182–3.

112 L. Zytkowicz, *Studia nad Gospodarstwem Wiejskim w Dobrach Koscielnich XVIw*, 2 vols (Warsaw, 1962).

113 ibid., II, p. 51.

114 J. Topolski, *Gospodarstwo Wiejskie w Dobrach Arcybiskupstwa Gnieznienskiego od XVI do XVIII Wieku* (Poznan, 1958), pp. 216–17.

115 J. Majewski, *Gospodarstwo Folwarczne we Wsiach Miasta Poznania w Latach 1582–1644* (Poznan, 1957), pp. 80–8.

116 A. Wyczański, 'Le niveau de la récolte des céréales en Pologne du XVIe au XVIIIe siècle' in *Première Conférence Internationale d'Histoire Economique (Stockholm, 1960). Contributions, Communications* (Paris–The Hague, 1960), pp. 585–90.

117 M. Małowist 'L'évolution industrielle en Pologne du XVIe au XVIIe siècle' in *Studi in onore di Armando Sapori*, I (Milan, 1957), pp. 589, 592; M. Małowist, 'The economic and social development of the Baltic countries from the fifteenth to the seventeenth centuries', *Economic History Review*, XII (1959). I am greatly indebted to my friend Professor Małowist for everything concerned with Poland in my article.

118 Slicher van Bath, op. cit., pp. 222–3.

119 ibid., pp. 223–4.

120 M. Bloch, *Les Caractères originaux de l'histoire rurale française* (Oslo, 1931), *passim* and especially pp. 131–53.

121 J. Costa, *Colectivismo agrario en España* (Madrid, s.d.); J. Klein, *The Mesta. A Study in Spanish Economic History* (Cambridge, Mass., 1920).

122 Kulischer, op. cit., pp. 131–43.

123 M. Dobb, *Studies in the Development of Capitalism* (London, 1950), especially p. 194, n. 2.

124 I. J. Brugmans, 'De Oost-Indische Compagnie en de welvaart in de Republiek', *Tijdschrift voor Geschiedenis*, LXI (1948), p. 230; Klerk de Reus, op. cit., p. 118.

125 N. W. Posthumus, 'The tulip mania in Holland in the years 1636 and 1637', *Journal of Economic and Business History*, I (1928–9), pp. 434–66.

126 G. Alivia, 'Di un indice che misura l'impiego monetario dell'oro relativamente a quello dell'argento e le sue variazioni dal 1520 ad oggi', *Giornale degli Economisti* (1911), p. 346.

127 E. J. Hamilton, 'Monetary inflation in Castile (1598–1600)', *Economic History*, II, pp. 177–212: the 'premiums on silver in terms of vellón', which rose somewhat between 1604 and 1623 (from 3 to 8.90 per cent), increased in 1624 to 22 per cent, and maintained a steady level throughout the period examined by Hamilton; see also E. J. Hamilton, *American Treasure and the Price Revolution in Spain, 1501–1650* (Cambridge, Mass., 1934), particularly pp. 93–4.

128 For this, see W. A. Shaw, *The History of Currency* (London, 1895); A. Despaux, *Les Dévaluations monétaires dans l'histoire* (Paris, 1936). For Danzig, see J. Pelc, *Ceny w Gdansku w XVI i XVII Wieku* (Lvov, 1937), pp. 4–5; for Milan: A. de Maddalena, *Prezzi e aspetto di mercato in Milano durante il secolo XVII* (Milan, 1949), pp. 151–2; for Strasbourg: A. Hanauer, *Etudes economiques sur l'Alsace ancienne et moderne*, I (Paris–Strasbourg, 1876), p. 257; for Amsterdam: N. W. Posthumus, *Nederlandsche Prijsgeschiedenis*, I (Leiden, 1943), p. cxix. In any article about the history of prices, there are references to fluctuations in the value of money, confirming much of what I said on pp. 166–8 above. In addition, purely monetary fluctuations are found also in places that are very far from western Europe: in Moscow (Spooner, op. cit., p. 239); in Ragusa (V. Vinauer, 'Monetarna kriza u Turskoj', *Istoriski Glasnik*, III–IV [1958], p. 143); in Constantinople (as my friend Halil Sahilloglu, of the University of Istanbul, has informed me). For a general account of the problem, see the major work of R. Gaettens, *Die Zeit der Kipper und Wipper der Inflationen* (Munich, 1955), pp. 74–99.

129 F. C. Spooner, *L'economie mondiale et les frappes monétaires en France (1493–1680)* (Paris, 1956), pp. 524–9.

130 C. M. Cipolla, *Mouvements monétaires dans l'Etat de Milan (1580–1700)* (Paris, 1952), pp. 43–4.

131 ibid., p. 35.

132 F. Mauro, *Le Portugal et l'Atlantique au XVIIe Siècle (1570–1670)* (Paris, 1960), pp. 415, 428 and 432.

133 ibid., p. 417.

134 J. D. Gould, 'The Royal Mint in the early seventeenth century', *Economic History Review*, V (1952), pp. 240–8. A good general examination may be found in R. Ashton, *The Crown and the Money Market (1603–1640)* (Oxford, 1960). See also B. E. Supple, 'Currency and commerce in the early seventeenth century', *Economic History Review*, X (1957).

135 Hamilton, *American Treasure*, pp. 42–3.

136 W. A. Shaw, *The History of Currency* (London, 1895), p. 144.

137 C. M. Cipolla, 'Note sulla storia del saggio d'interesse', *Economia Internazionale*, V (1952), p. 14.

138 ibid., p. 16.

139 L. de Rosa, 'Il banco dei Poveri e la crisi del 1622', *Rassegna Economica*, XXII (1958); C. di Somma, *Il Banco dello Spirito Santo dalle Origini al 1664* (Naples, 1960). And also M. de Stefano, *Banchi e Vicende Monetarie nel Regno di Napoli (1600–1625)* (Livorno, 1640).

140 de Rosa, op. cit., p. 57.

141 di Somma, op. cit., p. 89.

142 de Rosa, op. cit., p. 65.

143 N. Piccolomini, *Il Monte dei Paschi di Siena e le aziende in esso riunite*, II (Siena, 1891), pp. 308–9.

144 ibid., p. 215.

145 A. Hanauer, *Etudes economiques sur l'Alsace ancienne et moderne*, I (Paris–Strasbourg, 1876), pp. 560–6.

146 ibid., pp. 586–7.

147 J. G. van Dillen, *Bronnen tot de Geschiedenis der Wisselbanken (Amsterdam, Middelburg, Delft, Rotterdam)*, II (The Hague, 1925), p. 985. See also 'The Bank of Amsterdam' in *History of the Public Banks*, ed. J. G. van Dillen (The Hague, 1934), pp. 177ff.

148 Van Dillen, *Bronnen*, II, p. 1304.

149 ibid., p. 962.

150 ibid., p. 991.

151 J. Gentil da Silva and R. Romano, 'L'histoire des changes: les foires de "Bisenzone" de 1600 à 1650', *Annales E.S.C.*, XVII (1962).

152 See G. Luzzatto, 'Les banques publiques de Venise (siècles XVI–XVIII)' in *History of the Principal Public Banks*, ed. J. G. van Dillen (The Hague, 1934), p. 49.

153 There is a vast bibliography on this subject. See particularly G. Imbert, *Des Mouvements de longue durée Kondratieff* (Aix-en-Provence, 1959), pp. 194–202. See also W. Beveridge, 'Weather and harvest cycles', *Economic Journal* (1921), p. 452, and also the excellent analysis of G. Parenti, *Prezzi e mercato del grano al Siena* (Florence, 1942), p. 235.

154 In addition to what has been said about the agrarian contraction after the end of the century, see Parenti, op. cit., p. 216.

155 F. Braudel, P. Jeannin, J. Meuvret and R. Romano, 'Le déclin de Venise au XVII siècle' in *Decadenza economica Veneziana nel secolo XVII* (Venice–Rome, 1961), p. 33, n. 1: in Lyons, in 1619, 6,000 silk-weavers were receiving '*distribution de l'aumône générale*'.

156 A. de Maddelena, 'I bilanci dal 1600 al 1747 di una azienda fondiaria lombarda. Testimonianza d'una crisi economica', *Rivista Internazionale di Scienze Economiche e Commerciali*, II (1955). Confirmation may be found in another article by de Maddelena: 'Contributo alla storia dell'agricoltura della "bassa" Lombardia', *Archivo storico Lombardo* (1958), pp. 165–83. In addition to this it seems to me that, on another level, de Maddelena's article supports much of what I have said concerning the trend of agriculture on Italy, exemplified in the Company of Millers of Cesena.

157 de Maddelena, 'I bilanci', p. 44.

[*Editors' note:* many of the series of economic data discussed in this article are now available in G. Parker and C. H. Wilson, eds, *Introduction to the Sources of European Economic History, 1500–1800* (London, 1977).]

Chapter eight

The 'Maunder Minimum': Sunspots and Climate in the Reign of Louis XIV*

John A. Eddy

It has long been thought that the sun is a constant star of regular and repeatable behaviour. Measurements of the radiative output, or solar constant, seem to justify the first assumption, and the record of periodicity in sunspot numbers is taken as evidence for the second. Both records, however, sample only the most recent history of the sun.

When we look at the longer record – of the last 1,000 years or so – we find indications that the sun may have undergone significant changes in behaviour, with possible terrestrial effects. Evidence for past solar change is largely of an indirect nature and should be subject to the most critical scrutiny. Most accessible, and crucial to the basic issue of past constancy or inconstancy, is a long period in the late seventeenth and early eighteenth centuries when, some have claimed, almost no sunspots were seen. The period, from about 1645 until 1715, was pointed out in the 1890s by G. Spörer and E. W. Maunder. I have re-examined the contemporary reports and new evidence that has come to light since Maunder's time and conclude that this seventy-year period was indeed a time when solar activity all but stopped. This behaviour is wholly unlike the modern behaviour of the sun which we have come to accept as normal, and the consequences for solar and terrestrial physics seem to me profound.

The Sunspot Cycle

Surely the best known features of the sun are sunspots and the regular cycle of solar activity, which waxes and wanes with a period of about eleven years. This cycle is most often shown as a plot of sunspot number (Figure 8.1) – a measure of the number

* First published in *Science*, XCII (1976), pp. 1189–1202, and reprinted here by permission of the American Association for the Advancement of Science and the author.

of spots seen at one time on the visible half of the sun.[1] Sunspot numbers are recorded daily, but to illustrate long-term effects astronomers more often use the annual means, which smooth out the short term variations and average out the marked imprint of solar rotation.

There is as yet no complete physical explanation for the observed solar cycle. Modern theory attributes the periodic features of sunspots to the action of a solar dynamo in which convection and surface rotation interact to amplify and maintain an assumed initial magnetic field.[2] Dynamo models are successful in reproducing certain features of the eleven-year cycle, but with these models it is not as yet possible to explain the varying amplitudes of maxima and other long-term changes.

The annual mean sunspot number at a typical minimum in the eleven-year cycle is about six. During these minimum years there are stretches of days and weeks when no spots can be seen, but a monthly mean of zero is uncommon and there has been only one year (1810) in which the annual mean, to two-digit accuracy, was zero. In contrast, in the years around a sunspot maximum there is seldom a day when a number of spots cannot be seen, and often hundreds are present.

Past counts of sunspot number are readily available from the year 1700,[3] and workers in solar and terrestrial studies often use the record as though it were of uniform quality. In fact, it is not. Thus it is advisable, from time to time, to review the origin and pedigree of past sunspot numbers, and to recognize the uncertainty in much of the early record.

A Brief History

Dark spots were seen on the face of the sun at least as early as the fourth century BC,[4] but it was not until after the invention of the telescope, about 1610, that they were seen well enough to be associated with the sun itself. It would seem no credit to early astronomers that over 230 years elapsed between the telescopic 'discovery' of sunspots and the revelation of their now-obvious cyclic behaviour. In 1843, Heinrich Schwabe, an amateur, published a brief paper reporting his observations of spots on the sun for the period 1826 to 1843 and pointing out an apparent period of about ten years between maxima in their number.[5]

Rudolf Wolf, director of the Observatory at Bern and later at Zurich, noticed Schwabe's paper and shortly after set out to test the result by extending the limited observations on which the ten-year cycle was based. In 1848 he organized a number of European observatories to record spots on a regular basis and by a standard scheme, thus inaugurating an international effort which continues today. Wolf also undertook a historical search and re-analysis of old data on the sun in the literature and in observatory archives. More than half of the record of sunspot numbers in Figure 8.1, and all of it before 1848, is the result of Wolf's historical reconstruction. The most reliable part of the curve thus comes after 1848, when it is based on controlled observations. Wolf found descriptions and drawings of the sun which allowed him to reconstruct daily sunspot numbers thirty years into the past – to 1818 – although, unlike the real-time data, they came from a thinner sample and with less certain corrections for observers and conditions. He was able to locate sufficient information on the more distant past to allow reconstructed 'monthly averages' of the sunspot number (that is, a minimum of one observation per month) to 1749, and approximate 'annual averages' from more scattered data to 1700.[6] The reliability of the curve, and especially of its absolute scale, may be graded into four epochs: reliable from 1848 on, good from 1818 to 1847, questionable from 1749 to 1817, and poor from 1700 to 1748.

Wolf collected data to extend the historical curve the final ninety years to the telescopic discovery of sunspots in 1610.[7] He published estimated dates of maxima and minima for 1610 to 1699, but not sunspot numbers. That he elected to discontinue sunspot numbers at 1700 may be significant: perhaps he felt he had reached the elastic limit of the sparse historical record at the even century mark; it could also be that at 1700 he ran into queer results. In this article I shall point out that the latter probably applies. It seems fair to assume that, once he had confirmed and refined Schwabe's cycle, Wolf was biased towards demonstrating that the sunspot cycle persisted backward in time;[8] thus, when the cycle appeared to fade, especially in dim, historical data, he would have been inclined to quit the case and to call it proven. In any event we should be especially sceptical of the curve in its thinnest and oldest parts (1700 to 1748), and to question anew what happened before 1700.

Even though we are aware of the varying quality of the Wolf sunspot record, most of us probably take it as evidence of a truly continuous curve, much like the sample of a continuous

wave form that we see on the screen of an oscilloscope. We
assume that, just as Schwabe's seventeen-year sample was enough
to reveal the cycle's existence, so the 260-year record in Figure 8.1

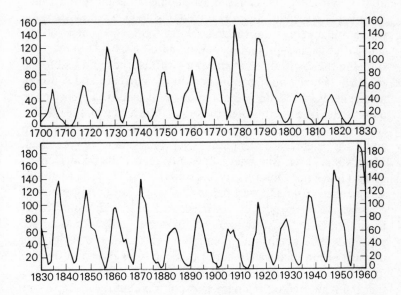

FIGURE 8.1 *Annual mean sunspot number,* R, *from 1700 to 1960*
(from n. 3, courtesy of M. Waldmeier)

is adequate to establish its likely perpetuation to the future and
extension through the past. Reconstructions of the solar cycle have
been estimated from indirect data to the seventh century BC in
the Spectrum of Time Project (STP) of D. J. Schove, but these
heroic efforts are of necessity based on far from continuous information and are built on the explicit assumption of a continued
eleven-year cycle.[9,10,11,12] Recent insights into the physical basis
for the sunspot cycle and its origin in the fluid, outer layers of the
sun give us new cause to suspect that at least some of the features
of the present sunspot cycle may be transitory. If we accept the
solar dynamo, we must allow that any of its coupled forces could
have changed enough in the past to alter or suspend the 'normal'
solar cycle. Indeed, there is now evidence that solar rotation has
varied significantly in historic time.[13]

The 'Prolonged Sunspot Minimum'

The possibility that sunspots sharply dropped in number before 1700 was pointed out rather clearly by two well-known solar astronomers in the late nineteenth century. In papers published in 1887 and 1889 the German astronomer Gustav Spörer called attention to a seventy-year period, ending about 1716, when there was a remarkable interruption in the ordinary course of the sunspot cycle and an almost total absence of spots.[14] Spörer was studying the distribution of sunspots with latitude and had found evidence that the numbers of spots in the northern and southern hemispheres of the sun were not always balanced. To check this observation he had consulted historical records, including Wolf's, and was surprised at what he found in the data of the seventeenth and early eighteenth centuries. Not long after, Spörer died. Meanwhile, E. W. Maunder, superintendent of the Solar Department, Greenwich Observatory, took up the case. In 1890 Maunder summarized Spörer's two papers for the Royal Astronomical Society and in 1894 gave a fuller account in an article entitled 'A Prolonged Sunspot Minimum'.[15,16] In his second paper Maunder provided more details and pointed out that to acknowledge this unusual occurrence was to admit that the solar cycle and the sun itself had changed in historic time, and could again. He stressed that the reality of a 'prolonged sunspot minimum' had important implications not only for our understanding of the sun but also for studies of solar–terrestrial relations.

It is not obvious that anyone in solar physics listened. In any case, nearly thirty years later, at the age of seventy-one, Maunder tried again with another paper of the same title on the same subject.[17] Included were quotations from a paper by Agnes Clerke who had claimed that during the 'prolonged sunspot minimum' there was also a marked dearth of aurorae.[18] Maunder offered as well the interesting conjecture that the long delay between the telescopic discovery of sunspots and Schwabe's discovery of the solar cycle may have been due in part to this temporary cessation of the solar cycle during a part of the interim.

In their five papers Spörer and Maunder made the following striking assertions: (1) that for a seventy-year period, from approximately 1645 to 1715, practically no sunspots were seen; (2) that for nearly half of this time (1672 to 1704) not a single spot was observed on the northern hemisphere of the sun; (3) that for sixty years, until 1705, no more than one sunspot *group* was seen on the sun at a time; and (4) that during the entire seventy-year period no more than 'a handful' of spots were observed and that these were mostly single spots and at low solar latitudes, lasting for a single rotation or less; moreover, the total number of spots observed from 1645 to 1715 was less than what we see in a single active year under normal conditions.

Maunder supported these claims with quotations from the scientific literature of the period in question. The editor of the *Philosophical Transactions of the Royal Society*, in reporting the discovery of a sunspot in 1671 (in the middle of the 'prolonged sunspot minimum'), had written that 'at Paris the Excellent Signior Cassini hath lately detected again Spots in the Sun, of which none have been seen these many years that we know of'.[19] (Following this, the editor went on to describe the last sunspot seen, eleven years before, for those who might have forgotten what one looked like.)

Cassini's own description of his 1671 sighting reads as follows: 'it is now about 20 years since astronomers have seen any considerable spots on the sun, though before that time, since the invention of the telescopes they have from time to time observed them.'[20] Cassini also reported that another French astronomer, Picard, 'was pleased at the discovery of a sunspot since it was ten whole years since he had seen one, no matter how great the care which he had taken from time to time to watch for them'.[21] And when the Astronomer Royal, Flamsteed, sighted a spot on the sun at Greenwich in 1684, he reported that '[t]hese appearances, however frequent in the days of *Scheiner* and *Galileo*, have been so rare of late that this is the only one I have seen in his face since *December* 1676'.[22]

Maunder did not have to look hard to find support for the strange case, for an absence of sunspots in the latter part of the seventeenth century had been matter-of-factly reported in astronomy books written before Schwabe's discovery of the cycle.[23] William Herschel had mentioned it in 1801.[24] Herschel's source of information was Lalande's three-volume opus, *Astronomie*, of 1792, in which dates and details are given of the anomalous absence of sunspots, including some of the quotations that Maunder later used.[25] Thus, neither Maunder nor Spörer had 'discovered' the 'prolonged sunspot minimum'. These authors, like myself, were simply pointing back to an overlooked and possibly important phenomenon which in its time had not seemed unusual but which looms large in retrospect.

Questions

Maunder's assessment of the significance of the 'prolonged sunspot minimum' was probably not an exaggeration. If solar activity really ceased or sank to near-zero level, it places a restrictive boundary condition on physical explanations of the solar cycle and suggests that a workable mechanism for solar activity must be capable of starting, and maybe stopping, in periods of tens of years. It labels sunspots as possibly transitory characteristics of the sun and, by association, also flares, active prominences, and perhaps the structured corona. One of the enigmas in historical studies of the sun is the long delay in the naked-eye discovery of the chromosphere[26] and the lack of any ancient descriptions of coronal streamers at eclipse.[27,28] It may be more than curious coincidence that the discovery of the chromosphere (1706), the first description of the structured corona (1715), and a lasting, tenfold jump in the number of recorded aurorae (1716) all came at the end of the 'Maunder Minimum', when, it seems, the solar cycle resumed, or possibly began, its modern course. If Maunder's 'prolonged sunspot minimum' really happened, it provides damning evidence[29] in the protracted debate over the production of sunspots by planetary gravitational tides, for through the years between 1645 and 1715 the nine planets were, as always, in their orbits. Finally, as Maunder stressed, this apparent anomaly in the sun's history, if real, offers a singularly valuable test period for studies of the connection between solar activity and terrestrial weather. If the 'Maunder Minimum' really occurred, it may define a minimum of a long term envelope of solar activity which could be more important for terrestrial implications than the eleven-year modulation that has for so long occupied attention in solar-terrestrial studies.[30]

It seems worthwhile to open, once again, the case of the missing sunspots, for it was never really solved. All the early work was based almost entirely on the same piece of evidence: the paucity of sunspot reports in the limited literature of the day. Spörer's original papers and Maunder's expansions of them leaned heavily on a lack of evidence in archival records and journals, and on contemporary statements that it had been a long time between sunspot reports. But in the words of a modern astronomer, absence of evidence is not evidence of absence.[31] How good were the observers in the seventeenth century, and how good the observing techniques? How constant a watch was kept? How many spots were missing, and when? New evidence has come to light in the fifty years since Maunder's time: we now have better catalogues of historical aurorae, compilations of sunspot observations made in the Orient, a fuller understanding of tree-ring records, and a new tool in atmospheric isotopes as tracers of past solar activity. New understanding of the sun since Maunder's day can sharpen our assessment of the facts in the case: we now know the relationship of sunspots to solar magnetic fields and something of the relation of magnetic fields to the corona, and can thus examine more critically the evidence from total solar eclipses during the time.

Solar Observations in the Seventeenth Century

History has left an uncanny mnemonic for the dates of the 'Maunder Minimum': the reign of Louis XIV, *le Roi Soleil* – 1643 through 1715. This was also the time of Milton and Newton; by 1642 Brahe, Kepler and Galileo were gone. Astronomical telescopes were in common use and were produced commercially; they featured innovations and important improvements over the original miniature models which in 1612 had sufficed to distinguish umbrae and penumbrae in sunspots and by 1625 had been used to find the solar faculae. During the 'Maunder Minimum' the Greenwich and Paris observatories were founded, and Newton produced the reflecting telescope; it was also the age of the long, suspended, and aerial telescopes with focal lengths that stretched to 60 metres and apertures of 20 centimetres and more.[32] The more usual telescopes turned on the sun had focal lengths of 2 to 4 metres and apertures of 5 to 10 centimetres, which would describe most solar telescopes used in the eighteenth and nineteenth centuries as well. To observe sunspots then, as today, one projected the solar image on a white screen placed at a proper distance behind the eyepiece. The image scale was adequate to permit one to see and sketch not only spots of all sizes but their features and their differences; observers recorded details of white-light faculae, penumbral filaments, satellite sunspots, and most of the observational detail known of sunspots today.

During the 'Maunder Minimum' the same astronomers who observed the sun discovered the first division in Saturn's ring (in 1675) and found five of Saturn's satellites (1655 to 1684); the former discovery attests to an effective resolution of almost 1 arc second and the latter to an acuity to distinguish an 11th-magnitude object less than 40 arc seconds from the bright limb of the planet. During the seventeenth century astronomers observed seven transits of Venus and Mercury, which implies a certain thorough-ness and a knowledge of other spots on the sun at the time. Römer determined the velocity of light (1675) from precise observations of the orbits of Jupiter's satellites. During the same century at least 53 eclipses of the sun – partial, annular or total – were observed, including some in Asia and the Americas. It is significant that not one solar eclipse that passed through Europe was missed.[33],[34]

Active astronomers of the time included Flamsteed, Derham, Hooke and Halley in England, both of the Huyghens in Holland, Hevelius in Poland, Römer in Denmark, the Cassinis, Gassendi, de la Hire and Boulliau in France, Grimaldi and Riccioli in Italy, and Weigel and von Wurzelbau in Germany, to name but a few. And astronomers of that era were generous in their definition of astronomy and still included the sun among objects of respectable interest. During the years when the Cassinis were pursuing their investigations of Saturn in Paris, they also wrote scientific articles on their observations of the sun and sunspots.[35] In 1630 Christopher Scheiner published a massive book, the *Rosa Ursina*, on sunspots and faculae and methods of observing them,[36] and Hevelius produced in 1647 a detailed appendix on sunspots and a chapter on solar observation in his *Selenographia*.[37]

In 1801 William Herschel commented that instrumental and observational shortcomings could explain most of the sunspot dearth between 1650 and 1713, and that, had more modern equipment been turned on the sun, many more spots would have been found;[38] but we have little cause to think that he had looked very far into the matter, which then seemed of minor import, long before the discovery of the sunspot cycle. Maunder did not cite Herschel's dissenting view, but trumped it anyway, with a quotation from the more contemporary English astronomer William Derham, who in 1711 had given his view on whether observers of the time could have missed the spots:

There are doubtless great intervals sometimes when the
Sun is free, as between the years 1660 and 1671, 1676 and
1684, in which time, Spots could hardly escape the sight of
so many Observers of the Sun, as were then perpetually
peeping upon him with their Telescopes in *England*, *France*,
Germany, *Italy*, and all the World over.[39]

It seems clear that on this question Derham was right and
Herschel wrong and that during the period of the 'Maunder
Minimum' astronomers had the instruments, the knowledge, and
the ability to recognize the presence or absence of even small spots
on the sun. And I might add that it does not take much of a
telescope to see a sunspot.

Was a continuous watch kept on the sun? This is quite another
question, and one for which direct evidence is lacking. Scheiner
(1575–1650) and Hevelius (1611–87) for at least a number of
years made daily drawings of the sun and sunspots, but we cannot
assume that this dutiful practice was continued by successors
without interruption for seventy years. There were no organized
or co-operative efforts, so far as we know, to keep a continuous
diary of the sun, as is done today. But the motives of astronomers,
then and now, are much the same: when a surprising dearth of
sunspots was reported, as it was on repeated occasions during the
span, we can expect that it would have inspired a renewed search
to find some. In this respect it is significant that new sunspots
were reported in the scientific literature as 'discoveries', and that
the sighting of a new spot or spot group was cause for the writing
of a paper.[40] This practice, were it followed today by even a few
owners of 5-centimetre refractors, would produce an intolerable
glut of manuscripts in the minimum years of the sunspot cycle and
an avalanche in the years of maximum.

Comparisons with the present time are dangerous: towards the
end of the seventeenth century the first learned societies were
founded and the first journals came into existence. These journals
were limited in number and scope and restricted in authorship,
and in that time bore little resemblance to the scientific
periodicals we read and rely on for thorough coverage today.
Absence of evidence may be a limited clue in such circumstances,
as may uncontested and possibly unrefereed reports. Moreover,
prevailing ideas of what something *is* influence how it is observed
and reported. Sunspots were not thought to be what we know they

are today. The original theological opposition to spots on the sun had been assuaged long before 1645, but, throughout the period of the 'Maunder Minimum' and until Wilson's observations in 1774,[41] a prevalent concept of sunspots was that they were clouds on the sun, and who keeps a diary of clouds? Finally, we can suspect that sunspots, like all else in science, went in and out of vogue as objects of intense interest. After the initial surge of telescopic investigation, sunspots may have drifted into the doldrums of current science. If this is so, Scheiner's massive tome may have been in part to blame: the *Rosa Ursina* must have been considered a bore by even the verbose standards of its day, and it may have smothered initiative for a time.[42,43]

Aurorae

Records of occurrence of the aurora borealis and aurora australis offer an independent check on past solar activity since there is a well-established correlation between sunspot number and the number of nights when aurorae are seen. The physical connection is indirect: auroral displays are produced when charged particles from the sun interact with the earth's magnetic field, resulting in particle accelerations and collisions with air molecules in our upper atmosphere. Aurorae register, therefore, those particle-producing events on the sun (such as flares and prominence eruptions) which happen to direct their streams toward the earth. Since these events arise in active regions on the sun, where there are also sunspots, we find a strong positive correlation between reported numbers of the two phenomena.

Aurorae are especially valuable as historical indicators of solar activity since they are spectacular and easily seen, require no telescopic apparatus, and are visible for hours over wide geographic areas. They have been recorded far back in history as objects of awe and wonder.

An increase in the number of reported aurorae inevitably follows a major increase in solar activity, and a drop in their number can generally be associated with the persistence of low numbers of sunspots, with certain reservations. As with sunspots, aurorae will not be seen unless the sky is reasonably clear, and an absence of either on any date in historical records could be due simply to foul weather. For the period of our interest we can exclude the possibility of years or decades of persistent continental overcast, since this would constitute a significant meteorological anomaly which would certainly have been noted in weather lore or cited by astronomers of the day.[44]

In fact, the period between 1645 and 1715 was characterized by a marked absence of aurorae, as was first pointed out by Clerke. 'There is', she wrote, '. . . strong, although indirect evidence that the "prolonged sunspot minimum" was attended by a profound magnetic calm'.[45] Historical aurora catalogues[46,47] confirm her assessment that there were extremely few aurorae reported during the years of the 'Maunder Minimum'. Far fewer were recorded than in either the seventy years preceding or following.

Auroral occurrence is a strong function of latitude, or more specifically of distance from the geomagnetic poles. Analyses of auroral counts in the modern era[48] lead us to expect a display almost every night in the northern 'auroral zone' – a band of geomagnetic latitude that includes northern Siberia, far-northern Scandinavia, Iceland, Greenland and the northern halves of Canada and Alaska. But this region is also an area of sparse historical record for the seventeenth century, and it should probably be excluded from consideration for the present purpose. In a more populous band just south of this zone – which includes Sweden, Norway and Scotland – we expect aurorae on 25 to about 200 nights per average year, the higher number at higher latitude. Progressively fewer are expected as we move south. For most of England, including the London area, we expect to see an average of 5 to 10 aurorae per year, or roughly 500 in seventy 'normal' years. In Paris we can expect about 350 in the same period, and in Italy perhaps 50. From England, France, Germany, Denmark and Poland, where astronomers were active during the 'Maunder Minimum', we might have expected reports of 300 to 1,000 auroral nights, by the statistics of today. Fritz's historical catalogue[49] lists only 77 aurorae for the entire world during the years from 1645 to 1715, and 20 of these were reported in a brief active interval, from 1707 to 1708, when sunspots were also seen. In thirty-seven of the years of the 'Maunder Minimum' not a single aurora was reported anywhere. Practically all reported aurorae were from the northern part of Europe: Norway, Sweden, Germany and Poland. For sixty-three years of the 'Maunder Minimum', from 1645 until 1708, not one was reported in London. The next, on 15 March 1716, moved the astronomer Edmund Halley to describe and explain it in a paper that is now classic.[50]

He was then sixty years old and had never seen an aurora before, although he was an assiduous observer of the sky and had long wanted to observe one.

The auroral picture, which seems clear at first glance, is muddied by subjectivity and by the obscurity of indirect facts from long ago. Historical catalogues cannot record aurorae but only reports of aurorae. Clerke did not mention that auroral counts from all centuries before the 18th are very low by modern standards. The 77 events noted during the 'Maunder Minimum' actually exceed the number recorded in any preceding century except the sixteenth, for which there are 161 in Fritz's catalogue. By contrast, 6,126 were reported in the eighteenth century and about as many in the nineteenth century.[51]

The really striking feature of the historical record of aurorae (Figure 8.2) is not so much the drop during the 'Maunder Minimum' but an apparent 'auroral turn-on' which commenced in the middle sixteenth century and surged upward dramatically after 1716. Were the historical record of uniform quality (and it is not), this apparent 'switching on' of the northern (and southern) lights would loom as the most significant fact of recent solar–terrestrial history. In truth, it must in part at least reflect the general curve of learning which probably holds for all of life in northern Europe at the time. The Renaissance came to auroral latitudes later than to the Mediterranean, and the envelope we see in Figure 8.2 may be but its shadow. The effect is large, however, and a part of it could well represent a real change in the occurrence of aurorae on the earth, and, by implication, a change in the behaviour of the sun. It is important that auroral reports do not increase monotonically with time as a learning curve might imply; the number reported rose in the ninth to twelfth centuries and then fell off.

The separation of the physical from the sociological in Figure 8.2. is a question of major importance in studies of the sun and earth. An acceptable solution would involve starting with a new and careful search for auroral data, particularly from northern latitudes, in the New World, Old World and Orient. It must include careful allowance for superstition and vogues and restrictions in observing aurorae, shifts of population, and the possibly important effects of single events, such as the development of the printing press (about 1450), or Gassendi's description of the French aurora of 1621[52] and Halley's paper in 1716.[53] One

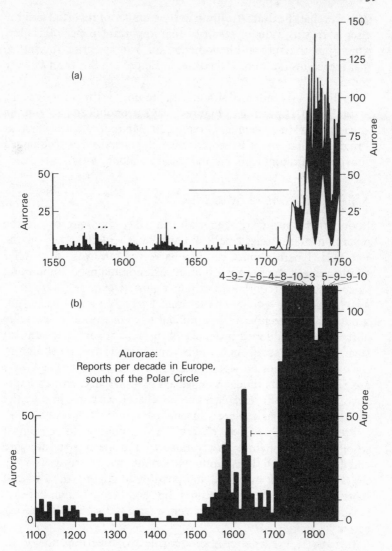

FIGURE 8.2 *Reported aurorae* (from Fritz, n. 46): (a) *All reports, from 1550 to 1750 by year, with the annual mean sunspot number superposed as white curves at the right and Far East aurorae* (see notes 55, 56, 62) *shown as solid squares.* (b) *Reports per decade in latitudes 0° to 66°N; counts after 1715 must be multiplied by the numbers shown at the top right of the plot. The period of the Maunder Minimum is shown in each diagram as a horizontal line*

suspects that the dramatic jump in the number of reported aurorae after 1716 was a direct result of this important paper of Halley, which put the auroral phenomenon on firm scientific footing so that more aurorae were looked for and more regular records were kept.

As for the 'Maunder Minimum', its presence in the auroral record is surely real, appearing in Figure 8.2 as a pronounced pause in the already upward-sweeping curve. Had Maunder looked first at Fritz's auroral atlas, he could have hypothesized a 'prolonged sunspot minimum' from auroral evidence alone.

Sunspots Seen with the Naked Eye

Spots on the sun were seen with the naked eye long before the invention of the telescope[54] and were particularly noted in the Far East, where a more continuous record survives. They offer another check on the reality of an extended sunspot minimum, since naked-eye reports of sunspots might be expected were there any strong solar activity at the time. Large spots and large spot groups can be seen with little difficulty when the sun is partially obscured and reddened by smoke or haze, or at sunset or sunrise; small groups or small spots are beyond the effective resolution of the eye and cannot be seen. Thus reports of naked-eye sightings are biased towards times of enhanced solar activity, and attempts have been made to establish the epochs of past maxima in the solar cycle from naked-eye sunspot dates.[55, 56]

Pre-telescopic sunspot observations probably come almost wholly from accidental observation. In Europe reports are rare and fragmentary.[57] It is from the Orient, where sunspots were deemed important in legend and possibly in augury, that we find more extensive and useful records. But here, too, the numbers are small and can only be used as a very coarse indicator of past solar activity.

In 1933 (five years after Maunder's death), Sigeru Kanda of the Tokyo Astronomical Observatory compiled a comprehensive list of 143 sunspot sightings from ancient records of Japan, Korea, and China, covering the period from 28 BC to AD 1743.[58] Most came after the third century, so that the long term average was about one sighting per decade. Were they distributed regularly (or just at solar maxima), we would thus expect six or seven events during the 'Maunder Minimum'. It is significant that none was recorded between 1639 and 1720 – a Far East gap that matches Western Hemisphere data very well.

As with aurorae, the evidence is necessary but not sufficient. Social practices or pressures could have suppressed observation or recording of spots during the time,[59] leading to an apparent but unreal dearth. Moreover, the sunspot gap from 1639 to 1720 is neither the only nor the longest in Kanda's span of reports: there were 84 years without any reports of sunspot sightings ending in 1604, 117 years ending in 1520, and 229 years ending in 808 (Figure 8.3a).

We may extend the naked-eye data in a sense by adding dates of reported aurorae in Japan, Korea, and China. All of these lands lie at low auroral latitudes, where displays are expected no more than once in ten years. As in the case of sunspots seen with the naked eye, aurorae reported in the Orient are presumed to sample only intense solar activity. And, as with the sunspot sightings, no Far East aurorae were reported during the 'Maunder Minimum', and more specifically between 1584 and 1770.[60,61,62] The oriental data (sunspots and aurorae) confirm that there were no intense periods of solar activity during the 'Maunder Minimum' and probably no 'normal' maxima in the solar cycle.

We may use the long span of oriental sunspot data as a coarse check on possible earlier occurrences of prolonged sunspot minima, or other gross, long term modulations of sunspot activity. Of particular note is an intensification of sunspot and aurora reports in the 200-year period centred around 1180, which is about halfway between the 'Maunder Minimum' and a more extended period of absence of Far East sunspots and aurorae in the seventh and early eighth centuries. As I will show below, the naked-eye maximum coincides with a similar maximum of solar activity in the ^{14}C record. If this is a real long-term envelope of solar activity, its period is roughly 1,000 years. We may be measuring only social effects, but, as with historical European aurorae, the subject is one of potential importance which deserves more specific attention by historians.

Carbon-14 and the History of the Sun

Modern confirmation for Maunder's 'prolonged sunspot minimum' may be found in recent determinations of the past abundance of terrestrial ^{14}C. Carbon and its radioactive isotopes

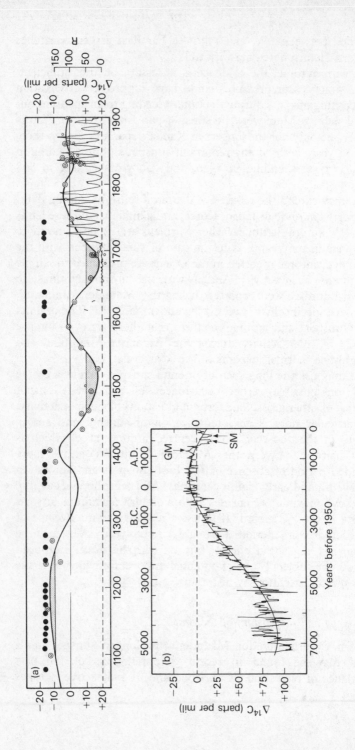

are abundant constituents of the earth's atmosphere, chiefly as carbon dioxide (CO_2). When CO_2 is assimilated into trees, for example, the carbon isotopes undergo spontaneous disintegration at well-known rates. Thus, by a technique now well established, it is possible to determine the date of life of a carbon-bearing sample, such as wood, by chemical measurement of its present ^{14}C content and comparison with a presumed original amount. The method requires a knowledge of the past abundance of ^{14}C in the atmosphere, and this value is found by analysing, ring by ring, the ^{14}C content of trees of known chronology. The history of relative ^{14}C abundance deviations is now fairly well established and serves as the basis for accurate isotopic dating in archaeology.[63,64,65,66]

The ^{14}C history is useful in its own right as a measure of past solar activity, as has been demonstrated by a number of investigators.[67,68] The isotope is continuously formed in the atmosphere through the action of cosmic rays, which in turn are modulated by solar activity. When the sun is active, some of the

FIGURE 8.3 (a) *History of deviations in the relative atmospheric ^{14}C concentration from tree-ring analyses for the period 1050 to 1900 (see n. 70): single open circles, Northern Hemisphere data; double open circles, Southern Hemisphere data (a heavy line has been drawn through the Southern Hemisphere data); closed circles, dates of reported sunspots seen with the naked eye from Kanda (n. 55). The annual mean sunspot number, R, is shown as a light solid line where known for the period after 1610, from Waldmeier (n. 3) and this study. Periods when the relative ^{14}C deviation exceeds 10 parts per mil are shaded. They define probable anomalies in the behaviour of the solar cycle: 1100 to 1250, Grand Maximum; 1460 to 1550, 'Spörer Minimum'; 1645 to 1715, 'Maunder Minimum'. (b) Measured ^{14}C deviation (in parts per mil) since about 5000 BC, with observed (smoothed) curve of sinusoidal variation in the earth's magnetic moment (from n. 80, figure 2). At about AD 100 the magnetic moment reached a maximum of about 10^{24} gauss per cubic centimetre. Shorter term ^{14}C excursions attributed in this article to solar cause are marked with arrows: M, 'Maunder Minimum'; S, 'Spörer Minimum'; GM, Grand Maximum in the twelfth to thirteenth centuries. The sharp negative ^{14}C deviation at the modern end of the curve is the Suess effect, due to fossil fuel combustion* incoming galactic cosmic rays are prevented from reaching the earth. At these times, corresponding to maxima in the sunspot cycle, less than the normal amount of ^{14}C is produced in the atmosphere and less is found in tree rings formed then. When the sun is quiet, terrestrial bombardment by galactic cosmic rays increases and the ^{14}C proportion in the atmosphere rises. There are other terms in the ^{14}C equilibrium process, as well as significant lags; but, if there had been a prolonged period of quiet on the sun, we would expect to find evidence of it in tree rings of that era as an abnormally high abundance of ^{14}C.

Such is the case. The first major anomaly found in the early studies of ^{14}C history was a marked and prolonged increase which reached its maximum between about 1650 and 1700,[69] in remarkable agreement in sense and date with the 'Maunder Minimum'. The phenomenon, known in carbon-dating as the DeVries Fluctuation, peaked at about 1690 and is the greatest positive excursion in the recent ^{14}C record – corresponding to a deviation of about 20 parts per mil from the norm. Subsequent studies have established the DeVries Fluctuation as a worldwide effect.

Figure 8.3 shows a curve (open circles and heavy line) of the relative deviation in the ^{14}C concentration based on recent measurements of tree rings,[70] plotted with increasing concentration downward for direct comparison with solar activity; also shown are sunspot numbers[71] (light line) including those from the present work, and years of early naked-eye sunspot sightings from Kanda (closed circles).[72] The three quantities give a wholly consistent representation of the 'Maunder Minimum'. We also note a clustering of naked-eye sunspot sightings at times when the ^{14}C record indicates greater than normal activity, and a general absence of them when the ^{14}C record indicates less than normal activity. Where annual sunspot numbers are plotted, the ^{14}C curve seems a fair representation of the overall envelope of the sunspot curve. It thus seems valid to interpret the ^{14}C record as an indicator of the long term trend of solar activity and of real changes in solar behaviour in the distant past, before the time of telescopic examination of the sun.[73,74,75]

We may calibrate the ^{14}C curve for this purpose by noting that the years of the 'Maunder Minimum' define a time when the relative deviation of ^{14}C exceeded 10 parts per mil. If we can make allowance for other effects on ^{14}C production and equilibrium, we may infer that, whenever the ^{14}C deviation exceeded $\pm$ 10 parts per mil, solar activity was anomalously high or low, with the 'Maunder Minimum' corresponding to a definition of 'anomalous'. We must remember that the ^{14}C indications will tend to lag behind real solar changes by periods of ten to fifty years, because of the finite time of exchange between the atmosphere and trees. By this criterion there have been three possible periods of marked solar anomaly during the last 1,000 years: the 'Maunder Minimum', another minimum in the early sixteenth century, and a period of anomalously high activity in the twelfth and early thirteenth centuries. We can think of these as the grand minima and a grand maximum of the solar cycle, although we cannot judge from these data whether they are cyclic features.

The erlier mimimum, which we might call the 'Sporer Minimum', persisted by our 10-parts-per-mil criterion from about 1460 through 1550. Its ^{14}C deviation is not quite as great as that during the 'Maunder Minimum', although that distinction is not a consistent feature of all representations of the ^{14}C history.[76] We can presume that the 'Spörer Minimum' was probably as pronounced as the 'Maunder Minimum' and that during those years there were few sunspots indeed. It appears to have reached its greatest depth in the early sixteenth century when there were also very few aurorae reported.

We noted earlier the possibility of an intensification of solar activity in the twelfth and thirteenth centuries, on the basis of naked-eye sunspot reports from the Orient. Evidence for the same maximum is found in the historical aurora record (Figure 8.2): the number of aurorae in Fritz's catalogue[77] is about constant for the ninth, tenth and eleventh centuries (23, 27 and 21 aurorae per century, respectively), rises abruptly for the twelfth century (53 aurorae), and then falls for the next three centuries (16, 21 and 7 aurorae). The ^{14}C record (Figure 8.3a) shows a similar anomaly in the same direction: a decrease in ^{14}C which could be attributed to a prolonged increase in solar activity.

We must take care in assigning any of the ^{14}C variations to a solar cause, for there are other important mechanisms. The overwhelming long-term effects on ^{14}C production are ponderous changes in the strength of the earth's magnetic field.[78,79] Archaeomagnetic studies have shown that in the past 10,000 years the earth's magnetic moment has varied in strength by more than a factor of 2, following an apparently sinusoidal envelope with a period of about 9,000 years, on which shorter-term changes are impressed. The terrestrial moment reached maximum strength at about AD 100, at which time we would expect to find a minimum in ^{14}C production because of enhanced shielding of the earth against cosmic rays.

The good fit of the observed (smoothed) curve of geomagnetic change to the long-term record of fossil ^{14}C is shown in Figure 8.3b, from a recent compilation,[80] here re-plotted with increasing ^{14}C in the downward direction to display increasing solar activity and increasing geomagnetic strength as upward-going effects. Damon[81] has stressed that the long-term trends in the radiocarbon content of the atmosphere have been dominated in the past 8,000 years by the geomagnetic effect, while the shorter-term fluctuations have probably been controlled by changes in solar activity. This point seems clear in Figure 8.3b, where, near the modern end of the curve, the 'Maunder Minimum' (M) and 'Spörer Minimum' (S) stand out as obvious excursions from the long-term envelope of geomagnetic change. And at about 1200 we find a broad departure in the opposite direction, which might fit the twelfth- and thirteenth-century maximum in sunspot and auroral reports. Whether the sun was indeed responsible is open to question, however, for Bucha[82] has pointed out that this ^{14}C decrease follows a similar short-term increase in the earth's magnetic moment (not shown in Figure 8.3b), which had its onset at about AD 900. Moreover, there is uncertainty in the fit of the smoothed archaeomagnetic curve to the radiocarbon data, and a shift to the right or left will change the apparent contrast of these shorter-term excursions.

We should like to know how solar activity in a possible twelfth-century Grand Maximum compares with the present epoch, but the present is an era of confusion in ^{14}C. The ^{14}C concentration has been falling steeply since the end of the nineteenth century, and the deviation (Δ ^{14}C) is now about -25 parts per mil. Were this a solar effect, it would be evidence of anomalously high solar activity. In fact, the sharp drop is an effect of human activity – the result of fossil fuel combustion, which introduces CO_2 with different carbon isotopic abundance ratios – the so-called Suess Effect.[83] If fossil fuel combustion is responsible for all of the modern ^{14}C trend, then during the twelfth-century Grand Maximum (when industrial pollution was not significant), the natural ^{14}C deviation may have been much greater than at present and the sun may have been more active than we are accustomed to observing in the modern era. There were possibly more spots on more of the sun during the twelfth-century Grand Maximum, and, if the eleven-year cycle operated then, there may have been higher maxima and higher minima than any we see in Figure 8.1.

The shallow dip and rise in the fourteenth and early fifteenth centuries (Figure 8.3a) suggest the presence of a subsidiary solar period of about 170 years, but these features seem for now too slight to warrant speculation; we may expect that additional ^{14}C data will clarify the case. The information available at present allows one to describe the history of the sun in the last millennium as follows: a possible Grand Maximum in the twelfth century, a protracted fall to a century-long minimum around 1500, a short rise to 'normal', and then the fall to the shorter, deeper 'Maunder Minimum', after which there has been a steady rise in the envelope of solar activity.[84]

This last phase, which includes all detailed records of the sun and the sunspot cycle, does not appear in the ^{14}C history as very typical of the sun's behaviour in the past, particularly if the *phase* of the long-term curve is important. During most of the last 1,000 years the long-term envelope of solar activity was either higher than at present, or falling, or at grand minima like the 'Maunder Minimum'. As with the present climate, what we think of as normal may be quite unusual. The possibility that solar behaviour since 1715 was unlike that in the past has already been proposed to help explain the sudden auroral turn-on. Another piece of evidence comes from records of the sun's appearance at eclipse.

Absence of the Corona at Eclipse

Historical accounts of the solar corona at total eclipse offer another possible check on anomalies in past solar behaviour. We know that the shape of the corona seen at eclipse varies with solar activity: when the sun has many spots, the corona is made up of numerous long tapered streamers which extend outward like the petals of a flower. As activity wanes, the corona dims and fewer and fewer streamers are seen. At a normal minimum in the solar cycle the corona seen by the naked eye is highly compressed and blank except for long symmetric extensions along its equator. We now believe that coronal streamers are rooted in concentrated magnetic fields on the surface of the sun, which in turn are associated with solar activity and sunspots. As sunspots fade, so do concentrated surface fields and associated coronal structures. Continuous, detailed, observations of the solar corona in X-ray wavelengths from Skylab have confirmed the association of coronal forms with loops and arches in the surface fields and have shown that in areas where there are no concentrated fields, loops, or arches there is no apparent corona.[85]

Were there a total absence of solar activity, we would still expect to observe a dim, uniform glow around the moon at eclipse: the zodiacal light, or false corona, would remain, since it is simply sunlight scattered from dust and other matter in the space between the earth and the sun. At times of normal solar activity the corona seen at eclipse is a mixture of the true corona (or K corona) and the weaker glow of the zodiacal light (or F corona). The latter is a roughly symmetric glow around the sun which falls off in brightness from the limb and is distended in the plane of the planets where interplanetary dust is gravitationally concentrated. If the F corona were ever seen alone, we would expect it to appear as a dull, slightly reddish, eerie ring of light of uniform breadth and without discernible structure.

In fact, first-hand descriptions of total solar eclipses during the 'Maunder Minimum' seem entirely consistent with an absence of the modern structured corona, but proof seems blurred by the customs of observing eclipses in the past and by the fact that scientists seldom describe what is missing or what is not thought to be important. The solar origin of the corona was not established until the late nineteenth century; before that it seemed equally well explained as sunlight scattered in our own atmosphere, or on the moon. Solar eclipses were regularly and routinely observed throughout the seventeenth century, but not to study the physical sun. They were occasions to test the then popular science of orbit calculation: careful measurement and timing of solar obscuration by the moon offered checks on lunar and terrestrial motions and opportunity to measure the relative sizes of solar and lunar disks. Such details are best obtained not at the eyepiece of a wide-field telescope in the open air but in a darkened room, by projection of the disks of the moon and sun upon a card, as we see in contemporary drawings from the time. Under these restrictive conditions a corona, structured or not, could escape detection, particularly since it appeared so briefly and at just the time when undivided attention was demanded to observe the precise minutia of obscuration.[86]

Nor was it so important to seek out geographic places on the central path of a total eclipse. The corona – K or F – is so faint that it cannot be seen except in exact totality. But if one's purpose were astronomical mensuration and timing, a partial or near-total eclipse was almost as good as a total eclipse and could be observed more accurately in the familiar conditions of permanent observatories. Since partial solar eclipses can be seen over large areas and thus can occur frequently at any location, there was not the impetus of today to travel far and wide to set up camp for one-time tries in distant, hostile lands. Eclipse expeditions are a modern fad that did not take hold until about the nineteenth century.[87]

These fundamental differences severely limit the number of cases we can test. There were sixty-three opportunities to see the sun eclipsed between 1645 and 1715,[88] but only eight of them passed through those parts of Europe where astronomers did their daily work (Figure 8.4). Another case (1698) comes from the

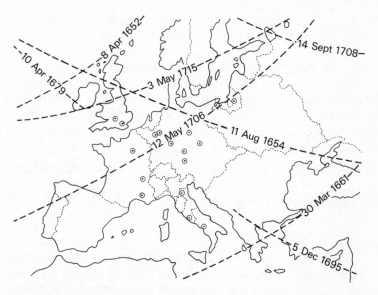

FIGURE 8.4 *Paths of totality for solar eclipses in Europe, from 1640 to 1715, from Oppolzer, n. 88. Sites of observatories which reported eclipse observations in the period are shown as double circles*

New World. Only a few of the European eclipses reached totality near any permanent observatory, and the three best observed occurred at the end of our period of interest – in 1706, 1708 and 1715, when spots had begun their return.

Nevertheless, from this list comes a handful of accounts that bear on the question and answer it consistently. They are descriptions of the corona from the eclipses of 1652, 1698, 1706 and 1708, the only contemporary first-hand descriptions of the sun eclipsed that I can find.[89] They were written, in general, by amateurs and nonconformists who watched the spectacle with eyes open to all of it. None describes the corona as showing structure. Not one mentions the streamers which at every eclipse in the present time are so easily seen with the naked eye to stretch as much as a degree or more above the solar limb. All describe the corona as very limited in extent: typically only 1 to 3 arc minutes above the solar limb. In each case the corona is described as dull or mournful, and often as reddish. No drawings were made. Every account is consistent with our surmise of what the zodiacal light would look like at eclipse, were the true corona really gone.

By 1715 the annual sunspot number had reached 26 and was climbing. At the eclipse of that year, at the end of the 'Maunder Minimum', the corona is fairly well described, and for the first time we have drawings of it. For the first time distinct coronal structures are described emanating from the sun. R. Cotes of Cambridge University described the corona (in a letter to Isaac Newton) as a white ring of light around the moon, its densest part extending about 5 arc minutes above the limb; he then added the following:

> Besides this ring, there appeared also rays of a much fainter light in the form of a rectangular cross. . . . The longer and brighter branch of this cross lay very nearly along the ecliptic, the light of the shorter was so weak that I did not constantly see it.[90]

We may presume that the light of the shorter branch was the polar plumes which we see today at times of sunspot minimum and that the longer, brighter branch was the familiar equatorial extensions seen at times of low sunspot activity. Thus by 1715 we find the corona described in modern terms and fitting a familiar form.

In her paper on the dearth of aurorae Clerke mentioned, without example, that it appeared to her probable that during the 'prolonged sunspot minimum' the radiated structure of the solar corona was also 'in abeyance'.[91] Recently Parker has repeated Clerke's conjecture.[92] The case for a disappearance of the structured corona during the 'Maunder Minimum' might seem more solid were it not for the fact that the earliest description yet found for the rayed or structured corona at *any* eclipse is that of Cotes in 1715.

R. R. Newton has expressed the situation very explicitly, on the basis of his own researches for definite accounts of the corona as positive documentation of historical solar eclipses:

> The corona is mentioned in most modern discussions of total solar eclipses, and to most people it is probably the typical and spectacular sight associated with a total eclipse. In view of this, it is surprising to see how little the corona appears in ancient or medieval accounts. . . .[93]
> . . . there is no clear reference to the corona in any ancient or medieval record that I have found. The most likely reference is perhaps the remark by Plutarch . . . but the meaning of Plutarch's remark is far from certain.[94]

I should add that here Newton is referring to *any* unambiguous description of the corona, K or F.

A misleading statement common in popular stories of eclipses is that the solar corona was seen in antiquity much as we would describe it today. Usually cited are two early accounts, one by Plutarch (about AD 46 to 120) and another by Philostratus (about AD 170 to 245). Both reports are ambiguous at best, and neither distinguishes between a structured or an unstructured appearance.[95] The situation in all subsequent descriptions before the eighteenth century seems to be no different. At the eclipse of 9 April 1567 Clavius reported seeing 'a narrow ring of light around the Moon' at maximum solar obscuration (although Kepler challenged this as possibly an annular eclipse). Jessenius at a total eclipse in 1598 reported 'a bright light shining around the Moon'. And Kepler himself reported that at the eclipse of 1604:

> The whole body of the Sun was effectually covered for a short time. The surface of the Moon appeared quite black; but around it there shone a brilliant light of a reddish hue,

and uniform breadth, which occupied a considerable part of the heavens.[96]

None of these or any other descriptions that I can find fit a rayed or structured corona; in many are the words 'of uniform breadth', and it seems to me most likely that we are reading descriptions of the zodiacal light, or of a K corona so weak that its radiance is overpowered by the glow of the F corona.

It could be that, until the scientific enlightenment of the eighteenth century, no one felt moved to describe the impressive structure of the solar corona at eclipse. Indeed, there are other examples from the history of eclipse observation where large and striking features were missed by good observers who were watching other things.[97] Perhaps the rays of the corona at eclipse were thought to be so much like the common aureole around the sun that they were not deemed worthy of description. Other excuses could be offered. It will be hard for anyone who has seen the corona with the naked eye to accept these explanations and to believe that, of the thousands of observers at hundreds of total eclipses, not one would have commented on a thing so breathtaking and beautiful. It thus seems to me more probable that, through much of the long period of the 'Maunder Minimum' and the 'Spörer Minimum', extending between perhaps 1400 and 1700, the sun was at such a minimum of activity that the K corona was severely thinned or absent altogether. The same may have been true for a much longer span before 1400 and for different reasons may apply as well to the Grand Maximum of the twelfth and thirteenth centuries and possibly earlier. But here the records are so dim and scant that conclusions seem unwarranted. In any case the corona as we know it may well be a modern feature of the sun. It is an interesting question, and another important challenge for historians.

Summary and Conclusions

The prolonged absence of sunspots between about 1645 and 1715, which Spörer and Maunder described, is supported by direct accounts in the limited contemporary literature of the day and cited regularly in astronomy works of the ensuing century. We may conclude that the absence was not merely a limitation in observing capability because of the accomplishments in other areas of astronomy in the late seventeenth and early eighteenth centuries, and because drawings of the sun made at the time show almost all the sunspot detail that is known today. Major books by Scheiner and Hevelius, published just before the onset of the Maunder Minimum, describe wholly adequate methods for observing the sun and sunspots. We may assume that a fairly steady watch was kept, since the dearth of spots was recognized at the time and since the identification of a new sunspot was cause for the publication of a paper. We can discount the possibility of seventy years of overcast skies, since there is no evidence of such an anomaly in meteorological lore and since night-time astronomy was vigorous and productive through the same period. Evidence that confirms the 'Maunder Minimum' comes from records of naked-eye sunspot sightings, auroral records, the now-available history of atmospheric ^{14}C, and descriptions of the eclipsed sun at the time.

I can find no facts that contradict the Maunder claim, and much that supports it. In questions of history where only a dim and limited record remains and where we are blocked from making crucial observational tests, the search for possible contradiction seems to me a promising path to truth. I am led to conclude that the 'prolonged sunspot minimum' was a real feature of the recent history of the sun and that it happened much as Maunder first described it.

Earlier in this article I reviewed the possible impact of a real 'Maunder Minimum' on theories of the sun and the solar cycle. For some implications the distinction between no sunspots and a few (annual sunspot numbers of one to five) is crucial; it is important to know whether during the great depression of the 'Maunder Minimum' the solar cycle continued to operate at an almost invisible level, with so few spots that they were lost in our fuzzy definition of 'zero'. Maunder held that there were enough instances of sunspot sightings through the period to make this case likely, and that the isolated times when a few spots appeared enabled one to identify the crests of a sunken spot curve:

> just as in a deeply inundated country, the loftiest objects will still raise their heads above the flood, and a spire here, a hill, a tower, a tree there, enable one to trace out the configuration of the submerged champaign.[98]

This explanation seems to me unlikely, since the known, visible crests are not at regular spacings. We can hope that more thorough investigation of contemporary literature will enable us to make this important distinction which for now seems beyond the limit of resolution.

The years of the 'Maunder Minimum' define a time in the ^{14}C record when the departure from normal isotopic abundance exceeded 10 parts per mil. If we take a ^{14}C deviation of this magnitude as a criterion of major change in solar behaviour, we may deduce from ^{14}C history the existence of at least two other major changes in solar character in the last millennium: a period of prolonged solar quiet like the 'Maunder Minimum' between about 1460 and 1550 (which I have called the 'Spörer Minimum') and a 'prolonged sunspot maximum' between about 1100 and 1250. If the prolonged maximum of the twelfth and thirteenth centuries and the prolonged minima of the sixteenth and seventeenth centuries are extrema of a cycle of solar change, the cycle has a full period of roughly 1,000 years. If this change is periodic,

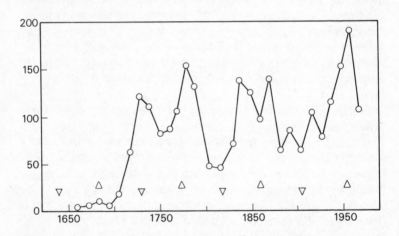

FIGURE 8.5 *Annual mean sunspot numbers at maxima in the eleven-year cycle, from 1645 to the present, to demonstrate long-term trends in solar activity. Evident is the well-known eighty-year cycle (extrema shown as triangles) imposed on a persistent rise since the 'Maunder Minimum'. The seventy-eight or eighty-year cycle was first noted by Wolf, n. 132, and later studied in detail by Gleissberg, n. 133. The solar constant may also have risen slowly through the period during which it has been measured, since about 1908 (see notes 30, 99)*

we can speculate that the sun may now be progressing toward a grand maximum which might be reached in the twenty-second or twenty-third centuries. The overall envelope of solar activity has been steadily increasing since the end of the 'Maunder Minimum' (Figure 8.5), giving some credence to this view. Moreover, throughout the more limited span during which it has been measured, the solar constant appears to have shown a continuous rising trend which during the period from 1920 to 1952 was about 0.5 per cent per century.[99]

The coincidence of Maunder's 'prolonged solar minimum' with the coldest excursion of the 'Little Ice Age' has been noted by many who have looked at the possible relations between the sun and terrestrial climate.[100] A lasting tree-ring anomaly which spans the same period has been cited as evidence of a concurrent drought in the American South-west.[101,102] There is also a nearly 1:1 agreement in sense and time between major excursions in world temperature (as best they are known) and the earlier excursions of the envelope of solar behaviour in the record of ^{14}C, particularly when a ^{14}C time lag is allowed for: the 'Spörer Minimum' of the sixteenth century is coincident with the other severe temperature dip of the Little Ice Age, and the Grand Maximum coincides with the 'medieval Climatic Optimum' of the eleventh to thirteenth centuries.[103,104] These coincidences suggest a possible relationship between the overall envelope of the curve of solar activity and terrestrial climate in which the eleven-year solar cycle may be effectively filtered out or simply unrelated to the problem. The mechanism of this solar effect on climate may be the simple one of ponderous long-term changes of small amount in the total radiative output of the sun, or solar constant. These long-term drifts in solar radiation may modulate the envelope of the solar cycle through the solar dynamo to produce the observed long-term trends in solar activity. The continuity, or phase, of the eleven-year cycle would be independent of this slow, radiative change, but the amplitude could be controlled by it. According to this interpretation, the cyclic coming and going of sunspots would have little effect on the output of solar radiation, or presumably on weather, but the long-term envelope of sunspot activity carries the indelible signature of slow changes in solar radiation which surely affect our climate.[105]

The existence of the 'Maunder Minimum' and the possibility of earlier fluctuations in solar behaviour of similar magnitude imply that the present cycle of solar activity may be unusual if not transitory. For long periods in the historic past the pattern of solar behaviour may have been completely different from the solar cycle today. There is good evidence that within the last millennium the sun has been both considerably less active and probably more active than we have seen it in the last 250 years. These upheavals in solar behaviour may have been accompanied by significant long-term changes in radiative output. And they were almost certainly accompanied by significant changes in the flow of atomic particles from the sun, with possible terrestrial effects. Our present understanding of the solar wind is that its flow is regulated by closed or open magnetic field configurations on the sun.[106] We can only guess what effect a total absence of activity and of large-scale magnetic structures would have on the behaviour of solar wind flow in the ecliptic plane. One possibility is that, were the sun without extensive coronal structure during the 'Maunder Minimum', the solar wind would have blown steadily and isotropically, and possibly at gale force, since high-speed streams of solar wind are associated with the absence of closed structures in the solar corona. During an intensive maximum, as is suggested for the twelfth and thirteenth centuries, the solar wind was probably consistently weak, steady, and with few recurrent streams.

The reality of the 'Maunder Minimum' and its implications of basic solar change may be but one more defeat in our long and losing battle to keep the sun perfect, or, if not perfect, constant, and if inconstant, regular. Why we think the sun should be any of these when other stars are not is more a question for social than for physical science.

Appendix: Sunspot Numbers

I have used contemporary accounts of telescopic observation of the sun to reconstruct estimated annual mean sunspot numbers for the period from 1610 to 1715 (Table 8.1 and Figure 8.6). Principal sources were Wolf's compilations.[107,108,109,110,111,112,113,114,115,116,117,118] The journal sources are, for the most part, the same as those that were used by Lalande, Spörer and Maunder; thus, except for the direct numerical data from Wolf, Scheiner and Hevelius, sunspot numbers given here are simply a literal quantification of Maunder's descriptive account. Full reliance has been

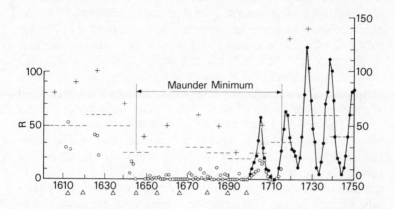

FIGURE 8.6 *Estimated annual mean sunspot numbers, from 1610 to 1750: open circles are data from Table 8.1; connected, closed circles are from Waldmeier, n. 3; dashed lines (decade estimates) and crosses (peak estimates) are from Schove (notes 9, 10, 11 and 12); triangles are Wolf's estimated dates of maxima for an assumed 11.1-year solar cycle (see notes 3, 7)*

placed on unchallenged statements in contemporary literature which specify periods in which no sunspots were seen, as, for example, between 1656 and 1660, 1661 and 1671, 1689 to 1695, 1695 to 1700, and 1710 to 1713.

Earlier I classified Wolf's historical sunspot data; by the same criteria the data in Table 8.1 should be given a reliability grade of 'poor', since they come from largely discontinuous sets and since allowance for observer and site can only be guessed. The estimated annual sunspot numbers are uncertain to at least a factor of 2, and zero as an annual average means 0 to perhaps 5. The fact that the telescopes of Flamsteed and Cassini were in less than perfect observing sites could have caused these observers to miss a class of tiny, isolated spots which might be detected and counted by keen observers today. The more important point is that their sites and instruments were certainly adequate to detect any level of activity higher than that at the minima of the present solar cycle; they might have missed a few spots but they could not have missed a large number.

My sunspot numbers for the period 1700 to 1715 are somewhat lower than those given for the same period by Waldmeier,[119] who took them from Wolf. Both values are shown in Table 8.1 and Figure 8.6. The general agreement seems heartening, but the difference may be important since it is in the only span of overlap with other direct numerical compilations. It is also in the least reliable part of Wolf's data and the period of recovery from the 'Maunder Minimum', for which a more gradual rise seems reasonable. Auroral data and eclipse observations from the period of overlap seem to me to support the more suppressed sunspot curve (Figure 8.6). I find it hard to justify Wolf's numbers for his first and possibly second cycles and suspect that his unusual-shaped maximum for 1705 was an artificiality of unrealistic correction factors. Wolf did not have confidence in most of the data for 1700 to 1749,[120] and his numbers towards the beginning of that period may represent, more than anything else, a wishful extrapolation of normalcy. I also show in Figure 8.6 and Table 8.1 Schove's estimates of decade-averaged and peak sunspot numbers from the STP,[121,122,123,124] which we can also expect to be systematically high.[125]

TABLE 8.1 *Estimated annual mean sunspot numbers, R, from 1610 to 1715; X, sunspots noted but not counted; XX, unusual number of sunspots noted but not counted; (X), unusually small number of sunspots noted but not counted. Schove's values are for the maxima of each supposed cycle.*

Year	R	Waldmeier[3]	Schove[10]	Year	R	Waldmeier[3]	Schove[10]
1610	X			1663	0		
1611	30	Minimum		1664	0		
1612	53			1665	0		
1613	28			1666	0	Minimum	
1614				1667	0		
1615	X			1668	0		
1616	X	Maximum	90	1669	0		
1617	X			1670	0		
1618	(X)			1671	6		
1619		Minimum		1672	4		
1620				1673	0		
1621	X			1674	2		
1622	X			1675	0	Maximum	6c
1623	X			1676	10		
1624	X			1677	2		
1625	41			1678	6		
1626	40	Maximum	100	1679	0		
1627	22			1680	4	Minimum	
1628				1681	2		
1629	(X)			1682	0		

TABLE 8.1. *continued*

Year				Year				
1630				1683	0			
1631				1684	11			
1632	(X)			1685	0		Maximum	50
1633				1686	4			
1634	(X)	Minimum		1687	0			
1635	(X)			1688	5			
1636				1689	4			
1637				1690	0		Minimum	
1638	X			1691	0			
1639	XX			1692	0			
1640		Maximum	70	1693	0		Maximum	30
1641				1694	0			
1642	6			1695	6			
1643	16			1696	0			
1644	15			1697	0			
1645	0	Minimum		1698	0		Minimum	
1646				1699	0			
1647				1700	2	5		
1648				1701	4	11		
1649		Maximum	40	1702	6	16		
1650	0			1703	8	23		
1651	0			1704	9	36		
1652	3			1705	18	58		50
1653	0			1706	15	29		
1654	2			1707	18	20		
1655	1	Minimum		1708	8	10		
1656	2			1709	3	8		
1657	0			1710	2	3		
1658	0			1711	0	0		
1659	0			1712	0	0		
1660	4	Maximum	50	1713	2	2		
1661	4			1714	3	11		
1662	0			1715	10	27		

Numbers given for 1625 to 1627 and 1642 to 1644 (from Scheiner and Hevelius) are probably more reliable than any subsequent data in Table 8.1, since they are based on more nearly continuous daily drawings. Data for 1611 to 1613 come from the observations of Galileo. Waldmeier[126] and Schove[127,128,129,130] have apparently followed Wolf in assuming that these three islands of data before 1650 sample extrema of the sunspot cycle: Galileo and Scheiner at maxima, Hevelius at minimum. If these periods are all nearer maxima, as I suspect, they give some hint of the fall to the long minimum that followed. The nature of the fall suggests that the telescope was invented barely in time to 'discover' sunspots before their numbers shrank to nearly zero. Had the invention of the telescope been delayed by as little as thirty-five years, the tele-scopic discovery and more thorough counting of sunspots could have been postponed a full century, burying forever the principal evidence for the 'Maunder Minimum'.

Notes

1 The Wolf sunspot number (or sunspot relative number) is defined as $R = k(10g + f)$ where f is the total number of spots (irrespective of size), g is the number of spot groups, and k is a normalizing factor to bring the counts of different observers, telescopes and sites into agreement.

2 R. B. Leighton, *Astrophys. J.*, CLVI (1969), p. 1.

3 M. Waldmeier, *The Sunspot-Activity in the Years 1610–1960* (Schulthess, Zurich, 1961).

4 R. J. Bray and R. E. Loughhead, *Sunspots* (Wiley, New York, 1965), p. 1.

5 H. Schwabe, *Astron. Nachr.*, XX (No. 495) (1843). For an interesting discussion of Schwabe, his lonely work, and the prejudice against the idea of cyclic solar behaviour before that time, see M. J. Johnson, *Mem. R. Astron. Soc.*, XXVI (1858), p. 196.

6 See n. 3 above.

7 R. Wolf, *Sunspot Observations, 1610–1715*, facsimile of a typescript from Eidgen Sternwarte in Zurich (in G. E. Hale Collection, Hale Observatory Library, Pasadena, Calif.). The eleven-page manuscript lists the days of each year on which spots were or were not seen, the numbers of spots (where known), and notes and references. Other more condensed accounts of the period by Wolf include: *Astron. Mitt. Zurich*, I (1856), p. viii; ibid., XXIV (1868), p. 111.

8 In (n. 3, p. 8) Waldmeier states that 'Wolf intended to prove for a longer interval the sunspot-periodicity discovered shortly before by ... Schwabe.' In one of his papers (*Astron. Mitt. Zurich*, I (1856), p. viii, Wolf explained that, in periods where data were sparse, he assumed continued operation of the 11.11-year cycle.

9 D. J. Schove, *Terr. Magn. Atmos. Electr.*, LII (1947), p. 233; *J. Br. Astron. Assoc.*, LXXI (1961), p. 320.

10 D. J. Schove, *J. Geophys. Res.*, LX (1955), p. 127.

11 D. J. Schove, *Ann. N.Y. Acad. Sci.*, XCV (1961), p. 107.

12 D. J. Schove, *J. Br. Astron. Assoc.*, LXXII (1962), p. 30.

13 J. A. Eddy *et al.*, *Sol. Phys.*, XLVI (1976), p. 3; *Science*, CXCVIII (1977), p. 824.

14 F. W. G. Spörer, *Vierteljahrsschr. Astron. Ges. (Liepzig)*, XX (1887), p. 323; *Bull. Astron.*, VI (1889), p. 60.

15 E. W. Maunder, *Mon. Not. R. Astron. Soc.*, L (1890), p. 251.

16 E. W. Maunder, *Knowledge*, XVII (1894), p. 173.

17 E. W. Maunder, *J. Brit. Astron. Assoc.*, XXXII (1922), p. 140.

18 A. M. Clerke, *Knowledge*, XVII (1894), p. 206.

19 See p. 173 of n. 16.

20 See p. 174 of n. 16.

21 See pp. 141–2 of n. 17.

22 See p. 174 of n. 16.

23 Late examples include: E. H. Burritt, *The Geography of the Heavens* (Huntington & Savage, New York, 1845), p. 180; R. A. Proctor, *The Sun* (Longmans, Green, London, 1871), p. 164.

24 W. Herschel, *Philos. Trans. R. Soc. London*, CCLXV (1801). In this wide-ranging and oft-cited paper Herschel reveals his belief in the influence of solar fluctuations on weather, based on his own observation of a correlation between the price of wheat in London and the number of visible sunspots. In making his point, he uses the extreme periods of spot absence of the Maunder Minimum, during which time the price of wheat rose. Herschel attributes the connection to reduced rainfall when the sun was less spotted, and to the inexorable workings of the law of supply and demand. This paper reveals, among other things, that the quest for a solar–weather connection predated the discovery of the solar cycle. It was not Herschel's worst mistake: in the same paper he tells of his belief in a habitable and possibly inhabited sun.

25 J. LaLande, *Astronomie* (Desaint, Paris, 1792; and Johnson Reprint Corporation, New York, 1966), III, pp. 286–7. This encyclopaedic work was probably the unacknowledged source of most of the nineteenth-century descriptions of past periods of prolonged sunspot absence. LaLande's references included original journal reports and Jacques Cassini's *Elements d'Astronomie* (Imprimerie Royale, Paris, 1740), pp. 81–2, 182. Jacques Cassini was the son of G. D. (Jean) Cassini, who discovered the sunspot of 1671 and the moons of Saturn.

26 G. E. Hale, 'Photography of the solar prominences' (thesis, Massachusetts Institute of Technology, 1890); reprinted in *The Legacy of George Ellery Hale*, H. Wright, J. Warnow, C. Weiner, eds (MIT Press, Cambridge, Mass., 1972), p. 117; C. A. Young, *The Sun* (Appleton, New York, 1896), p. 193.

27 R. R. Newton, *Ancient Astronomical Observations and the Acceleration of the Earth and Moon* (Johns Hopkins Press, Baltimore, 1970), p. 39.

28 R. R. Newton, *Medieval Chronicles and the Rotation of the Earth* (Johns Hopkins Press, Baltimore, 1972), pp. 99, 600–1.

29 C. M. Smythe and J. A. Eddy, *Nature*, CCLXVI (1977), p. 434.

30 J. A. Eddy, *Bull. Am. Astron. Soc.*, VII (1975), p. 365; ibid., p. 410.

31 Attributed to M. J. Rees, in *Project Cyclops*, J. Billingham, ed. (NASA publication CR 114445, Stanford/NASA Ames Research Center, Moffett Field, Calif., 1973), p. 3.

32 H. C. King, *The History of the Telescope* (Sky Publishing, Cambridge, Mass., 1955), pp. 50–9.

33 A. H. Pingré (and M. G. Bigourdan), *Annales célestes du dix-septième siècle* (Gauthier-Villars, Paris, 1901).

34 This invaluable year-by-year diary (see n. 33) of astronomical advance in the seventeenth century was begun by Pingré in 1756 and completed by Bigourdan in 1901. It illuminates a most

interesting century in astronomy and by length alone (639 pages) attests to the vigour of observational work at the time.

35 See, for example, G. D. Cassini, *Anc. Mem.*, X (1688), p. 727; J. Cassini, *Hist. Acad. R. Sci.* (Amsterdam) (1701), pp. 132, 356; ibid. (1702), pp. 185, 194; ibid. (1703), pp. 18, 141, 148, 151.

36 C. Scheiner, *Rosa Ursina sive Sol ex Admirando Facularum* (Apud Andream Phaeum Typographum Ducalem, 1630).

37 J. Hevelius, *Selenographia sive Lunae Descripto* (Gedani, Danzig, 1647).

38 See n. 24 above.

39 See pp. 143–4 of n. 17.

40 See n. 35 above.

41 A. Wilson, *Philos. Trans.*, LXIV (1774), p. 6.

42 The *Rosa Ursina* (n. 36), although large (25 by 36 by 8 cm) and beautifully set, has not enjoyed kind reviews; comments on the book range from 'voluminous', 'enormous' and 'ouvrage considérable renfermant plus de 2000 observations' to the less couched words of astronomer Jean Delambre: 'There are few books so diffuse and so void of facts. It contains 784 pages; there is not matter in it for 50 pages' (*Histoire de l'Astronomie Moderne* (Imprimerie de Huzard-Courcier, Paris, 1821), vol. I, p. 690; cited in n. 43 below).

43 R. Grant, *History of Physical Astronomy* (H. and G. Bohn, London, 1852), p. 216.

44 The 'Maunder Minimum' coincided with a prolonged period of distinct climatic anomaly – years of severe winters and abnormal cold – but there is no evidence of unbroken overcast. Astronomers are neither so mute nor so long-suffering that they would have kept quiet through year after year of continuous, frustrating cloud cover. The time was one of vigorous growth and discovery in observational astronomy, as, for example, in the important revelations of Saturn already cited. Throughout the seventy years of the 'Maunder Minimum' comets were regularly discovered and observed. We may conclude that during these years skies were at least tolerably clear, and certainly adequate to allow at least sporadic if not normal sampling of aurorae and sunspots, had they been there to see.

45 See p. 206 of n. 18.

46 For this study I have used H. Fritz, *Verzeichniss Beobachter Polarlichter* (C. Gerold's Sohn, Vienna, 1873), which is still probably the most thorough published compilation of ancient aurorae. If criticized, it is more generally for sins of commission than omission; some of the ancient aurorae listed may not have been aurorae at all but meteors or comets (C. Stormer, *The Polar Aurora* (Oxford University Press, New York, 1955), p. 14; n. 47, p. 20).

47 S. Chapman, in *Aurora and Airglow*, B. M. McCormac, ed. (Reinhold, New York, 1967).

48 E. H. Vestine, *Terr. Magn. Atmos. Electr.*, XLIV (1944), p. 77.

49 See n. 46.
50 E. Halley, *Philos. Trans. R. Soc. London*, XXIX (1716), p. 406. Halley mentions that the aurora borealis had rarely been seen since the early seventeenth century.
51 Schove (notes 9–12 above) has noted a tendency for auroral counts to alternate by century with more in even centuries (such as the sixteenth and eighteenth) and fewer in odd, in which most of the 'Maunder Minimum' took place.
52 See p. 15 of n. 47.
53 See n. 50 above.
54 Galileo and the other 'discoverers' of sunspots were well aware of the existence of sunspots and naked-eye reports of them before they looked at the sun with telescopes (G. Abetti, in *IV Centenario della Nascita di Galileo Galilei* (Barbèra, Florence, 1966), p. 16).
55 For example, see S. Kanda, *Proc. Imp. Acad. (Tokyo)*, IX (1933), p. 293. Kanda's compilation is more valuable in its own right than as a clue to past epochs of maxima, since large spots have been known to occur during years of minimum activity.
56 More recent studies of specific ancient oriental sunspot reports have been carried out by D. J. Schove and P. Y. Ho (*J. Br. Astron. Assoc.*, LXIX (1958), p. 295; *J. Am. Orient. Soc.*, LXXXVII (1967), p. 105.
57 See n. 4 above.
58 See n. 55 above.
59 S. Nakayama (in *A History of Japanese Astronomy* (Harvard University Press, Cambridge, Mass., 1969), pp. 12–23) has discussed the limitations of the 'Institutional Framework of Astronomical Learning' in early Japan and the resultant repression of ideas and research. I have found no evidence that the 'Maunder Minimum' was a unique period in this regard, however, and the almost precise coincidence with other evidences from Europe make the Far East sunspot gap seem real to me.
60 See n. 55 above.
61 See n. 56 above.
62 S. Matsushita, *J. Geophys. Res.*, LXI (1956), p. 297. I have taken from Matsushita's list only those auroral reports that he deemed 'certain' or 'very probable'.
63 H. E. Suess, *J. Geophys. Res.*, LXX (1965), p. 5937.
64 P. E. Damon, A. Long, D. C. Grey, ibid., LXXI (1966), p. 1055.
65 I. U. Olson, ed., *Radiocarbon Variations and Absolute Chronology* (Almqvist & Wiksell, Stockholm, 1970).
66 P. E. Damon (personal communication) has compiled radiocarbon data from five laboratories (University of Arizona; State University of Groningen, Netherlands; University of California, San Diego; University of Pennsylvania; and Yale University).
67 M. Stuiver, *J. Geophys. Res.*, LXVI (1961), p. 273; *Science*, CXLIX (1965), p. 533; J. R. Bray, ibid., CLVI (1967), p. 640;

P. E. Damon, *Meteorol. Monogr.*, VIII (1968), p. 151; J. A. Simpson and J. R. Wang, *Astrophys. J.*, CLXI (1970), p. 265.

68   H. E. Suess, *Meteorol. Monogr.*, VIII (1968), p. 146.

69   H. DeVries, *Proc. K. Ned. Akad. Wet. B*, LXI (No. 2) (1958), p. 94.

70   J. C. Lerman, W. G. Nook, J. C. Vogel (n. 65, p. 275). There are several available compilations of relative ^{14}C concentration; the most commonly cited is probably that of Suess (n. 63) for Northern Hemisphere trees. P. E. Damon has kindly provided a compilation of ^{14}C data from five world radiocarbon laboratories (see n. 66), which has been very helpful in establishing real features. I have used the recent Groningen data cited here since they include a large sampling from trees of the Southern Hemisphere, where the larger ocean surface might be expected to bring about, in effect, faster tree response to real changes in atmospheric concentration. Fluctuations in ^{14}C atmospheric concentration are severely damped out in tree-ring concentrations because of the finite time of exchange between the atmosphere and the trees; the time constant is on the order of ten to fifty years. The presence of absorbing oceans in the equilibrium process acts as an added sink, or leak, and, since the problem is analogous to that of determining changes in the rate of water flow into a bucket by noting its level, a leaky bucket makes a slightly more responsive system. In fact, there are only minor differences between the historical curve of Lerman *et al.* and that given by Suess and others; they show the same extrema at about the same times.

71   See n. 3 above.

72   See n. 55.

73   The use of ^{14}C data to deduce solar changes in the past and the possible relation of these changes to the history of the terrestrial climate have been the subject of numerous papers (for example, see notes 67, 68 and 74); J. R. Bray, *Nature (London)*, CCXX (1968), p. 672; P. E. Damon, A. Long, E. J. Wallick, *Earth Planet. Sci. Lett.*, XX (1973), p. 300.

74   J. R. Bray, *Science*, CLXXI (1971), p. 1242.

75   P. E. Damon (n. 65, p. 571).

76   The earlier compilations by Suess (n. 63) and by Damon (notes 64 and 66) show that the deviation at 1500 is approximately equal to that of the 'Maunder Minimum' period.

77   See n. 46.

78   V. Bucha, *Nature (London)*, CCXXIV (1969), p. 681 (in n. 65, p. 501).

79   R. E. Lingenfelter and R. Ramaty (in n. 65, p. 513).

80   Y. C. Lin, C. Y. Fan, P. E. Damon, E. J. Wallick, *14th Int. Cosmic Ray Conf.*, III (1975), p. 995.

81   See n. 65, p. 571.

82   See n. 78.

83   See n. 63.

84   See n. 30.

85 G. S. Vaiana, J. M. Davis, R. Giaconni, A. S. Krieger, J. K. Silk, A. F. Timothy, M. Zombeck, *Astrophys. J.*, CLXXXV (1973), p. L47.

86 The seventeenth-century style of observing solar eclipses is well described throughout Pingré's compendium (n. 33). A principal result from each eclipse was a table giving times of obscuration and the amount of the disk covered in 'digits' – 12 digits corresponding to the solar diameter and total obscuration.

87 A. J. Meadows, *Early Solar Physics* (Pergamon, London, 1970), p. 9.

88 T. R. von Oppolzer, *Canon of Eclipses* (reprinted by Dover Publications, New York, 1962).

89 V. Wing, *Astronomia Instaurata* (R. and W. Laybourn, London, 1656), pp. 98–102; (n. 43, pp. 364, 376–91); (n. 33, p. 570); J. Cassini, *Mem. Acad. Sci. (Amsterdam)* (1706), p. 322.

90 Cited in A. C. Ranyard (*Mem. R. Astron. Soc.*, XLI (1879), p. 503). Cotes might have given a more thorough account had he been free of a perennial eclipse nuisance, for, according to Halley, Cotes 'had the misfortune to be oppressed with too much company' (n. 43, p. 379). Halley's own description of the 1715 corona, from the same reference, follows: 'a few seconds before the sun was all hid, there discovered itself round the moon a luminous ring . . . perhaps a tenth part of the moon's diameter in breadth. It was of pale whiteness . . . and concentric with the moon.'

91 See n. 18 above.

92 E. N. Parker, in *Solar Terrestrial Relations*, D. Venkatesan, ed. (University of Calgary, Calgary, 1973), p. 6; *Sci. Am.*, CCXXXIII (September, 1975), p. 42.

93 See p. 99 of n. 28.

94 See p. 601 of n. 28.

95 The Plutarch reference is to his account of the solar eclipse of 27 December AD 83; his description follows, as given by R. R. Newton (n. 27, p. 114; n. 28, pp. 99–100): '[during a solar eclipse] a kind of light is visible about the rim which keeps the shadow from being profound and absolute.' Newton feels that Plutarch's 'kind of light' could be the rim of light visible during an annular eclipse or light from solar prominences, but that, if it is the corona, this is the earliest extant account. In any case it does not help us in answering whether the K corona was seen, since Plutarch's description could as well or better be the zodiacal light. The reference to Flavius Philostratus is from a passage in his fictional and controversial *Life of Apollonius of Tyana*, written about AD 210. Newton avoids it completely, but we should probably expose it to light: 'About the time that [Apollonius] was busy in Greece a remarkable phenomenon was seen in the sky. A crown like a rainbow formed around the sun's disk and partly obscured its light. It was plain to see that the phenomenon portended revolution and the Governor of Greece [the tyrant Domitian] summoned Apollonius . . . to expound it. "I hear,

Apollonius, that you have Science in the supernatural"'
[translation of J. S. Phillimore (Clarendon, Oxford, 1912) of
book VIII, chap. 23]. In Philostratus' story the 'crown'
(stephanos) portends the name of Stephanus who later murdered
Domitian. The use of the word is thus couched in symbolism
and gives no evidence that Philostratus had ever seen either a
total solar eclipse or the structured corona.

96 R. Grant (n. 43, pp. 377–8) gives the Clavius, Jessenius, and
Kepler accounts.

97 J. A. Eddy, *Astron. Astrophys.*, XXXIV (1974), p. 235.

98 See n. 17.

99 E. Opik, *Irish Astron. J.*, VIII (1968), p. 153; see also n. 30. A
change in solar luminosity of 0.5 per cent per century corresponds
to 0.005 stellar magnitude per century and is thus outside the
limits of practical detection in other G stars.

100 For example, see G. Manley, *Ann. N.Y. Acad. Sci.*, XCV (1961),
p. 162; Suess (n. 68); Bray (n. 74); *Adv. Ecol. Res.*, VII (1971),
p. 177; S. H. Schneider and C. Maas, *Science*, CXC (1975), p. 741.

101 See n. 92 above.

102 A. E. Douglass, *Climatic Cycles and Tree Growth* (Publication
289, Carnegie Institution of Washington, Washington, D.C.),
I (1919), p. 102; II (1928), pp. 125–6. Douglass found
that from 1660 to 1720 the curve of south-west tree growth
'flattens out in a striking manner' and, before knowing of
Maunder's work, he described the end of the seventeenth century
as a time of unusually retarded growth in Arizona pines and
California sequoias.

103 A good review of past climate history is given in n. 104 from which
the climate incidents cited here were derived. The Little Ice Age
lasted roughly from 1430 to 1850; it was marked by two severe
extremes of cold, roughly 1450 to 1500 and 1600 to 1700, if we
take H. H. Lamb's index of Paris–London Winter Severity as a
global indicator.

104 W. L. Gates and Y. Mintz, eds, *Understanding Climate Change*
(National Academy of Sciences, Washington, D.C., 1975),
appendix A.

105 If changes in the solar constant are reflected in the envelope of
solar activity, and if the rate of change has held to the 0.5 per
cent per century rate cited earlier (n. 99), then we can estimate
that during the 'Maunder Minimum' the solar flux was about
1.4 per cent lower than at present – a number not inconsistent
with temperature estimates during that coldest period of the
Little Ice Age (n. 104 above).

106 A. Hundhausen, *Coronal Expansion and the Solar Wind*
(Springer-Verlag, Berlin, 1972); A. S. Krieger, A. F. Timothy,
E. C. Roelof, *Sol. Phys.*, XXIX (1973), p. 505.

107 See n. 7 above.

108 See n. 14 above.

109 See n. 15 above.

110 See n. 16 above.

111 See n. 17 above.

112 See n. 24 above.

113 See n. 25 above.

114 See n. 33 above.

115 See n. 34 above.

116 See n. 35 above.

117 See n. 36 above.

118 See n. 37 above.

119 See n. 3 above.

120 See n. 7 above.

121 See n. 9 above.

122 See n. 10 above.

123 See n. 11 above.

124 See n. 12 above.

125 The solar emphasis of the Spectrum of Time Project (STP) was first directed at fixing the epochs of presumed eleven-year maxima of the past solar cycle (n. 11). Amplitudes of past cycles (ten-year averages) and of past maxima of the cycle were estimated on the basis of the best information available: auroral counts and other unspecified data, with an arbitrary correction for what fraction of aurorae was recorded in a given century (n. 12). Moreover, in the STP there was a built-in constraint to generate nine solar cycles in each 100 years, regardless of whether there was evidence for them or not (n. 10). These and other assumptions tend to dilute possible drastic changes in the past (like the 'Maunder Minimum') and to nullify possible long-term drifts in the amplitude of solar activity. The 'Maunder Minimum' shows up as a significant drop in the number of sunspots in the STP, but with $R_{max} = 30$ at its weakest 'maximum' in 1693, which falls in the middle of a five-year period for which direct accounts from the contemporary literature report that no spots were seen. It is unfair to press the comparison since the STP covers a much longer span than the 'Maunder Minimum' and, more to the point, it should be noted that the STP shows Maunder's 'prolonged sunspot minimum' in figure 1 and table 2 of n. 10 above.

126 See n. 3 above.

127 See n. 9 above.

128 See n. 10 above.

129 See n. 11 above.

130 See n. 12 above.

I am indebted to the libraries of Harvard College, the US Naval Observatory, and the Hale Observatories for privilege of access. I thank O. Gingerich, H. Zirin, T. Bell, J. Ashbrook, D. MacNamara, G. Newkirk, M. Stix, M. Altschuler, L. E. Schmitt, and P. E. Damon for help and suggestions. I am most indebted to E. N. Parker for calling my attention to Maunder's papers, and for personal encouragement in all the work reported here. This research was funded entirely by NASA contract NAS5-3950. The National Center for Atmospheric Research is sponsored by the National Science Foundation.

Index

Abel, Wilhelm, 30, 31

absolutism: anti-absolutism and Puritan Revolution, 153; impossibility of enforcing, 141; pre-Fronde legalism and, 153; problem of, 44–8; revolts against, 42

Acton, John Acton, 1st Baron, 122

agriculture: and animal-rearing, 197; cereal cultivation, 195, 197; Company of Millers of Casena, 198; Dutch and English prosperity, 203–4; Dutch reclamation of land, 201; and economic life, 204, 213–14; evaluation of trends, 29–31; harvest failures, 12, 39, 91, 92, 213; interaction between crises and, 215; lack of statistics, 195; Polish grain, 178; Polish rural economy, 198–9; and population flow, 9; and recession, 35; 'refeudalization', 196–7; serf labour, 99; seventeenth-century agrarian society, 91; seventeenth-century dependence on, 7–8; sixteenth-century expansion, 196; sugar and tobacco cultivation, 94; taxation and, 40, 41; and trade and industry, 201–2; and vagrancy, 10; yield ratios, 9, 30–1

Aitzema, Lieuwe van, 1, 2

Alba, Ferdinand Alvárez de Toledo, third Duke of, 127

Aleppo, 175

Alexandria, 175

Alexis I, Romanov, Tsar of Russia, 19

Algiers, 65, 173–4, 178

Algiers, King of, 60

America: customs regulations, 181–2; Dutch activity in, 69–70; evidence of drought, 255; mining industry, 184, 192–4; Spanish exploitation of, 94; trade with Seville, 34–5, 93–4, 168–70, 182

American Revolution, 136, 143, 158

Amsterdam, 86, 103; banking situation, 211; centre of commerce, 98; city hall, 98; industry, 190–2; metropolis, 104; population migration to, 191; wealth of, 100

Anabaptists, 118

animal husbandry, 195, 197

Anjou, François, Duke of, 62

Anna of Saxony, *wife of* William I of Orange, 59

Anne of Austria, Queen Regent of France, 3, 19

Antwerp, 61, 140

Argentine Pampas, 197

Arminianism, 15

art, 85, 86, 89–90

Asia, 35–6, 94, 96, 99, 182

Assarino, Luca, 115